D1519663

Nasser at War

Nasser at War

Nasser at War

Arab Images of the Enemy

Laura M. James

First published 2006 by
PALGRAVE MACMILLAN
Houndmills, Basingstoke, Hampshire RG21 6XS and
175 Fifth Avenue, New York, N.Y. 10010
Companies and representatives throughout the world

PALGRAVE MACMILLAN is the global academic imprint of the Palgrave
Macmillan division of St. Martin's Press, LLC and of Palgrave Macmillan Ltd.
Macmillan® is a registered trademark in the United States, United Kingdom
and other countries. Palgrave is a registered trademark in the European
Union and other countries.

ISBN 13: 978–0–230–00643–0   hardback
ISBN 10: 0–230–00643–4   hardback

This book is printed on paper suitable for recycling and made from fully
managed and sustained forest sources.

A catalogue record for this book is available from the British Library.

Library of Congress Cataloging-in-Publication Data

James, Laura M., 1978–
   Nasser at war : Arab images of the enemy / Laura M. James.
      p. cm.
   Includes bibliographical references (p.   ) and index.
   ISBN 0–230–00643–4
      1. Egypt–History–1952–1970. 2. Nasser, Gamal Abdel, 1918–1970. 3.
   Egypt–History, Military–20th century. I. Title.

   DT107.83.J234 2006
   962.05′3092–dc22   2006046444

10   9   8   7   6   5   4   3   2   1
15   14   13   12   11   10   09   08   07   06

Printed and bound in Great Britain by
Antony Rowe Ltd, Chippenham and Eastbourne

Contents

Acknowledgements

So many people assisted in the writing of this book that to thank each as he or she deserves would make the acknowledgements longer than the work itself, 'contrary to usage'. I owe a great debt to the constant good advice and interest of my supervisor, Philip Robins. My editor, Michael Strang, was unfailingly helpful. Avi Shlaim's feedback shaped the original direction of my research. I am also immensely grateful to Louise Fawcett, Clive Jones, Deirdre Parsons, Barry Rubin, Noa Schonmann, Rachel Scott, Michael Thornhill, Dominik Zaum and one splendid anonymous reader, who commented on all or part of the manuscript. Valuable advice was provided at various stages by Hassan Abu Talib, Richard Aldrich, Nigel Ashton, Patrick Belton, Peter Catterall, John Ciorciari, Dominic Coldwell, Paul Dresch, Henry Frendo, Roy Giles, Anthony Glees, Galia Golan, Salwa Sharawi Gomaa, Bahgat Korany, Karma Nabulsi, Michael Oren, Richard Parker, William Quandt, Ya'acov Ro'i, Abdel Monem Said, Mustapha al-Sayyid, Amy Scott, Avraham Sela, Mohammad Selim, Ahmed al-Shahi, Jennifer Welsh, Jon Wilks and Ahmad Youssef-Ahmad. The original doctoral research was funded by the Economic and Social Research Council; and some of the material appeared in my article, 'Nasser and his Enemies', in MERIA Journal (2005).

This project would have come to nothing without the patience and good humour of those individuals who consented to be interviewed, and I would like to express my gratitude to all of them. In particular, I am indebted to the Helal family and to Sir John and Lady Graham, for their generous hospitality; to Mohsen Alaini, Abdel Hamid Abubakr, Tharwat Okasha and Ahmed Said, who provided me with additional research materials; and to Ahmad Hamrush, Amin Howeidy and Sami Sharaf, each of whom answered my questions on more than one occasion. I am also very grateful to staff at the UK National Archives, the Al-Ahram Centre for Political and Social Studies, Dar el-Kutub and the Egyptian Foreign Ministry; as well as to many individuals in Oxford, including Robin Darwall-Smith, Lucie Ryzova, Debbie Usher and Marga Lyall. In Cairo, I owe special thanks, for introductions and advice, to Mostafa Elwi-Saif, Yasser Elwy, Tariq Habib, Iman Hamdy, Samer al-Karanshawy, Gamil Matar, Summer Said, Gamal Shaheen, Mohammed Shokeir and Hisham Radwan. I am likewise indebted to Walid Abdelnasser, Khaled

Abubakr, Hadeel Alaini, Yoav Alon, Jehan Attia, Richard Belfield, Ian Boag, Jeremy Bowen, Simone de Brincat, Richard Crampton, Laura Engelbrecht, Gamal Hamed, James and Caroline Hanks, Charles Holmes, Abdalla Homouda, Mike Lattanzi, Charles Levinson, Abdel 'Aaty Mohamed, Sarah Mosad, Gamila 'Ali Raga'a, Mohamed Abdel Rashid, Kevin Rosser, Magda Shafei, James Vaughan and Ali Abdel Wahab.

Without the dedication of Abeer Heider, my Arabic would never have reached the necessary standard. Additional linguistic support was provided by Iman, Shima'a and Rose; as well as by the Hawamdeh family in Amman, the Ibrahim family in Damascus, Cynthia Dearin, Clive Holes, Ahmed Sidahmed and Jan Taaks. I owe much to my former teachers, especially Richard Wilkinson. Finally, for impressive patience and practical assistance of all kinds when I was in the throes of research, I owe a more-than-honourable mention to my long-suffering flatmates and friends, Josie Delap, Mariana de Castro, Michael Horton and Sophie Pownall; to my kind hosts, Lindsay Wise, Rachel Ziemba and Gerard van Rootselar; and, most of all, to my family.

I need hardly add that all errors remain my own.

Abbreviations

ANA	Arab News Agency
ACPSS	Al-Ahram Centre for Political and Social Studies (Egypt)
ASU	Arab Socialist Union (Egypt)
BBC-SWB	*British Broadcasting Corporation: Summary of World Broadcasts*
CIA	Central Intelligence Agency (USA)
FLOSY	Front for the Liberation of South Yemen
FO	Foreign Office (UK, later Foreign and Commonwealth Office)
FRUS	*Foreign Relations of the United States*
FYW	*The Fifty Years War: Israel and the Arabs* (Interview Transcripts)
IDF	Israel Defence Force
IDP	*International Documents on Palestine*
KGB	Komitet Gosudarstvennoi Bezopasnosti (Soviet Intelligence)
MEDO	Middle East Defence Organisation
MP	Member of Parliament (UK)
NA	National Archives (UK, formerly Public Record Office)
NATO	North Atlantic Treaty Organisation
NLF	National Liberation Front (Aden)
NSC	National Security Council (USA)
PFLP	Popular Front for the Liberation of Palestine
PLA	Palestine Liberation Army
PLO	Palestine Liberation Organisation
RCC	Revolutionary Command Council (Egypt)
SAF	South Arabian Federation
SAS	Special Air Service (UK)
SCUA	Suez Canal Users' Association
SEC	Supreme Executive Committee (of the ASU)
SIS	Secret Intelligence Service (UK, also called MI6)
SOE	Special Operations Executive (UK)
UAC	United Arab Command
UAE	United Arab Emirates
UAR	United Arab Republic
UNEF	United Nations Emergency Force
USAID	United States Agency for International Development
YAR	Yemen Arab Republic
YFM	Yemeni Free Movement

Introduction

The Nasser era in Egypt marked a critical turning point in modern Middle Eastern history.[1] From his 1956 triumph at Suez to the tragedy of the 1967 War, President Gamal Abdel Nasser became the ultimate symbol of Arab revolution. 'Nasserist' Arab nationalism, through a combination of new radio technology, radical rhetoric and personal charisma, changed the political face of the region and defined a common Arab identity. A common identity can be fortified by a common enemy, and this book assesses how Nasser's changing adversaries affected the nature of Arabism. It explains the failure of initial Egyptian attempts to improve relations with Britain, the former colonial power; the bitter dynamics of inter-Arab competition; and how the Arab-Israeli conflict at last reached an uncompromising impasse. Most significantly, it explores Nasser's gradual redefinition of the United States, from sympathetic collaborator to imperialist archenemy – an image that the USA seems unable to discard in the Arab arena.

Nasser's initial consolidation of power in Egypt following the Free Officers' *coup d'état* of 23 July 1952 soon came to be based on a more anti-Western foreign policy attitude, culminating in the Suez Crisis of 1956. Thereafter, Cairo began to promote revolution in the wider Arab region, through such adventures as the experimental union with Syria of 1958–61 and a lengthy intervention in the 1962–67 Yemeni Civil War. However, crushing defeat in the June 1967 'Six Day War' with Israel eventually exposed the hollowness of Arab nationalist pretensions. In the aftermath, the Egyptian leaders attempted to come to terms with their new environment through limited domestic reform and a national focus on the renewed War of Attrition with Israel. Nasser's death on 28 September 1970 abruptly terminated this epoch.

As a leading light of the Non-Aligned Movement, the Egyptian President was an important player on the world stage from the mid-1950s. He also dominated the Arab countries, as the political stances of rulers and revolutionaries alike came to be defined in terms of their attitude towards him. At home, Nasser's pre-eminence was evident. He was the regime's principal decision-maker in matters of war and peace.[2] There was a limited circle of people he might consult – former revolutionary colleagues, confidential aides, a very few respected experts – but he was never bound by their advice.[3] When he wanted assistance in formulating a policy, Nasser used to send a neat conference agenda to the people he meant to invite, remembers one such aide. The agenda specified place, time, purpose, attendance and the date by which the President expected to receive their written positions. The meeting itself would never last more than an hour or so, since Nasser believed 'the conference is not for discussing the problem, it is for taking a decision'.[4]

It may have been a brisk and militarily efficient management style; it was probably not conducive to a full and frank exchange of views among advisors. And there were no other routes through which the President was likely to be exposed to diverse opinions. He attached a high importance to knowledge, spending much of his time each day reading the foreign newspapers and secret internal reports.[5] But Nasser's personal control of the apparatus of government created every incentive for subordinates to tell him what they thought he wanted to hear.[6] In any case, his charismatic – and incredibly lengthy – speeches soon enabled him to shape the political preconceptions of a generation for whom he could do no wrong. The President's orations were continually lauded and disseminated by the state-controlled press.[7] Political parties were banned and the influence of interest groups was minimal. Thus Nasser's own decided views regarding the international situation were subject to few checks and balances as they guided the formation of Egyptian foreign policy in the 1950s and 1960s.

Any attempt to understand these views must address the problem of identifying reliable sources. Among Arab countries, Egypt is now relatively open to historical research. Nonetheless, access to archives remains difficult. Formal records of policy discussions, such as minutes of meetings and internal memoranda, are largely unavailable – except when they are reproduced, not necessarily accurately, in memoirs. Indeed, in the most critical cases, the documents may never have existed. It has therefore been necessary to compare an eclectic range of more partial accounts. This book draws on tapes, transcripts and contemporary translations of Nasser's keynote speeches, as well as the weekly *Al-Ahram* newspaper editorials by his close confidant Mohammed Hassanein Heikal, who was often perceived as the informal voice of the Nasser regime.[8] Over 30 first-hand interviews with former Egyptian and Yemeni insiders – including a vice president, prime ministers, ministers, generals and ambassadors – were performed in Cairo, Alexandria and London. Recently published Arabic memoirs, Western archives and a range of secondary materials have also been useful.

Taken in isolation, most of these sources are problematic. Archived foreign diplomatic documents only contain second-hand accounts of

Egyptian decision processes. Contemporary statements intended for public consumption have obvious incentives to mislead. *Ex post facto* reconstructions of events, as narrated in memoirs and interviews, tend to be distorted by the universal human habit of rewriting the past, consciously or unconsciously.[9] Effective analysis thus depends on comparing a range of sources, with painstaking reference to the original context.[10] In the case of each contention made in a primary source, one must consider whether it might be better explained than by the theory that it is simply true. It is necessary to ask both why an assertion might be unintentionally inaccurate (due, for example, to lack of first-hand knowledge or the passage of time) and why it might be deliberately misleading.[11] Nonetheless, when assessed, analysed, compared, contrasted and generally taken with a hefty pinch of salt, the available sources shed a fresh light on Nasser's legacy of confrontation.

During Nasser's lifetime, he tended to be viewed in the West as an irresponsible rabble-rouser: wilfully undermining British and French interests in the Third World; siding with the USSR against the USA in the Cold War; and refusing to come to any reasonable compromise with Israel. Shortly after his death, however, both the journalist Robert Stephens and the politician Anthony Nutting published sympathetic biographies, which set the tone for most subsequent analysis. Each author had met the Egyptian President several times and experienced many of the events related at first hand.[12] Nevertheless, much new information on the Middle East in the 1950s and 1960s has since become available, some of which is exploited in the latest biography by Saïd Aburish.[13] In contrast to Stephens' explicit focus on political minutiae, the key strength of Aburish's work lies in his use of personal detail. His major purpose, however, is to explore the importance of Nasser's ideology in a contemporary context, arguing that Western opposition to Arab nationalism caused modern Islamic fundamentalism. In the end, perhaps none of these works entirely manages to avoid the biographer's snare of accepting at face value the subject's rationalisations of his own decisions.

Consequently, despite the existence of some excellent studies of Egyptian domestic politics under his rule, Nasser's periodic – and highly dramatic – foreign policy crises have never been systematically assessed in light of modern research.[14] The omission is particularly remarkable since the perspectives of Nasser's adversaries in these crises have been the focus of much attention in recent years. There is a lively current debate on Anglo-American involvement in Egypt prior to the Suez affair.[15] Several ground-breaking studies of secret British opposition to

Nasser in Yemen have been inspired by newly released archival material.[16] Finally, the enhanced international profile of the Israeli-Palestinian problem has reignited interest in the 1967 War and its aftermath, which defined the parameters of the present *impasse*.[17] This book draws on such fresh insights into the US, UK and Israeli viewpoints, in order to integrate them with recent revelations from the Egyptian side, previously published – if at all – only in Arabic.

The book analyses conflict decision-making in Egypt during the Nasser era by focusing on changing images of the enemy. When a country faces war, attention becomes sharply concentrated on the opponent.[18] Leaders make foreign policy decisions with primary reference to the enemy's intentions and capability.[19] In fact, however, they can only respond to their *idea* of the enemy, which will necessarily be a simplified and selective representation of a complex reality.[20] Nonetheless, it is possible to identify regularities in the way such images of the enemy develop, interact and endure. 'Perceptions of the world and of other actors,' avers Robert Jervis, 'diverge from reality in patterns that we can detect and for reasons that we can understand.'[21] For example, adversaries' actions tend to be seen as more deliberate, centralised and co-ordinated than is in fact the case, encouraging the formulation of elaborate conspiracy theories.[22] Furthermore, images of the enemy are resistant to change, since policy makers tend to interpret incoming information in line with their existing beliefs.[23]

That raises an obvious problem. 'We have no eternal allies and we have no perpetual enemies,' Lord Palmerston told the House of Commons more than a century and a half ago. But how, if images are fixed, does the one transform into the other?[24] This book explores how conflicts can act as catalysts for shifting perceptions. Describing how Nasser and his regime viewed their various adversaries in an ongoing series of hostile confrontations – the Suez War, the Yemen War, the 1967 War and the War of Attrition – it demonstrates how such images help to explain choices that have long baffled historians. At the heart of the analysis, the rapid and resentful deterioration in relations between Egypt and the United States emerges as a constant theme. In a Middle East divided by internal rivalries and Cold War commitments, Nasser's rising star kindled the growth of a common Arab identity that defined itself in firm opposition to the West. It was to prove his most lasting legacy.

1
The Coming and the Going: Friends and Enemies of the Egyptian Revolution

America can win our friendship by acting in accordance with the principles of the American liberation revolution.[25] – Gamal Abdel Nasser

Colonel Gamal Abdel Nasser sent a message to the United States Embassy in Cairo on 23 July 1952, in the early hours of the morning. The message was carried by an officer named Ali Sabri, and was ultimately received by Ambassador Jefferson Caffery. So much is agreed, amid the confusion of claim and counter-claim. Colonel Nasser was then 34 years old, a provincial post office clerk's son who had made good in the army – quiet and a good listener. That night, he was busy directing a somewhat hurried *coup d'état*, slipping occasionally into English as he gave his orders, on the grounds that 'Arabic was not a suitable language to express the need for calm'.[26] The rebellion had been brought forward unexpectedly when the conspiracy of his Egyptian Free Officers' Movement had been discovered by agents of King Farouk. Later known as the July Revolution, Nasser's coup would inspire a series of inferior imitations by cells of 'Free Officers' across the Arab world – in Iraq, a bloodbath; in Yemen, a façade; in Libya, a farce. It remains the foundation of the present Egyptian regime.

The messenger, Ali Sabri, was Chief of Air Force Intelligence under the monarchy. He was also a Free Officer, who later became one of Nasser's most powerful lieutenants. Like several of his co-conspirators, Sabri had studied in the USA, attending a six-month course in Colorado normally reserved for NATO officers.[27] In the months preceding the July Revolution, he kept up his US contacts, particularly with the assistant Air Force Attaché, David Evans.[28] Once again, the exact nature of this relationship is controversial. According to the official

1

Egyptian version, Sabri and Evans discussed only routine air force business until suddenly, on the night of the coup, it occurred to Nasser
that the 80,000 British troops stationed in the Suez Canal Zone Base
might present something of a problem if they chose to intervene – as
they had, under comparable circumstances, in 1882. The solution, he
decided, was to inform the Americans that the revolution was a purely
internal affair, and hope they would dissuade the British. But this presented a delicate social dilemma. Nasser and his coterie were not
acquainted with the US Ambassador. To everyone's relief, up popped
Ali Sabri with his fortuitous friendship, and he was at once sent speed-
ing through the roadblocks of a city in revolution.[29]

There are indications, however, that this may not be the whole story.
The ongoing meetings between Sabri and Evans are said to have been
used as a mechanism to keep the United States in touch with the Free
Officers' Movement, providing assurance that the latter was not a
Communist front, and that the former would therefore discourage
British interference.[30] Some sources even portray the entire coup as a
CIA plot, masterminded by the resourceful and ubiquitous Kermit
Roosevelt, the Agency's foremost 'crypto-diplomat'. Roosevelt, whose
hand was last seen in the murky Mossadegh affair in Iran, is alleged to
have met Ali Sabri and other Free Officers on at least three occasions,
in Egypt and in Cyprus.[31] Although most of the former revolutionaries
deny any knowledge of such contacts, one does concede that Nasser
might have authorised them (for informational purposes) without
telling his co-conspirators, who would have doubted his intentions.[32]
Soviet Intelligence, as well as significant sections of Egyptian opinion,
certainly believed that the US had sponsored the coup.[33] On balance,
however, it seems that although the CIA took pains to keep itself
informed on a friendly basis, it played a minimal active role in the conspiracy and was surprised by its timing – which may in fact have been
the most important reason for Ali Sabri's message.[34]

The final recipient of the message, 'our confidant' Jefferson Caffery,
has also been linked to the Free Officers' conspiracy.[35] Indeed, Hassan
Touhami (alias 'Junior', a key contact between the CIA and the new
Egyptian regime) later implied that the elderly Ambassador was posted
to Cairo in 1949 based on his experience of managing military
upheavals.[36] However, US Embassy records indicate no specific foreknowledge of the coup.[37] Once he received Nasser's message, Caffery
openly exerted his influence in a plea against bloodshed, persuading
the new leaders to allow the King to go into exile.[38] Nevertheless,
Nasser's eventual successor Anwar Sadat (a Free Officer who nearly

missed the revolution because he was at the cinema, but turned up in the nick of time to announce it on the radio) may protest a little too much when he states firmly: 'This was the only part which the United States Ambassador played in this last episode of Farouk's reign.'[39]

Certainly, there was great goodwill between the Free Officers and the US Embassy immediately after the Revolution.[40] On 20 August, Caffery was invited to dine with the regime's figurehead, General Mohammed Naguib, and nine principal officers, who emphasised their friendly intentions and hopes of assistance, especially over financial aid and relations with the British.[41] They used to ask the Ambassador's advice on international affairs. Given the ongoing negotiations, this may have been partly disingenuous, but it was indeed a bewildering transition for the new Revolutionary Command Council (RCC), mostly officers of low to middle rank with no experience of government. Seventeen years later, Nasser would empathise with the Libyan revolutionaries' 'feelings of anxiety and nervousness, combined probably with acute sleeplessness'. They would, he remarked feelingly, be 'much too terrified to leave their offices'.[42]

On a daily basis, however, the new leaders' most important negotiations with the United States tended to be mediated by the CIA. Under James Eichelberger, the local CIA station assisted the Egyptian internal security forces.[43] Wilbur Eveland recalls joking with one of Nasser's CIA contacts that he was teaching the Egyptians to dominate the Arab world:

> More seriously than I'd expected, Chuck said that this had been the original CIA plan but that now the agency was attempting to direct Egypt into fields compatible with US objectives.[44]

Nasser's own association with the United States at this time was so strong that Egyptians sometimes disparagingly called him 'Colonel Jimmy'.[45] He developed a particular friendship with the Embassy's Second Secretary, William Lakeland. This worried British diplomats, who dismissed Lakeland as 'notable for his youthful enthusiasm and idealistic, even sentimental approach to the Egyptians untempered by realism and uncoloured by any feeling of solidarity with us'.[46] Nasser also got on well with US Secretary of State John Foster Dulles, whom he met in May 1953.[47] At this stage, the United States was not naturally ranked among Egypt's imperialist enemies – indeed, Nasser had deliberately avoided mentioning the Americans in such a context in either the original Free Officers' manifesto or his subsequent book, *The*

Philosophy of the Revolution.[48] He still saw the US as representing the non-imperialist future (*al-gāyin*, 'the coming'), in contrast to the colonial British past (*al-rāyin*, 'the going').[49]

***

Before the revolution, the Free Officers had considered the British to be their 'chief enemy', blamed for all the failings of the monarchy, especially the poor state of the army.[50] 'She occupies our country,' shouted the Free Officer Salah Salem to general approval in 1951, when a visiting general attempted to direct his attention towards the Israeli threat instead, 'we must get rid of her first'.[51] The eviction of the British was a more important goal for Nasser than the overthrow of the King; and he remembered the encirclement of the Abdin Palace by British tanks in 1942, which forced Farouk to choose a new Prime Minister, as a defining moment.[52] In the early years, the concept of 'imperialism' was identified primarily with Britain. It was her past sins to which Nasser was referring when he declared:

> Imperialism closed our factories, trimmed the wings of our army, destroyed our navy, and closed the door of honour in our faces. Therefore the revolution undertook to liberate the country from occupation and the assistants of occupation.[53]

After the revolution, however, the Egyptian conception of imperialism was focused on the issues of foreign military bases and alliances. It denoted the actions of Western states, rather than their intrinsic nature. Thus the possibility was apparently left open for Britain to escape this damning label.[54]

It was true that, immediately after the revolution, the new military regime would 'have nothing whatever to do with' the British, fearing sabotage.[55] The Egyptian General Staff still maintained that 'the British are the main enemy while the Israelis are a secondary threat'.[56] The dispute over whether Sudan should be a part of Egypt fostered mutual distrust. After the two countries agreed on Sudanese independence in February 1953, the principal focus of resentment came to be the massive presence of British troops in the Suez Canal Zone Base. 'We cannot feel free and sovereign until they go,' Nasser complained. 'We have a record of sixty-five promises that they were going to be withdrawn but they are still there.'[57] He threatened holy war if they refused to evacuate, and guerrilla fighters (*fidā'iyūn*) were trained, funded, equipped and more or less openly sent to attack the British.[58] When Dulles attempted to persuade him of the need to form a Middle East Defence Organisation (MEDO) against the Soviet threat, Nasser asked:

> How can I go to my people and tell them I am disregarding a killer with a pistol sixty miles from me at the Suez Canal to worry about somebody who is holding a knife a thousand miles away?[59]

At least one British Embassy observer believed that the young officers had 'a real hatred for us politically in their hearts'.[60] Similarly, Winston Churchill's envoy Robin Hankey concluded in June 1953 that Nasser had 'a deep emotional dislike of the British'. However, he added that it seemed to be conflicting with 'a very considerable admiration of us', and this theme is echoed elsewhere.[61] Amid all the hostile rhetoric and commando operations, unpublicised 'contacts with the British were maintained calmly', remembers RCC member Khaled Mohieddin.[62] In January 1953, Cairo Radio approvingly broadcast Nasser's words to the *Daily Mirror*:

> I am not against the British people, but I am opposed to the British forces' occupation of the Canal Zone. If this question were settled, a great friendship would exist between us.[63]

It was finally settled on 27 July 1954, when a timetable for British evacuation of the Canal Zone was agreed, and so Nasser's prediction was put to the test. Sir Evelyn Shuckburgh, a member of the British delegation, was initially impressed by the 'friendly and confident atmosphere', as Minister of Guidance Salah Salem confided to him that:

> He had not slept, he had instructed his broadcasting stations to stop anti-British propaganda. He, who had made so many speeches against us, would become our best friend in the Middle East.[64]

Nasser repeatedly expressed the hope (which regime insiders claim was sincere) that Britain and Egypt could work together at last.[65] 'Co-operation between Egypt, Britain and every peace-loving nation,' he announced after signing the final agreement, 'will consolidate Egypt's freedom, strengthen its sovereignty and not commit or hinder it in any way.'[66] Esmat Abdel Magid, who assisted Foreign Minister Mahmoud Fawzi in hammering out the terms, was then optimistic about the prospect of establishing good relations.[67] Twelve years later,

Nasser reminisced: 'We hoped, after a long period of British occupation and domination which lasted about eighty years, to begin new relations based on equality and respect.'[68]

***

The issue of British evacuation had important implications for the relationship between Egypt and the United States. Nasser was concerned about American 'support for the imperialist powers in order to win them over to her side in her dispute with communism'.[69] He began, recalls one of his staff, to believe that the US was 'just fooling around'.[70] 'Do not believe that the USA will ever help us,' Nasser warned his countrymen, 'for she and her ally, Britain, have one plan and their policy is determined in advance.'[71] In early 1954, he told the new Ambassador to Washington, Ahmed Hussein, to focus on acquiring American support over British evacuation.[72] However, he continued to complain to Lakeland that the United States was losing out because it 'always sides with Britain'.[73] In particular, the US was seen as bowing to British pressure not to provide weapons to Egypt. Unfortunately, when US Deputy Secretary of Defence William Foster visited Cairo in November 1953, he promised more arms than could ever be given. Parker Hart, then Director of Near Eastern Affairs in the State Department, recalled: 'suddenly we were presented with the picture of Ali Sabri immediately jumping on a plane... with a long list of items to buy'.[74] None were forthcoming, and many Egyptians recall the incident with deep rancour.[75] When Eisenhower eventually refused additional aid, Nasser remarked upon the fulfilment of the prophecy of those who criticised his regime: 'The only thing Egypt will get back from America will be Ali Sabri.'[76]

Relations improved again in 1954, for two reasons. First, the Free Officers' regime, like many a revolution before it, was torn by internal power struggles. (It was, however, unusually prone to exile rather than to execute alienated colleagues, and they tended to be welcomed back later from Paris or Geneva with cultural responsibilities and renewed access, turning up in people's offices at critical moments to give unheeded advice.) President Naguib, an overly popular figurehead, had begun to take an independent line, and the CIA supported Nasser in his struggle to assert control. He consolidated his victory after becoming the target of a failed assassination attempt at Alexandria in October 1954, which enabled him to crack down on the Muslim Brotherhood and link it to Naguib. Eight revolver shots, all of which missed, were fired at the Egyptian leader, and Hassan Touhami later claimed that the

CIA helped to orchestrate the incident, providing Nasser with a bullet-proof vest just before his speech.[77] However, there is no other evidence for this allegation, and it is noteworthy that Nasser's initial reaction, in the shock of the moment, was to blame an imperialist rather than a domestic conspiracy.

CIA co-operation over the Naguib issue was partly due to Nasser's secret offer of concessions in the Evacuation Agreement with Britain – the signing of which constituted a second reason for reduced tensions in the US-Egyptian relationship.[78] Unfortunately, the effect was only temporary. This was largely because Nasser believed (genuinely, in the opinion of the CIA) that the United States was committed in return 'to give him some military help'.[79] He was offered an arms deal worth $20 million in October 1954, but this was barely one fifth of what he had been expecting.[80] In any case, he argued that domestic pressures made it impossible for him to accept the supervisory military mission required by US legislation. The CIA's attempt to get round this obstacle by handing over the paltry sum of $3 million in a suitcase was taken as an insult by the increasingly suspicious Nasser, who used it to build the 'folly' of Cairo Tower.[81] Eveland, who was sent to discuss the issue and met Nasser (accompanied by his commander-in-chief, Abdel Hakim Amer, and a highly unrealistic list of desired weapons) at Touhami's house in November 1954, recalls: 'I felt that he either expected the CIA to produce a miracle or he'd agreed to see us merely out of Arab hospitality.' But during the fruitless discussions, Nasser sounded a separate warning note. He stated that he 'considered American attachment to Israel dangerous for us in the long run'.[82]

***

Before the revolution, the question of Israel was not a high priority for the Free Officers.[83] Nasser is said to have told a CIA representative that the conspirators' enemies were 'our own superior officers, other Arabs, the British and the Israelis – in that order'.[84] Their problematic neighbour was not mentioned in the revolutionary charter, which focused on expelling the British and fostering domestic development.[85] Moreover, in RCC meetings just after the revolution, according to a senior Free Officer:

> We did not even mention Israel... We didn't even realise that we didn't mention it... It wasn't even in our agenda... We did not ever think to attack Israel because we know that if we attack Israel we are attacking the whole world.[86]

The question remains: should this lack of attention be taken to indicate a more open attitude toward Israel; or did it merely constitute a pragmatic decision to deal with one enemy at a time?

'The idea of throwing the Jews into the sea is propaganda,' Nasser told Richard Crossman in December 1953.[87] Mahmoud Riad, his Foreign Minister, claimed much later that the Egyptian leader 'had always been flexible on the subject of Israel'.[88] Nasser had fought in Palestine in 1948, which at least taught him the dangers for any Egyptian regime of a military confrontation with the Jewish state. It also allowed him to develop reasonable relationships with individual Israelis, through routine negotiations over the repatriation of dead bodies and small gifts of oranges and chocolate.[89] He admitted to having been inspired by conversations with one particular captain about how the Jewish secret resistance movement was organised and world opinion mobilised against the British.[90] Later, he confirmed to a US diplomat:

> that in addition to his friend in Israel he has contacts in Paris and in Turkey through whom he attempts to keep informed about the situation in Israel. He said that, although an eventual settlement with Israel is in his mind, his present contacts are for informational purposes only.[91]

It is generally agreed that Nasser was 'open to contact' by the Israelis on the subject of peace.[92] In early 1953, Foreign Minister Fawzi told Ambassador Caffery that Nasser was considering the 'possibility of eventual agreement with Israel'.[93] When Israel had suggested secret talks to the Free Officers in August 1952, Nasser was the most ready to respond, and although overruled at the time, he was in surreptitious contact with Tel Aviv through a number of intermediaries until 1955.[94] Most significant were the regular meetings between Paris Embassy representatives Shmuel Divon and Abdel Rahman Sadeq, personally authorised by Nasser in January 1953, through which he explicitly sought to strengthen Prime Minister Moshe Sharett in his battle against David Ben Gurion's hardliners.[95] However, Nasser's patience with this strategy ran out in late 1954, and when Sharett used the channel to ask him to save Jewish saboteurs, he concluded that the hardliners had 'the upper hand', telling Sadeq: 'Go and damn him'.[96]

Key insiders, such as Interior Minister Zakaria Mohieddin, are inclined to play down the importance of these contacts on the grounds that 'the Israelis were not serious' – and, in any case, Egypt could not be seen at that time to neglect the Palestinian cause.[97] One aide states that Nasser intended merely:

> to keep the Palestinian issue alive because our generation could not agree with Israel, because they lived the crisis. Maybe the generation following us could solve this tragedy... Abdel Nasser did not have the intention to attack Israel... he wanted the whole matter to freeze, and to remain as it is.[98]

Hoda Abdel Nasser agrees that her father 'knew the Israelis did not want peace', safely accepting proposals only to expose their hypocrisy.[99] Nasser frequently suggested that he saw Zionist Israel as actively 'aggressive and expansionist', seeking to expand 'until it possessed the Nile Valley, part of Iraq and part of the Kingdom of Saudi Arabia'. Nevertheless, he continued to assert that Egypt did not want war.[100]

Whether or not Nasser ever felt that some kind of accommodation with Israel might be possible, developments from July 1954 made it seem increasingly unlikely. Sections of the Israeli military, unknown to Sharett, instigated Egyptian Jews to sabotage Western institutions in order to make it appear that the regime had lost control of the Muslim Brotherhood, deterring British evacuation. Zakaria Mohieddin denies that this was an important factor. 'The sabotage did not cut the contacts. It is the unseriousness of the offers which we had that prevented our reaching a solution.'[101] However, Nasser did lay increasing emphasis on Israeli 'aggression' in his public speeches at that time, and one of his security officers claims he thought the aim was to force him out of office.[102] 'Israel is a friend of no one but Israel,' broadcast the Egyptian leader in September 1954.[103] The following month Caffery reported that although 'up to a few months ago', they had been discussing the 'possibility of eventual agreement with Israel', that had been changed by 'what Egyptians consider to be recent Israeli aggressive tactics'.[104]

However, this does not imply that the leaders now expected a major confrontation, still less that they sought one. Captured Egyptian military documents suggest that, although they saw the probability of some sort of armed clash with Israel as increasing from 1954, they continued to believe that it would be strictly limited in scope.[105] On 23 December, Kermit Roosevelt was apparently still urging Nasser toward secret meetings with an Israeli official in a personal letter:

> It appears to many of us in Washington you are in danger of walking into some well laid Israeli traps... which will handicap seriously

the ability of your friends in the United States to counter Zionist pressures here. As you are aware, these pressures are steadily mounting.[106]

Even after Ben Gurion had replaced Sharett as Minister of Defence in January 1955, Nasser continued to maintain: 'War has no place in the constructive policy which we have prepared for our people.'[107]

***

Nevertheless, 1955 was the year in which the foundations of war were to be laid, and in which Egypt's relations with all its enemies deteriorated sharply. The initial trigger was the Baghdad Pact, signed by Turkey and Iraq on 24 February. Nasser believed that this mutual defence agreement 'was an attempt, led by Britain, to suck in the other Arab states and isolate Egypt'.[108] Remembering previous British treaties, Cairo saw it as a means of renewing the colonial presence under another guise: 'They have aims, and we will be treated as we were treated before.'[109] These tensions were brought to the fore in Sir Anthony Eden's sole meeting with Nasser, at a British Embassy dinner in Cairo in February 1955. Their radically different perspectives were barely concealed by the surface bonhomie. Eden felt Nasser seemed friendly, but was vexed when he seized the chance of 'suddenly holding hands' for the photographer.[110] Nasser thought Eden, slipping more or less appropriate Arabic proverbs into the conversation at every opportunity to impress his new wife, behaved like 'a prince dealing with vagabonds'.[111] The British Foreign Minister suggested that Nasser should not treat the Baghdad Pact as a crime; the Egyptian leader laughed as he retorted, 'No, but it is one.'[112]

Unsurprisingly, the two men failed to come to any agreement over Middle East defence. Nevertheless, Nasser still thought they might be able to do business. Even after Eden had become Prime Minister, and Britain had acceded to the Baghdad Pact in April, the Egyptians saw an advantage in trying to improve relations.[113]

Perhaps neither side tried very hard. The British Ambassador's failure to meet Nasser at the airport on his return from the Bandung Afro-Asian Conference that spring caused a small controversy, and contacts remained uneasy. That October, Egypt signed a Mutual Defence Agreement with Saudi Arabia, then involved in the Buraimi border dispute with the UK. The following month, Nasser did praise the 'constructive attitude' Eden displayed in his Guildhall speech on the Arab-Israeli conflict.[114] US Intelligence suggested that although Egypt retained her strong hatred of British 'imperialism', nevertheless:

> Egypt continues to have important economic and military ties with the UK. Egyptian leaders not only retain a certain respect for UK advice, but also recognize that the UK continues to exercise influence in Jordan...[115]

It was precisely the question of Jordan, however, that was to upset this fragile balance. Nasser thought that he had received assurances from both the Foreign Secretary, Harold Macmillan, and the British Ambassador, Sir Humphrey Trevelyan, that Britain was prepared to 'freeze' the Baghdad Pact as it was, inviting no new Arab members.[116] But in December 1955, the Templer military mission was sent to Jordan in almost open contravention of this assurance. Nasser decided Eden 'was no longer to be trusted'.[117]

Nasser's deep distrust of the Baghdad Pact may be explained in the context of Arab regional rivalries. The existence of an anti-Soviet defence agreement in the Middle East did not in itself disturb the Egyptian President. However, he suspected that it constituted a Western attempt to sideline Cairo in favour of Baghdad.[118] Nasser and the Iraqi leader, Nuri Said, were in direct competition for both Arab legitimacy and Western assistance, and their interests inevitably clashed.[119] Nuri particularly objected to the Egyptian *Voice of the Arabs* radio station, launched in July 1953, which he condemned to the Egyptian Minister of Guidance, Salah Salem, as far too lowbrow. Salem, known as 'the Dancing Major' and the butt of many a joke, hurried home to demand that the great Egyptian author Taha Hussein be put on the air immediately. It had to be gently explained to him that Nuri was in fact resentful of the massive popularity of *Voice of the Arabs*, and the way in which it promoted the Arab nationalist idea, in simple terms, to Arabs everywhere. Nuri would also have disapproved of the radio station's strong links with Egyptian Intelligence's regional networks.[120]

The Iraqis claimed that Salah Salem and later Nasser himself had said that they understood the need for Iraq to join the Baghdad Pact. But when it was finally announced in early 1955, the Egyptians responded with an Arab summit and hostile propaganda.[121] In early March, Egypt, Syria and Saudi Arabia hastily agreed their own alternative, all-Arab alliance.[122] The Egyptian press was full of personal attacks on Nuri Said, who was quoted as announcing: 'I am no longer one of you, I have become a Zionist. I have no relationships with the Arabs anymore!'[123]

The Egyptian Ambassador to London claimed the Pact was 'a Turkish-Iraqi plot for the eventual dismemberment of Syria'.[124] On 1 March, Nasser's first meeting with the new US Ambassador, Henry Byroade, was entirely devoted to discussion of the Baghdad Pact. Byroade noted that the Egyptian leader's hatred of his Iraqi counterpart seemed personal, based on the feeling that he had been 'cast aside' by the US in Nuri's favour.[125] 'Nasser is convinced,' reported the British Ambassador in March 1955, 'that Nuri in concluding the Pact with Turkey is working to isolate Egypt and thus fulfil his original conception (dating from 1942) of an Arab League in which Egypt would have no part.'[126] Nasser's own speeches painted the Iraqi leader as utterly, foolishly dependent on the United States and Britain. He accused Nuri of trying to unite the countries of the Fertile Crescent, excluding Egypt as 'outside the Arab field'.[127]

In June, again speaking to Byroade, Nasser equated Iraq with Israel as an enemy seeking to humiliate Egypt.[128] The difference, of course, was that Nasser saw the Iraqi people as part of his own Arab constituency, and was always careful to express in his rhetoric how 'Egypt holds in respect the Arab people of Iraq'. For their sake, he would 'put up with anything the Iraqi government may venture'.[129] Throughout his political career, Nasser's triumvirate of enemies was to consist of imperialism, Zionism and Arab reaction. In his early conception, however, the third term had generally been applied to hostile groups *within* Egypt. By 1956, the Egyptian regime was clearly beginning to use the image of a triangular imperialist-Zionist-reactionary enemy against Iraq. 'Britain and the USA – the perpetrators of the Palestine tragedy – are today the cherished allies of Nuri al-Said.'[130]

***

This context also affected reactions to the major Israeli reprisal raid on a military camp in Gaza of 28 February 1955, which has been repeatedly identified, by Nasser and others, as a critical 'turning point'.[131] Some authors suggest that this is misleading, arguing that it merely intensified the existing Egyptian priority of battling the Baghdad Pact.[132] However, the Raid did have a dramatic effect on Egyptian images of Israel. Nasser had always seen Israel as potentially aggressive, but the Gaza Raid came as a nasty shock, because it implied an imminent threat.[133] He told the British Ambassador that although he had previously felt there was 'a reasonable chance of peace', afterwards he lived 'in constant fear of an Israeli attack'.[134] Described by

Egyptians as 'violent', 'butchery', a 'sneak attack' and an 'insult', the Gaza incident was viewed as part of a longstanding plot to weaken the Arabs. As a result, the Palestine issue became 'a matter of life or death'.[135]

This was because the Gaza Raid caused major internal difficulties for the Egyptian regime. 'It was impossible,' explains one insider, 'a military government coming out after revolution and not being able to defend itself'.[136] The incident caused extreme anger in the army, forcing Nasser to step up his own rhetoric.[137] Egypt had not been defeated in 1948, he announced as he opened a new military college the following month; and today, 'let me tell Israel that we are ready for her'.[138] The Egyptians turned their primary attention to seeking arms from any available source – a response so obvious that they did not even need to discuss it.[139] 'Now we are asking for them to save our lives,' Nasser told Byroade, comparing Israel to those other temporary interlopers, the Crusaders. 'The situation has changed completely. Now I can't wait.'[140] Cairo also stepped up support for the *fidā'iyūn* striking at Israel across the Gaza border.[141]

US difficulties sustaining an alliance with both Egypt and Israel were crystallised by the Gaza Raid. The *Al-Ahram* newspaper suggested that America 'shares the guilt for the Gaza attack, for it planned it as a way of forcing the Arabs to conclude peace with Israel'.[142] Members of Nasser's circle, such as Ali Sabri and Salah Salem, claim that he saw the raid, together with the coolness developing between Egypt and America, as evidence the US had been co-operating with Israel throughout, and was using her to blackmail Nasser into line with Western defence requirements and the Baghdad Pact.[143] When he returned from the Bandung Conference in late April 1955, Nasser was clearly extremely suspicious of Ambassador Byroade.[144] He complained that:

> US personnel in Egypt and Arab states were spreading rumours about the Revolutionary Command Council's instability, the American representative in the Sudan was conspiring against Egypt, the Eisenhower Administration was sabotaging foreign support for the High Aswan Dam and undermining the Egyptian economy through its cotton policy, and the Americans were intending to pressure Egypt into making peace with Israel.[145]

The arms issue, however, was the crux of the problem. Nasser blamed 'Jewish and Zionist influence' for the failure of negotiations with the USA, concluding 'it would be a miracle if we ever obtained any arms from this direction'.[146] He warned Byroade that, while he sincerely wished to retain his friendship with the United States, he had concluded that he should seek arms from the USSR, since 'if Israel really started a war the Western powers would again boycott the Arab world as they did before, but still let Israel obtain equipment'.[147] And on 27 September, Nasser duly announced the 'Czech' Arms Deal, despite what he called the 'uproar in Washington'.[148] This was principally expressed through the visits of a plethora of CIA envoys, including Kermit Roosevelt. The agents occupied themselves in sending home emergency telegrams to undermine the US Ambassador, or gleefully writing controversial speeches for Nasser in a back room while the stately British Ambassador fretted outside, but they did nothing to change the Egyptian decision.[149] Explaining his position to American diplomats, Nasser referred once more to the Gaza Raid. He was now convinced that the US Government 'was trying to keep Egypt weak and that this resulted from Jewish influence'.[150]

***

'It's off,' Nasser told his negotiator Salah Gohar after the Gaza Raid, ruling out further Egyptian-Israeli talks.[151] Nevertheless, the possibility continued to be discussed for a surprisingly long time. Nasser certainly emphasised repeatedly that he did not want war with Israel, which might 'mean his destruction'.[152] In early April 1955, Foreign Minister Fawzi, claiming to be speaking with Nasser's secret authority, told Byroade that the 'iron was now hot' for Arab-Israeli peace: next year would be too late. Nasser himself, a few days later, was less forthcoming, but agreed to discuss the question further.[153] He gave a *Newsweek* interview suggesting that peace was possible if Israel showed goodwill 'by accepting the UN resolutions with regard to refugees, by paying just compensation to them, and by internationalising Jerusalem'.[154] But in August, Fawzi tentatively suggested to the US ('don't quote me,' he begged) that even the refugee right of return might be abandoned in return for territorial concessions in the disputed Negev region.[155] At the end of the year, the Egyptian leader came to a secret agreement with the CIA to make peace with Israel.[156] He later characterised it, rather grandiosely, as the 'most tremendous and difficult decision of any Arab leader this generation'. But he still emphasised that it would be a slow process.[157] Even within the regime, only Ali Sabri and Zakaria Mohieddin could be informed.[158]

These successive peace initiatives (Projects 'Alpha' and 'Gamma', as they were known to Western diplomats) in retrospect had no chance of success. Neither did the secret shuttle diplomacy of US Special Envoy Robert Anderson in early 1956. Nasser wanted the whole of the Negev in return for recognition of the Jewish state; while Israel, seeking full peace, refused to give up any land.[159] Moreover, concessions to Israel would have been extremely risky for Nasser in the Arab context. On this basis, many historians argue that the Cairo entered the negotiations in bad faith, seeking merely to gain time and tactical advantage *vis-à-vis* the West.[160] But although Nasser probably had low expectations of 'Alpha', they were founded on the image that he had developed after the Gaza Raid of an actively aggressive Israel: 'a sword pointed at our dignity and liberty' seeking 'domination from Nile to Euphrates'.[161] Egyptian military documents from early 1956 reveal a marked emphasis on Israel's suspected covert activities.[162] Zakaria Mohieddin, who was Anderson's conduit to Nasser, recalls his own perception that 'the Israelis were not serious' and were 'extremists in their solutions'. He used to ask Anderson for specific proposals, but 'nobody used to specify anything'.[163]

However, this does not mean that the Egyptians perceived Israel as likely (or even able) to express her hostility through a full-scale war. The US Embassy found that:

> Nasser appeared decidedly relaxed about the military aspects of a major Israeli attack. He seemed quite positive that his force in the Sinai was capable of conducting a delaying action for two months after which time his striking force now forming in the rear would be available for General Amer to 'play with'.[164]

Nasser told Byroade that he knew he could not win a war against Israel if he started one, but only because, under those circumstances, 'you would feel you had to move in'. Similarly, Ali Sabri reported to the Americans that Nasser felt they were trying to push him too hard with the Anderson mission. Although he believed the Israelis were not seeking a settlement in good faith, he did *not* think they would launch a preventive war. That was simply rhetoric to scare the United States.[165] In line with this belief, from 4 June 1956 Egypt began to reduce her military deployments on the Sinai border. The purpose was to integrate the new Soviet arms, which made Egypt's neighbour seem even less of a threat.[166] 'Israel will not enjoy supremacy again,' announced Nasser.

'We shall have absolute supremacy in all arms.'[167] Amer proclaimed that the Egyptian army could wipe out Israel in 48 hours.[168]

***

Unfortunately, Egyptian relations with both the United States and Britain had come to depend on the prospect of an Arab-Israeli peace. The CIA's last-ditch attempt at the end of 1955 seems to have been a *quid pro quo* for serious discussion by the Western powers and the World Bank of the possibility of financing the ambitious Aswan High Dam project.[169] Nasser was suspicious, seeing even the Dam as a device to increase American influence in Egypt and overthrow him.[170] He feared that any direct contacts with Israel might be used against him, while a personal meeting with Ben Gurion would be 'suicidal'.[171] Most particularly, he thought the lack of realism of the whole enterprise showed the Americans were playing the Israeli game.[172] This seemed to be confirmed when the despatch of US arms to Israel was debated in February 1956. Cairo painted it as a direct and deliberate incitement of further border attacks. 'We think you have been conducting a comic opera in the Middle East during the past two weeks,' exclaimed Nasser angrily.[173] By March, it was clear that the Anderson mission was over and Dulles was blaming Egypt. Washington began to implement the alternative 'Omega' plan to 'contain' Nasser, delaying aid to Egypt and assisting Baghdad Pact countries.[174]

The original initiative behind 'Omega' appears to have been British. Immediately after the Czech Arms Deal, the senior British diplomat Evelyn Shuckburgh 'wrote a paper setting out the various alternatives before us, and concluding that we must first try to frighten Nasser, then to bribe him, and if neither works, get rid of him'.[175] On 28 November 1955, he sent a top secret telegram to Sir Ivone Kirkpatrick, the Permanent Under-Secretary of State for Foreign Affairs, which made it clear that the idea was not new to the Foreign Office. The original draft contained a paragraph that was later deleted:

> It looks very much as if the only possible ways of disrupting the present course of the Egyptian régime were:-
> (i)   the death of Nasser;
> (ii) a free hand to the Israelis.

On the same day, a telegram to the British Ambassador in Washington explained that Nasser 'was dangerously committed to the Communists', advocating the advantages of a joint Anglo-American initiative 'to overthrow him if possible'.[176]

The situation degenerated further after the new British Foreign Secretary, Selwyn Lloyd, visited Cairo in February 1956. The meeting was marred by a misunderstanding over the Jordanian King Hussein's dismissal of General Glubb, his British Chief of Staff. Each side apparently believed the other had arranged the timing, but Nasser's inability to stop laughing at Lloyd's expression (like a 'puzzled fish') hampered his efforts to convince the Foreign Secretary of his lack of complicity.[177] Sir Anthony Eden, hearing the reports back in London, was furious. He telephoned Foreign Office Minister Anthony Nutting, raging: 'I don't want him neutralised. I want him murdered.'[178] (Eden expressed the same sentiment to Ivone Kirkpatrick, who apparently responded: 'I don't think we have a department for that sort of thing, Prime Minister. But if we do, it certainly is not under my control.'[179]) Meanwhile, a privileged intelligence source codenamed LUCKY BREAK was reporting that Nasser, under increasing Soviet influence, planned to take over the Arab world.[180] On 8 March, Shuckburgh remembers, 'both we and the Americans really gave up hope of Nasser and began to look around for means of destroying him'.[181]

***

But was Nasser aware of the Anglo-American attitude? He certainly did not fail to notice the general deterioration in relations. On 15 March 1956, Ambassador Trevelyan wrote a long letter to Shuckburgh, reporting the words of Nasser's confidant Mohammed Hassanein Heikal, who claimed to be 'greatly perturbed' by the widening gap between Egypt and the United Kingdom.[182] Towards the end of the month, Nasser gave conciliatory interviews to the *Sunday Times* and the *Observer,* once again suggesting a moratorium on the Baghdad Pact, but when he received no response from Eden other than a dismissive Foreign Office statement, he took it (as Nutting suggests that Eden intended it) as an open declaration of war.[183] The Foreign Office wrote in April 1956 of the importance of 'keeping Nasser guessing', pending a final policy decision. But it may already have been too late.[184]

On 31 March, Secret Intelligence Service (SIS) officers allegedly revealed plans to kill or depose Nasser to CIA agents Eveland and Eichelberger, who were sufficiently alarmed to leak the information back to the Egyptian leader.[185] Nasser was, Ali Sabri told American officials in Cairo the following day, 'extremely upset' that the USA and

UK had embarked on 'some secret policy decision' aimed at his destruction. Relations with Britain, Sabri said, were deteriorating so much that 'I don't know what's going to happen'.[186] On 5 April, Ambassador Trevelyan wrote to Shuckburgh expressing concern at the rumours going round Cairo. 'Nasser's suspicions of us must have been raised to the greatest possible extent.'[187] That month, Egypt entered into the 'Jeddah Pact' with Saudi Arabia and Yemen, based largely on common opposition to the UK.[188] In May, the Egyptian leader reached new (and, in retrospect, ironic) heights of hyperbole when he wondered aloud to the US Ambassador whether things might have reached the point where the British 'would even spur Israeli aggressions against Egypt' – although subsequent developments suggest that he still failed to see this as a genuine possibility.[189]

Nevertheless, Nasser may not have been aware of the murkier aspects of the second stage of the 'Omega' plan, according to which the United States began to build up Saudi Arabia as a rival to Egypt and planned a pro-Iraqi coup in Syria ('Operation Straggle'). He certainly paid relatively little attention to tales of British covert shenanigans, even doubting US motives for relaying the information. 'Is this intended to frighten us or to worsen our relations with the British?' he minuted Eichelberger's report of the CIA-SIS meeting.[190] The Egyptian leader seems to have been much more deeply concerned by his battle against the British press, which raged throughout 1956. Nasser made a point of keeping up with foreign press cuttings and radio transcripts, and was always thin-skinned about their contents, but in April he complained to US Ambassador Byroade that the British newspapers 'were now treating him publicly as an enemy.'[191] He was so angry that, according to the Libyan Prime Minister, the mere mention of the UK 'made him go purple in the face and start pacing round the room like a wild animal'.[192]

Nasser did not necessarily see the newspaper war as a fight to the death, however. Occasionally it even amused him, as when he cut out a *Daily Telegraph* article entitled 'The Master Plan of Nasser' and sent it to his Intelligence Chief with a note: 'If they are accusing us of doing all that then we had better do it.'[193] In May, he apparently assured Trevelyan that Egyptian propaganda attacks on the UK and her allies would stop, 'and for a while this was done'.[194] And in a speech in June following the evacuation of the last British soldier, although Nasser once more excoriated the British press, his tone was relatively mild:

> In regard to Britain, she has fulfilled her obligations under the Evacuation Agreement. Britain had 80,000 troops in the Canal Zone.

They have all left. In connection with Britain we have no aggressive aims against them at all.[195]

On the eve of the Suez Crisis, the UK was seen as an enemy to be treated with caution, but Nasser did not seem to realise the full extent of the personal hostility directed against him in London.

***

This was nothing, however, beside his disregard of France. Given the importance of French enmity toward Egypt in the development of the Suez affair, it is remarkable how little emphasis Cairo had previously placed on France as an adversary – despite open threats from the French side. There are suggestions that the French Secret Service made an attempt on Nasser's life in 1954, and Paris was known to be deeply opposed to Cairo, seeing Egyptian support for the Algerian rebels as a principal cause of the ongoing battles in that North African colony.[196] In January 1956, Tharwat Okasha, a former Free Officer stationed at the Paris Embassy, claims to have told Nasser that the French would attack Egypt that year. But the Egyptian leader, together with the rest of the RCC, still rejected the possibility. France was never seen as a crucial enemy because her hostility was interpreted almost entirely in relation to other actors. When, in February 1954, the exiled Okasha was first sent to Paris as a military attaché, he was asked 'to do certain jobs'. The first was to find out about French arms exports to Israel; the second was to seek information on the Algerian situation.[197]

France was seen as Israel's most dedicated Western supporter, and the Egyptians were particularly sensitive to the French supply of weapons to the Jewish state.[198] By May 1956, Nasser was working himself up over the issue, noted Byroade, referring perhaps to his speech of 13 May:

France yesterday gave Israel twelve new planes. I want them to know that such a step does not terrify us nor does it cause us to lose confidence in ourselves... France, which is giving Israel arms, wants to lure us away from supporting the right of self-determination for the struggling peoples of North Africa.[199]

Egyptian solidarity with the Algerian nationalist insurgents constituted the other great grievance between the two countries. In March 1956, the French Foreign Minister, Christian Pineau, had visited Egypt in a final effort to seek a rapprochement. It failed. As a result, French troops in Algeria increased by 100,000, and additional arms were shipped to Israel.[200] The very nature of these two disputes, however, led Cairo to underestimate Paris as an independent enemy. France was seen as hostile inasmuch as she was an important ally of Israel and opposed to the Arab nationalist struggle in her colonies. But in neither of these capacities was it believed she could present a *direct* threat to Egypt. Six months later, the Treaty of Sèvres would prove this to have been a major miscalculation.

2
Eliminate the Past: Nationalising the Suez Canal Company

> *We shall eliminate the past by regaining our right to the Suez Canal... At this moment as I talk to you some of your Egyptian brethren are proceeding to administer the canal company and to run its affairs.*[201] – Gamal Abdel Nasser

On 24 July 1956, at precisely 12.32 pm, a young man named Abdel Hamid Abubakr arrived for an appointment with the President of Egypt. He was accompanying his boss, Mahmoud Younis, who was in charge of the Revolutionary Command Council's Technical Division. The two men expected to be congratulated on the successful opening of their new pipeline, and were surprised at the unusually tense atmosphere in Nasser's office. Two minutes late for their meeting (relatively prompt by Cairo standards), they were roundly scolded. When they were shown in to see the President, his opening gambit was equally disconcerting. 'What do you know about the Suez Canal?' he asked.

They did not know much, although Abubakr had sometimes entertained friends at a rather good club nearby. Nasser then let them in on a state secret. In two days' time, he intended to make a historic speech in Alexandria, when he would announce the nationalisation of the Suez Canal Company. Younis kissed and congratulated the President. It was 'like a dream', recalls Abubakr. The Canal Company, owned by British and French shareholders, was the ultimate symbol of foreign domination in Egypt. The massive building project, directed in the 1860s by the French engineer Ferdinand de Lesseps, had reputedly killed 125,000 Egyptian workers. The Khedive's default on his loan had been used to justify the British 'temporary occupation', which had only truly ended the previous month, on 13 June, when the last British soldier left the Canal Zone base.

Having hailed the President with great enthusiasm, the two men turned to leave, but Nasser stopped them. 'Where are you going?' he asked. 'You will go and nationalise the canal.' He gave them some books so they could read up on it, and 48 hours in which to come up with a comprehensive plan. It was to be a top-secret operation. They must choose trusted men to assist them in taking over the company offices, but even these would be held at gunpoint as they received the fatal information, or issued with sealed orders, not to be opened until the appointed time. The signal was a particular codeword in Nasser's speech: the name of 'de Lesseps'. In the event, this final flourish caused more trouble than it was worth. Nasser was so afraid that the officers listening to his broadcast on their radios would miss the name that he repeated it incessantly, to the bewilderment of the massed crowds, who knew little and cared less about the French engineer. Since there was at this stage no possibility of a last-minute cancellation, they might just as well have synchronised their watches. But that would have destroyed the legend.[202]

***

Unfortunately, the legend surrounding this defining moment in modern Egyptian history tends to obscure the actual sequence of events. The summer of 1956 is often described like a slow-motion table tennis match. President Nasser, offended by Western hostility as expressed through the 'Omega' plan, granted diplomatic recognition to communist China on 16 May. In response, the United States decided to withdraw its offer to help fund the Aswan High Dam. This was finally made clear in a meeting between the US Secretary of State, John Foster Dulles, and the Egyptian Ambassador to Washington, Ahmed Hussein, on 19 July. Unsurprised but deeply offended, Nasser's knockout riposte was a highly dramatic speech at Alexandria a week later, nationalising the Suez Canal Company in the teeth of the Western Powers, in order to use the revenues to pay for the Dam.

It is a compelling tale, but it raises more questions than it answers. For example, when was the decision to nationalise the Suez Canal actually made, and who was involved? Initially, the story seems to imply that the nationalisation was a straightforward response, by the President, to the withdrawal of Aswan Dam funding. Nasser heard the news of Dulles' refusal on 19 July, in an aeroplane with the Indian premier, Jawaharlal Nehru. They were returning together from a Non-Aligned summit at Brioni in Yugoslavia. The well-informed journalist

Mohammed Hassanein Heikal claims in one account that Nasser had already decided to nationalise the canal by the time he landed in Egypt.[203] In other books, he dates the decision to the morning of 20 July, recounting the President's words to him on the telephone:

> he said that the theme of his speech would be that Egypt would build the High Dam even if we had to build it with shovels... I asked him if he remembered his idea of having half the revenue of the Suez Canal... and using that money to build the Dam. He replied in a very tense voice: 'But why only half?'[204]

Nehru, however, who remained in Cairo until 21 July, believed that Nasser's first reaction had been to abandon the Aswan Dam project.[205] Nasser himself later stated that he did not begin researching the issue until Nehru left. He claimed to have made his final decision on 23 July, after various meetings, discussions and studies.[206] However, other regime members are unanimous that the President made the decision at an earlier stage, assisted by just a few close aides. Perhaps 14 people were given advance notice of the nationalisation.[207] Abdel Latif Baghdadi, a member of the RCC, went to Nasser's house on the evening of 21 July. In the garden, he met Ali Sabri, who informed Baghdadi of the national-isation plans, presenting them as finalised, and the President himself shortly confirmed it.[208] The RCC, which had been disbanded on Nasser's recent election as President, was specially reconvened for consultation on the morning of 24 July. Immediately afterwards, as we have seen, the President set Younis his task. Finally, just two hours before the speech, the Cabinet was informed. Although 'many of them were very perturbed', Nasser allowed no real discussion, confining them to his house in Alexandria to preserve secrecy.[209]

However, even if we take the earliest date given, 19 July, it raises certain problems. First, almost all sources suggest that when Nasser sent Ambassador Hussein to Washington to convey his full acceptance of the long-disputed US conditions for the Aswan Dam loan, it was in the belief that he would be refused. Heikal claims that Nasser expected the United States to back out of funding the Dam as early as April, and stories to that effect were soon current in Cairo.[210] Nasser was aware of the potential fallout in the US from his diplomatic recognition of China in May, which confirmed growing Congressional opposition to the Aswan Dam project.[211] That recognition therefore suggests that Nasser had already given up hope of fruitful alliance with Washington – which must be taken to include funding for the Aswan Dam.

Ambassador Byroade was informed as early as 15 June that Nasser no longer believed in the possibility of a US loan, and was considering acceptance of a Soviet offer instead.[212] Afterwards, it was confirmed to him that the President had not been surprised by Dulles' refusal, having expected all along that the United States 'would not follow through'.[213] Ten years later, Nasser himself agreed: 'I was sure that Mr Dulles would not help us by financing the Aswan Dam.'[214] Under these circumstances, it beggars belief that the Egyptian President would not have made plans in case he was proved right. 'Of course,' exclaims regime insider Amin Howeidy, Nasser was already planning the nationalisation when he sent Hussein back to Washington. 'If it happens that they will give us what we want, he will cancel it. If not, he will act.'[215] It seems that Nasser even hinted to his horrified Ambassador that he might nationalise the Canal Company in the probable event of a US withdrawal of funding. He said to Hussein 'that he felt there was really no chance' that the loan would materialise, but 'quietly told him that if he kept his nerve, everything would turn out all right'.[216]

***

However, there is also strong evidence that the Egyptian regime had been planning – or at least contemplating – the nationalisation of the Suez Canal Company for some time. It had been on the agenda from the inception of the revolution: it was written down, according to Howeidy, in Nasser's 'black notebook', waiting for an opportunity to be put into action.[217] The case is not absolutely proven by the fact that preparations were being made as early as 1955 to enable Egypt to manage the canal. The concession was in any case to revert to Egypt in 1968, and this was the ostensible target.[218] Asked, in a press conference following the announcement of the Evacuation Agreement, whether Egypt would nationalise the canal after the British left, Nasser replied: 'I think we can wait fifteen years.'[219] Soon after, he gave a talk on Cairo Radio to mark the anniversary of the opening of the canal.

> Compatriots, I announce in your name the beginning of the period that leads to Egypt's taking over the Suez Canal establishment when the period of the concession expires... We are beginning this period now because we want to avoid falling into the errors of the past, when problems caught us unprepared ... I am happy on this occasion to be able to praise the good and friendly relations existing between the Republic's Government and the Suez Canal Company.[220]

Years later, Nasser continued to insist that there had been no national-isation plans prior to the Aswan Dam refusal, although 'we studied the management by our mobilisation department of the army in order to be ready to take over the canal by the time of the end of the concession'.[221]

However, given the scale of the studies, the assertion of such long-term thinking does not ring true. Ever generous in sharing his experi-ence of fighting colonialism, Nasser later told President Kaunda of Zambia that the prerequisite for successful nationalisation was detailed preparation. 'Before nationalising Suez Canal, we were sure that we were able to run Suez Canal.'[222] Although much of this preparation was practical, readying Egypt to manage the canal itself (and thus might in theory have been aimed at the expiry of the concession), work was also done on specific legal and historical justifications for nationalisation. From 1955, almost every branch of the Egyptian government had its Suez Canal research unit, including the army, the Foreign Ministry and Military Intelligence, not to mention the actual Office of Suez Canal Affairs.[223] Ali Sabri headed a top-secret committee in the Prime Minister's Office devoted to consideration of this issue.[224] President Tito of Yugoslavia would later assert that Nasser had informed him of plans to nationalise the canal as early as February 1955.[225] Given this wealth of evidence, there is little credibility to Heikal's remarkable claim that Nasser *falsely* suggested he had been planning the move for two years, in order to absolve Dulles of the guilt of provoking the crisis, and so to help him restrain the British and French.[226]

In summary, nationalisation was on Nasser's agenda at some future point, it was closely linked in his mind to the departure of the British, he no longer expected the United States to fund the Aswan Dam, and he may even have toyed with the idea of nationalising the canal as a response. However, there is no evidence that he had a deliberate plan or timetable leading to nationalisation in July 1956. Most of the canal management studies do seem to have been triggered by the signature of the Evacuation Agreement with the British in 1954.[227] On this basis, it is tempting to link the timing of the nationalisation to the departure of the last British soldier from the Canal Zone, just over a month previ-ously. But the obvious fact that the presence of UK troops inhibited nationalisation does not show that their absence immediately necessi-tated it. As late as 8 June, the Egyptian government had reached a new agreement with the Canal Company, arranging for the continuation of the concession and training of more Egyptian pilots.[228] Nasser may have been awaiting a suitable opportunity, but he was 'not in a hurry' – indeed, one source identifies 1960 as his 'target date'.[229]

It seems unlikely, therefore, that Nasser deliberately provoked the July crisis to provide a timely excuse to make his move. There is too much evidence of genuine anger within the Egyptian regime, and an *ad hoc* flavour to the decision-making in the week preceding the nationalisation speech.[230] Members of the Egyptian elite were largely surprised by Nasser's announcement. Abubakr's likening of it to a 'dream' is echoed by Sayyid Mar'i, the Agriculture Minister, who experienced the greatest shock of his life. 'This was not a decision; it was a bombshell – it was more than a bombshell.'[231] Awed astonishment was the keynote of the massive public rejoicing, when huge crowds mobbed the President, trying to kiss his 'feet, hands and face', while the harassed Interior Minister, Zakaria Mohieddin, was forced 'to shield Nasser from the adulations of devotees who persisted in climbing into [his] automobile'.[232]

Foreign observers were similarly blindsided by the nationalisation. The US State Department barely mentioned the Suez Canal when considering likely Egyptian responses to the refusal of Aswan Dam funding.[233] The day before the much-heralded speech at Alexandria, which Nasser had publicly promised would answer all Western provocations, Byroade's best guess was that the President might terminate the moribund American aid programme.[234] 'The art of diplomacy is not dead,' purred Selwyn Lloyd, congratulating himself on Egypt's quiet reception of the Aswan Dam funding withdrawal – although it is unclear precisely what he thought British diplomacy had to do with it.[235] Even the USSR seems to have been taken aback.[236] On balance, nationalisation of the Suez Canal Company cannot be considered the most obvious riposte for Nasser at this stage. Thus his decision requires further explanation.

***

'It is not so much the withdrawal of the money which we mind,' Zakaria Mohieddin told the British Ambassador, Sir Humphrey Trevelyan. 'We can find other ways of financing the High Dam. It is the way in which it was done.'[237] It may be, therefore, that the explanation lies in the press statement issued by Dulles on 19 July, in which he announced and explained the funding withdrawal. One of his stated reasons concerned the rights of Sudan, part of which would be flooded as a result of the scheme. Another was that the enterprise might overload the Egyptian economy. Nasser deeply resented these 'insincere' justifications.[238] In his nationalisation speech, he accused the US of seeking 'to sow dissension between Egypt and the Sudan' for its own ends.[239] The insult to the Egyptian economy stung particularly.[240] This was a 'slap in the face' to Egypt, decided Nasser and his advisors, when they met to discuss a response.[241] 'If a shameful clamour, raised in Washington..., announces by lies, deceit and delusion that the Egyptian economy is impotent and unstable,' the President announced, 'I look at them and tell them: "Die in your rage. You shall not dominate or tyrannise over us."'[242]

Nasser's first reaction, however, related to a different aspect of Dulles' statement. Showing it to Heikal and Fawzi on the way home from Brioni, he exclaimed: 'This is not a withdrawal... it is an attack on the regime and an invitation to the people of Egypt to bring it down.'[243] From the point of view of a sensitive dictator, the phrasing could be seen as highly inflammatory. Nasser complained in his nationalisation speech:

> The US Secretary of State addressed the Egyptian people saying... What we are talking about concerns only Gamal Abdel Nasser and not the Egyptian people. They addressed themselves directly to the Egyptian people. This method was quite clear and obvious. We have had many years of experience of it.[244]

Nasser's understanding of the funding withdrawal as a direct attempt to undermine his regime explains his dramatic reaction. The purpose, he later told Nutting, was 'to show that Egypt was not going to be pushed around by the West'.[245] In the wider context of 'Omega', the wording of Dulles's statement could itself be interpreted as an aggression.

***

Images of a hostile West thus played a key role in Nasser's decision to nationalise the Suez Canal Company. Britain and America 'suck the blood of peoples and usurp their rights', he declared, linking all his principal enemies in a grand alliance:

> America, the leader of the free world, supports imperialist France in murdering the Algerians in Algeria. Britain also supports her... Israel is America's protégé and gets assistance – because Israel without assistance cannot live.[246]

'You fellows are out to kill me,' he told the US Ambassador. 'And all I can do is protect myself. I tell you this, I am not going to be killed.'[247] To his confidant Heikal, Nasser complained that Dulles and Eden had been deceiving Egypt all along. 'They pressed us for peace with Israel, they pressed us for pacts, they pressed us to extend the Suez Canal concession and all they wanted to do was to increase their own influence.'[248]

This raises a puzzle. If Nasser was indeed so convinced that the West was hostile and seeking to overthrow him, why did he provide a perfect pretext? In order to answer this question, it is necessary to delve more deeply into the thinking of the Egyptian leader during the week preceding the nationalisation, and especially his estimations of his enemies' capabilities. As he wrestled with his choice on the night of 20 July, Nasser, ever the methodical staff officer, wrote a detailed 'appreciation of the situation'. This document shows that the President was indeed thinking in terms of active enmity from the Western powers. However, he also believed that they would be unable to attack him openly. He related this in the short term to their lack of an immediate military capability in the region; and in the long term to anticipated support for Egypt from the Third World and Soviet bloc. Nasser thought that the danger of intervention would peak at 80 per cent in early August, 'decreasing each week through political activities' to a mere 20 per cent by the end of September. He relied on his Foreign Minister, Mahmoud Fawzi, musing:

> How can we make the political situation swim? Fawzi can do that. He is an expert in floating things... Can we gain two months by politics? If we succeed we shall be safe. So much will depend on Fawzi.[249]

The percentages alone are implausible. Had Nasser genuinely believed that nationalising the canal would lead to four chances in five (more, if one takes the figures as cumulative) of invasion by a massively superior force, it is impossible to believe that he would have gone ahead. Moreover, other evidence suggests that the President was more optimistic than otherwise about the possibility of avoiding conflict. Troop deployments at the end of July did not suggest preparations to face a Western operation.[250] 'There will be no war,' Khaled Mohieddin quotes Nasser as asserting flatly.[251] 'I did not ask you to fight,' the President retorted to an anxious Sayyid Mar'i, two hours before his speech. 'If war breaks out it will be Abdel Hakim Amir who is fighting, not you.'[252] Nasser told his aides that the West would begin with threats:

Political threats, psychological threats. And then at last, military threats, which can be changed to a real war. We have to escape war as we can. We don't want war. And we have to avoid it, by changing our priorities except for one thing: the nationalisation of the Suez Canal.[253]

Nasser believed that the upcoming elections and international public opinion would restrain the Americans from participating in any attack, although they would probably 'give their blessing under the table'.[254] They 'could not resort to force because that would show them up as vindictive bullies, and in any case the Saudis would restrain them'.[255] To help them along, he shifted the focus of his rhetorical bile to Britain and France. 'The uproar which we anticipated has been taking place in London and Paris,' he declared two days after his bombshell, carefully avoiding any mention of Washington.[256] He attempted to win Byroade's sympathy by presenting the nationalisation as a straightforward fund-raising measure: a relatively pro-Western alternative, in other words, to the acceptance of Soviet aid for Dam.[257]

Nasser's 'appreciation of the situation' predicted that Eden would react violently, and that this violence would 'take the form of military action'.[258] However, he did not behave as though he expected a British attack, believing they would be deterred by fear of the Arab world's anger.[259] The key to this apparent contradiction lies in the timing. In his 'appreciation', written on 20 July, Nasser clearly stated that the British would have to intervene immediately. 'It must appear as a direct reaction.' Thus the *real* possibility of violence would depend 'on how many troops the British have ready for quick intervention from the Mediterranean, Aden, Cyprus or Malta'.[260] That day, Nasser apparently asked Cypriot and Maltese dissidents for a report on British military forces in the area. These reports were so important to him that he delayed his nationalisation announcement from 24 July to receive them. When they arrived, they convinced him that the British would require two months to assemble a force strong enough to intervene. 'All I need is one month, so this is long enough for me,' noted Nasser.[261] Later, he recalled the timing slightly differently, but the general idea was the same:

It was clear to us that Britain would not be ready to have any military movement before three or four months. We studied the deployment of the British troops and... thought at that time that it would be possible to reach a sort of settlement during those three months.[262]

Nasser also thought that the French would react strongly, 'because the Company was a French company'.[263] But while he noted that the Algerian rebellion might encourage France to move against him, he also seems to have believed that it would effectively tie up her forces. Thus he estimated she would need as much time as Britain to prepare.[264] Finally, he believed that although Israel might well try to participate, the US would 'order her not to interfere.'[265] Nor would Eden welcome her involvement. 'He will prefer to keep it European.'[266] When the Egyptian President made the announcement to his Cabinet, one member did raise this possibility, but Nasser ruled it out as impossible and self-destructive for Britain's role in the Middle East. 'It was, he said, a taboo which Britain could not touch'.[267] Nasser wondered briefly whether Israel might 'take the chance alone and attack Syria or Jordan'.[268] But he took the speculation no farther.

***

As long as nobody suggested that Egypt should reverse the nationalisation, Nasser's behaviour from July to October 1956 was sweetly reasonable. He would not back down. 'It was obvious that Nasser had made his decision and the matter was closed.'[269] But winning over world opinion was his highest priority, and this depended on displaying the maximum possible political flexibility, particularly with regard to effective canal management. He promised full compensation to shareholders, and when his initial refusal to allow foreign canal employees to resign caused international anger, Ali Sabri soothingly confirmed that they were merely required to give due notice.[270] Not one ship – even when the British and French, in an attempt to undermine confidence, began to send as many as they could find, all refusing to pay dues to the new authority – was turned away from the Suez Canal.[271] The core of Nasser's strategy depended on his perception that the United States could be separated from her European allies. He 'believed that the United States aspired to replace Britain and France in the region, and he sought to exploit these rivalries'.[272] Ali Sabri privately approached US representatives to assert that 'force was only a primitive way and there was no sense in it, because Egypt stood ready to work out a reasonable and just solution to the canal problem'.[273]

The initial British response to the Suez Crisis had been to organise an international conference, which convened in London on 16 August. Nasser, in statesman mode, originally planned to attend, but was soon convinced that the extreme bias displayed in the agenda and location meant it could only detract from his dignity.[274] Nevertheless, he continued to play with compromise solutions, such as the Indian suggestion of a dual-sponsored conference, until the British Prime Minister's 'violent personal attack' of 8 August.[275] 'Our quarrel is not with Egypt, still less with the Arab world; it is with Colonel Nasser,' stated Eden.[276] So Nasser stayed at home, instead sending Ali Sabri to London as an observer, to lurk on the sidelines and receive daily briefings from the Indian and Soviet delegates.[277]

On 23 August, the London Conference agreed on a set of proposals for international control of the canal. A delegation headed by the Australian Prime Minister, Robert Menzies, was sent to present them to Nasser in Cairo. It was a disaster. Menzies found Nasser illogical (a characteristic which, in the opinion of the Australian premier, he shared with most Arabs and Indians) and 'rather gauche, with some irritating mannerisms'.[278] The Egyptian leader, muttering darkly of 'collective colonialism', did not take kindly to Menzies' private warning that Britain and France would fight. He later told his Cabinet that 'he had started the meeting with the intention of reaching a compromise', but the Prime Minister was so arrogant, provoking him time after time, that at last 'he had no alternative but to rise from his chair and expel Menzies from his office'.[279] It is a pleasing image, although wildly at variance with Menzies' own report that 'Nasser took this calmly and said he was well aware that he could not assume that forcible measures would not be used.' In reality, however, the personality clash was relatively unimportant. Nasser would never have welcomed the London Conference proposals; while President Eisenhower's simultaneous statement ruling out the military option ('received with glee' by the Egyptians, according to Menzies) confirmed the impossibility of intimidating him into acceptance.[280]

Nasser gave equally short shrift, on 12 September, to the Western proposal for a Suez Canal Users' Association (SCUA). Any faint illusion that he might consider this option was dispelled by his speech three days later deriding 'the sabre-rattling of the big powers':

In these decisive days in the history of humanity, in these days when justice struggles to defend its existence in the face of the falsehoods of aggression, evil, international chaos, domination, tyranny and imperialism, in these days Egypt, your homeland, stands firm in safeguarding its sovereignty.[281]

To 'stand firm' ('*ṣamada*') was the keynote of Nasser's policy at that time. He was 'quite unyielding', reported a British journalist who also met him on 15 September.[282] Such an attitude seemed justified in retrospect by developments at the second London Conference, which began on 19 September. Delegates were increasingly opposed to the use of force, and Britain and France became isolated from their usual allies.

This was a testimony to the success of Nasser's US policy. From the very beginning, the Americans focused on mediation and legal measures to reverse the nationalisation, suggesting that military action was unwarranted. The CIA allegedly stayed in touch, reactivating old links between Kermit Roosevelt and Zakaria Mohieddin – although the State Department, which had abandoned hope of co-operation with Nasser, took a harder line.[283] After the London Conference, Dulles declined to associate himself with the Menzies mission, told President Eisenhower that there was a considerable chance of a peaceful settlement, and was even ambivalent regarding his own brainchild, the SCUA. Nevertheless, in early September, Nasser remained sceptical. Eisenhower's statement ruling out the use of force provoked the private comment: 'That man puzzles me; which side is he on?'[284] He still linked Britain and the United States. 'I have read a statement by Sir Anthony Eden, or it may have been Mr Dulles, that he didn't trust Gamal Abdul Nasser. I must confess that I don't trust them either.'[285] On 15 September, he complained: 'I don't know what America's stand is. The American President speaks of peace. The American Secretary of State makes proposals which mean war.'[286]

The following week, the Suez dispute was referred to the UN Security Council. It was at this point that Nasser finally decided to negotiate, and made some carefully measured concessions. Foreign Minister Mahmoud Fawzi gave an unusually conciliatory speech in New York, and direct private discussions followed, in an atmosphere of renewed international optimism. Fawzi offered substantial concessions to the British and French Foreign Ministers, Selwyn Lloyd and Christian Pineau. He accepted both the existence of the SCUA and the impartial arbitration of its disagreements with the Egyptian government. On 13 October, assisted by UN Secretary-General Dag Hammarskjöld, both sides agreed on 'Six Principles' as a basis for further negotiations, which were scheduled in Geneva at the end of the month. Eisenhower, in the middle of an election campaign, greeted the news with rather premature enthusiasm: 'it looks like here is a very great crisis that is behind us'.[287]

***

Britain and France, however, had long been preparing for war. Both governments were starkly determined that the nationalisation of the Suez Canal Company should not succeed. 'Nasser must be compelled to disgorge,' Eden wrote to his Chancellor of the Exchequer, Harold Macmillan.[288] '*Il faut coloniser le canal ou canaliser le colonel*,' was the more elegant French rendition.[289] France was ready to go with Britain 'to the end' in dealing with Nasser, Pineau told Lloyd on 29 July. Four days after Nasser's fateful speech in Alexandria, the British Chiefs of Staff were instructed by the newly convened Egypt Committee to assume French involvement as they prepared 'an outline plan for possible operations against Egypt'.[290] Nasser's other great enemy, Nuri Said, approved. 'Hit Nasser, and hit him hard', he had told the British Foreign Minister over dinner when news of the canal nationalisation came in – and he repeated the advice at every subsequent opportunity.[291]

Dulles, for his part, had rushed straight to London to find out what his allies were up to, only to be informed on 1 August of the British doomsday scenario. If Nasser got away with it, warned the British Foreign Secretary, 'we should lose the pipeline and our oil supplies,' and the British economy 'would then be slowly strangled'. With no apparent irony, Lloyd described the Egyptian President as 'a paranoiac' with 'the same type of mind as Hitler'.[292] Macmillan, switching analogies, called him 'an Asiatic Mussolini'.[293] Were Nasser not toppled within the year, wrote Press Secretary William Clark in his diary, 'the Eden government is doomed and British (and probably Western) influence in the Middle East is destroyed'.[294] Eden believed that 'Colonel Nasser's action had presented us with an opportunity to find a lasting settlement of this problem, and we should not hesitate to take advantage of it.'[295] However, the Egyptian leader had been correct in his belief that UK forces were not ready to act immediately. 'The question that Eden put perfectly clearly was when we can take military action to topple Nasser, free the canal,' recorded his Press Secretary. 'The answers that he got, which were slightly horrifying, were that we could not do this.'[296] It was some time before the plans for 'Operation Musketeer' got laboriously underway.

Eden's basic goal was now to destroy Nasser's regime. He believed this could be accomplished by military means, or by forcing the Egyptian leader to back down. He was prepared to follow the US suggestion of economic pressure, 'provided the results show themselves without delay'.[297] He also seems to have sanctioned various covert alternatives. 'We'll bump Nasser off,' the new head of SIS was cheerfully told by his Middle East chief, and tales abound of unlikely plots to poison the Egyptian President's coffee, rig his razor with explosives, flood his office with nerve gas, or simply shoot him.[298] (KGB advisors were called in to improve Nasser's personal security, memorably suggesting that he should keep a canary with him at all times.)[299] An SIS spy ring based in Cairo's Arab News Agency (ANA) is alleged to have had all sorts of interesting plans. Government committees worked on 'black propaganda' and arrangements for a successor government.[300] Sir Douglas Dodds-Parker, who chaired the committee set up to consider 'ungentlemanly' alternatives to military force, claims it was merely cosmetic – but adds that he did discuss such options with former SOE colleagues, 'not in official committees but meeting in various places, a club or coming along here and having a chat'.[301] SIS, assisted by certain 'Suez Group' MPs, who had been in contact with former Wafd Party notables and Naguib supporters since the spring, reportedly began setting up an Egyptian 'shadow government' in the South of France, even contacting the Muslim Brotherhood.[302] One Beirut agent is said to have spent £162,500 recruiting the Egyptian Deputy Chief of Air Force Intelligence to organise a military coup.[303]

***

At least some of these activities must have been known in Cairo. The ANA spy ring was uncovered at the end of August, and the Deputy Chief of Air Force Intelligence turned out to be a double agent, a fact Nasser later publicised with relish. Based on newspapers alone, the Egyptian leader could hardly have failed to realise that Britain and France were in belligerent mood, and making co-ordinated plans.[304] Even *Punch* proclaimed:

> But we'll Hang Out the Washing on the palace of Abdin
> And knock this dastard Nasser to the middle of next week![305]

Military movements of the scale required for 'Operation Musketeer' could not be hidden. Although he may have doubted they would be used, Nasser was informed by multiple sources that General Keightley was assembling Anglo-French forces in Mediterranean. Even the CIA, alleges Heikal, deviously 'warned Egypt that Eden was in a highly unpredictable condition and in a state of mind that made him ready to undertake the most dangerous of gambles'.[306] Dulles himself is said to have sent similar information through the ambassadors of Baghdad Pact countries.[307]

Nasser announced to the world on 12 August that he expected an assault from France (which 'wants to solve the Algerian problem') and

Britain (which 'wants to reassure itself that it is "Great Britain"').[308] However, most of his attack predictions seem to have been directed at a global audience. 'I may have a war on my hands,' he told Menzies.[309] 'The British and French are going to stay out there in the Mediterranean until they find a pretext to come in,' he predicted to the departing Byroade.[310] In mid-September, he informed one British journalist that 'if people thought that the war would be over in forty-eight hours, they were very much mistaken,' detailing plans for guerrilla operations.[311] A month later, he told another reporter, Tom Little, that no compromise was possible. 'Sir Eden intends to attack me and there is nothing I can do about it.'[312] Unfortunately, none of these utterances can be taken at face value. It was politically important to assure the world that Egypt was the bewildered victim; and the British that they were prepared for an attack. The last source is particularly dubious, since it has been claimed that Little was 'a senior SIS agent' (heading the blown spy ring); and that the Egyptians, knowing this, chose to feed him disinformation rather than arresting him.[313]

Privately, on 30 August, Nasser was reported 'to have estimated the chances of invasion at 10–1 against'.[314] Former Egyptian officials tend to agree with this assessment.[315] Nasser clung tenaciously to his original estimation that the likelihood of war would decrease over time and that he could avoid it entirely by careful diplomacy.[316] Agriculture Minister Sayyid Mar'i thought it was obvious that 'the idea of war was not uppermost in his thoughts and that war itself did not enter his plans as a serious possibility'. He perceived that 'Nasser's assessments were made on the basis that the possibility of a solution to the crisis by peaceful means was far greater than through war' – although he could not tell 'whether this assessment was based on political analysis or on information which reached him at the time'.[317] In fact, several of the sources of information available to Nasser may have given him the impression that he could avoid war. Polls showed that British public opinion was becoming more averse to the use of force.[318] Nasser had been proved right in his belief that the Commonwealth (apart from the Dominions) would not support military action.[319] He felt that powerful world opinion was on his side:

> No longer does the Suez Canal problem concern only Egypt, Britain, France, and the USA. No, it has become the problem of the whole world, which is defending the freedom for which it has struggled in the face of the use of aggressive force and the policy of force pursued by the big Powers.[320]

By the end of September, Nasser's conviction that the danger was over had been bolstered by additional evidence. Diplomatic reports from Washington suggested that a military confrontation was now unlikely.[321] Once the UN negotiations began to produce results, it was felt that 'the steam had gone out of the situation,' as Heikal put it. 'The train has passed the station,' Hammarskjold told Fawzi.[322] Insiders claim that the Egyptian government had 'great faith' in the follow-up negotiations planned in Geneva, and was hopeful about the prospects of 'solving the problem diplomatically'.[323] Nasser himself stated in a subsequent interview that he 'got the impression they were willing to reach agreement.'[324] In consequence, he virtually ruled out the prospect of an Anglo-French invasion.

The Egyptian High Command was initially less certain. 'It is expected that some Western states will carry out hostile actions against Egypt as a result of the Suez nationalisation,' stated an 'Operation Order' issued on 1 September. The assumption was that Egyptian forces would be unable to withstand the Western attack. Plans focused on delaying battles, retreat and subsequent guerrilla warfare rather than active defence or counter-attack.[325] 'They probably expect that the Egyptian armed forces would be defeated in a short period,' Trevelyan reported in August, 'and plan, in that case, to disrupt the security forces and Administration and for many of the Free Officers to go underground'. ('Tell him to cheer up!' Eden scribbled in a quick minute. But the Foreign Office, with customary diplomacy, somehow neglected to relay the message until the moment had passed.)[326]

'One should not,' the 'Operation Order' even added, 'ignore what action may be taken by Israel in these circumstances.' However, the context suggests that, as far as Israel was concerned, the High Command was still thinking in terms of covert action and localised border raids.[327] The Soviet-equipped Egyptian army was now believed to be superior in terms of overall strength. Nasser remained convinced that the British would perceive the assistance of Israel as a liability, while Egyptian Intelligence noted how recent broadcasts from Tel Aviv 'emphasized that Israel should not allow itself to be used as a catspaw by the imperialist powers.'[328] By October, therefore, the army reduced its level of alert.[329] Concerns over the possibility of war in the Middle East began to centre on the Israel-Jordan border.

3
When the Bombs Started Falling: Suez and the Arab Hero

Even Nasser, when told of the attack, could not believe it until he stood on the roof of his house and saw that the planes buzzing Cairo had French and British insignias on their wings.[330] – Jehan Sadat

It started out as such a good day. Nasser, on 29 October 1956, had just returned from four days' relaxing holiday. The military danger appeared to be over. Talks to settle the Suez Canal issue once and for all were soon to take place in Geneva. Foreign Minster Fawzi was busy working on an Egyptian plan to implement the Six Principles agreed in New York, based on a draft submitted by Hammarskjöld the week before. Provided that he could go to Geneva on equal terms with Eden, this might present an opportunity for Nasser himself to play a more personal part in the grand international drama as it drew to a close. That morning he had an amiable meeting with the new American Ambassador, Raymond Hare. President Eisenhower was calling for restraint as usual, although this particular appeal seemed puzzlingly ill-timed. Nasser made it plain that he didn't understand what all the fuss was about. 'Could it be that Israel really wanted war? If so, he could not see why.'[331] At last, following a brief but significant noon meeting with the Paris Embassy press attaché, he took the afternoon off to enjoy his son's birthday party.

There is no indication that Nasser's unconcern was anything other than genuine. But given the number of ominous signals he had been receiving recently, it almost begins to resemble wilful blindness. Apart from the US Ambassador's visit, Arab embassies in Washington were also warning of an extensive Israeli military operation. Nasser himself had noticed the radio broadcasts from Tel Aviv alter in tone over the past week, although he claimed not to have thought it significant. The Egyptian 3rd Infantry Division reported large troop concentrations near the border.[332] And there had been an additional, highly significant set of secret reports from Paris and Istanbul, as discussed below. Nonetheless, the Egyptian regime still believed that Israel's target would be Jordan. So sure was Nasser that he had sent his military chief, Abdel Hakim Amer, to Amman to co-ordinate an Arab alliance against the expected offensive. Even there, the Jordanian General Ali Abu Nuwar confided his belief that the positions of the Israeli divisions suggested they would attack Egypt instead. Amer remained unconvinced.[333]

In the middle of the birthday party, Nasser received an urgent report. Israeli paratroopers were landing in the Mitla Pass in Sinai, just 30 km east of the Suez Canal.[334] This was a tremendous shock. The Egyptian army was 'completely surprised', remembers Amin Howeidy, who was in the Operations Room when the news first came in. 'It was two o'clock. I can't forget it. I was the officer in charge, I was a Major. Two o'clock.'[335] It all seemed so illogical. There had been no attempt to neutralise the Egyptian air force, while the Israeli troops were moving in without any sort of air cover. 'Something very strange is happening,' Nasser told his journalist friend Mohammed Hassanein Heikal, telephoning him at six o'clock that evening. The Israelis in Sinai were 'occupying one empty position after another'. It looked as though 'all they want to do is to start up sandstorms in the desert'.[336]

The initial assumption, therefore, was that the Israel attack would be strictly limited. It could be a feint, with Jordan or Gaza remaining the real target. Alternatively, Israel might be trying to stir up trouble before Britain and France could reach an agreement over the Suez Canal. Although the RCC had been disbanded in July, Nasser seemed to feel in need of support from his old colleagues. At 10.30pm, he and General Amer (recently returned from Jordan) consulted with Zakaria Mohieddin, Abdel Latif Baghdadi, Kamal al-Din Hussein and Hussein Shafei at the Military Headquarters. As the night drew on and new information continued to come in, it became clear, as Baghdadi put it, 'that the operation was much larger than just an Israeli military attack on one of our posts, as had been its habit until now'.[337] Nevertheless, it seems that for several hours the leaders were still thinking in terms of a larger revenge attack rather than an all-out Israeli invasion. Orders were given to move troops back into Sinai, and the air force prepared for action. The possibility of Anglo-French involvement was never even raised.[338]

***

The next afternoon's events were consequently disconcerting. London and Paris presented the Egyptian and Israeli governments with a joint ultimatum, ordering both to stop fighting and withdraw ten miles from the Canal. Egypt was further required to 'accept the temporary occupation by Anglo-French forces' of key positions at Port Said, Ismailiyya and Suez – failing which, British and French forces would in any case 'intervene in whatever strength may be necessary'.[339] Since the last British 'temporary occupation' of Egypt, beginning in 1882, had only come to an end four months previously, it is hard to imagine a more offensive choice of phrase. The Egyptian regime, which had previously ignored all indications of Anglo-French collusion with Israel, was instantly convinced of it. Although details of the tripartite talks at Sèvres had not yet emerged, the rest of the world took little longer.

In Cairo, the ultimatum came as a 'terrible shock'.[340] It was 'received with astonishment bordering on disbelief'.[341] Nasser had been utterly convinced that Britain could not endanger her position in the Middle East by aligning with Israel against the Arabs. Of course, most international observers were surprised too. The Soviets, who had taken no prior measures to protect their personnel in Egypt, evacuated in a panic.[342] Even Douglas Dodds-Parker, a junior minister at the British Foreign Office, could not believe his eyes when first shown the ultimatum. 'Of all the alternatives put to the decision-makers,' he marvelled, 'this seemed, and was to prove, the most disastrous combination of the unworkable and the unbelievable'.[343] The initial reaction of Evelyn Shuckburgh was similar, if pithier. 'We think A.E. has gone off his head,' he scribbled in his diary.[344]

Nasser's incredulity, however, requires further explanation. He had resolutely ignored several warnings of the possibility of collusion. The Egyptian military attaché in Istanbul had long emphasised the sinister significance of the French arms that were being sent to Israel, and on 6 October he sent his conclusion to Cairo. 'England and France will present a final ultimatum to Egypt,' he predicted. This would be followed by 'a tripartite attack (England, France and Israel) in the middle of November' – and he soon correctly amended the date to 'before the end of October'.[345] Khaled Mohieddin relayed a report from a Paris friend that France would co-operate with Israel in attacking Egypt. It was interpreted as a deliberate false leak aiming to concentrate Egyptian forces in the Sinai, away from Alexandria.[346] The Egyptian Ambassador in Paris was given similar information by Eastern Bloc colleagues at a cocktail party, but never passed it on.[347] An unidentified man who came to the Paris Embassy seeking payment for intelligence on the joint military planning at Sèvres was turned away without ceremony.[348]

With hindsight, of course, it is possible to find significance in all sorts of small indications that were justifiably ignored at the time. But there were further, more credible warnings. By 28 October, the CIA was certain that the French at least were colluding with the Israelis, and allegedly asked Ambassador Hussein to inform Nasser.[349] On the very morning of 29 October, while the Egyptian President was telling Ambassador Hare about his holiday, reports were coming in of puzzling reconnaissance missions by British planes in Sinai.[350] Perhaps the most notable example is that of the Egyptian military attaché at the Paris Embassy, the former Free Officer, Tharwat Okasha. He had a very highly placed French friend, who shared his love of Mahler and Wagner and had previously passed on secret information regarding French policy in Algeria.

At seven o'clock on the morning of 27 October, Okasha was woken by a telephone call from this contact, who arranged an immediate meeting in a Paris suburb. Here he passed on the 'exact plan' formulated at Sèvres. On returning to the Embassy, Okasha summoned the press attaché, who knew Nasser personally, gave him verbal details to memorise and sent him straight to Cairo to inform the President.[351] Nasser met him at noon on 29 October, shortly after seeing the US Ambassador. As the press attaché entered Nasser's office, he saw him standing casually, one foot on a chair. He passed on the whole story. 'This is very strange,' remarked Nasser, and asked him to repeat it. The man complied. But the President did not believe him. 'Look here, my son,' he said. 'Israel, France can do it, but the British cannot at all co-operate with the Israelis. They have dignity, and they will hesitate 100 times to co-operate with the Israelis.'[352] And then, at last, Nasser went on to his party, armed with this fixed image that improbably survived until the actual announcement of the Anglo-French ultimatum.

***

It may even have survived a little longer. Nasser's enemies understood his regime would fall if he accepted the ultimatum. That was its purpose. But they also believed it would fall if he refused it. Nasser would have agreed with them in the former case, but the latter seemed less clear. Such an apparently irrational policy, which risked denying British access to Arab oil and her historic spheres of influence in the Middle East, could surely only be a bluff? Even after the ultimatum, an actual attack by the British was 'something beyond imagination'.[353] Heikal suggests that the problem was that the Egyptian President still believed in the myth of the 'British gentleman'. Although the whole affair 'reeked of hypocrisy and double dealing', he could not credit that there might really be a Western intervention, and it troubled him. 'This is all a lie,' he said. 'How can they lie? Is Eden a liar?'[354]

Therefore, Nasser wrote soon afterwards, they estimated that 'British invasion was only a possibility, although we reckoned that the possibility was then 70 percent,' and when the government met on the evening of 30 October, they chose to reject the Anglo-French terms.[355] Other attendees later put it more strongly. 'Nasser did not in any way estimate that this ultimatum was serious.'[356] He seemed to think the British aim was merely to keep Egyptian forces out of Sinai, 'giving Israel a chance to gain a victory'.[357] When asked whether Egypt was prepared to fight Britain and France, the President displayed 'signs of unease'. His eventual decision to reject the ultimatum 'whether it is genuine or merely a threat' was simplified by the fact that he thought it was probably the latter.[358] Finally, at nine o'clock, he sent for the British Ambassador, Sir Humphrey Trevelyan, and delivered a decisive refusal. The Egyptian President, noted Trevelyan, still seemed 'completely relaxed and at his ease'.[359]

The Egyptian regime did make some preparations for a Western offensive. There were plans for a civilian evacuation of the Canal Zone and a naval redeployment from the Red Sea to safety in Saudi Arabia.[360] But until the following day, Nasser later confirmed, 'all our estimations were based on the idea that Britain would not participate in any attack'.[361] Had they taken the ultimatum seriously, the obvious move would have been to pull their troops out of the Sinai Peninsula. However, when the RCC core met to discuss the course of the war on the morning of 31 October, remembers Baghdadi:

we expressed our fear of the possibility that the English and the French would drop forces in the Canal Zone in order to cut off our forces in Sinai. But Gamal [Abdel Nasser] looked upon this as an unlikely possibility...[362]

Thus he did nothing to halt the military reinforcement of the Sinai troops. Although Heikal claims that Nasser argued all night with Amer, trying to persuade him to withdraw, it is hard to accept that the President could not have prevailed by some means, had he genuinely believed the need to be urgent.[363]

***

There was one final unpleasant surprise in store for the Egyptian regime. On 31 October, in the early evening, British and French planes began bombing Egyptian territory. Even then, Nasser's first assumption was that they were Israeli.[364] But soon he was no longer able to deny the evidence of his own eyes. The Western powers had entered the war. 'Suddenly,' recalls Baghdadi, 'we were overcome by confusion and many of us were paralysed'.[365] Nasser appears to have joined in the initial panic. 'On the day of the air raids against us, I was worried,' he later confessed, 'and asking myself what would be the reaction of the people'.[366]

By midnight, the situation at Military Headquarters was 'tense and nervous'. There were reports of paratroopers dropping nearby, aiming to assassinate the Egyptian leadership.[367] Nasser's advisors vainly attempted to persuade him to go to a safe house.[368] The leaders' disarray reinforces the point that they had not genuinely expected Western intervention and found themselves unprepared, with many troops still concentrated in Sinai, at risk of being cut off by an Anglo-French landing. Army units' orders were repeatedly changed, apparently at random.[369] 'There was no preparedness, no planning, no training nor anything else,' writes Mar'i. 'We were surprised,' he concludes, 'by a war at a level far higher than our direct capability'.[370]

Officially, surrender was never an option. 'I saw the Egyptians!' Howeidy remembers. 'I saw them in the streets here. The bombings were coming, and they were in the streets. And they will have no idea about capitulation.'[371] On the other hand, from the moment that Britain and France entered the war, there was no chance of a conventional military victory, and the Cairo regime knew it. Baghdadi recalls:

> The question which bothered each one of us at that moment was whether to continue with the war and bear the consequences of destruction and devastation, or to save our country from ruin by surrendering and going underground in order to maintain the struggle against this conquest which would be thrust upon us.

Most were in favour of the latter option. The President remained 'confused', expressing no opinion as yet.[372] The following day, CIA Chief Allen Dulles estimated that Nasser was 'pretty well on the ropes' and might accept a ceasefire.[373] But when Foreign Minister Fawzi suggested sustained political efforts to persuade the UN to impose such a ceasefire, Nasser was angry. 'Egypt,' he declared at last, 'must resist force with force'.[374]

In practical terms, this decision had two facets. First, if somewhat belatedly, Nasser ordered the army to be withdrawn from Sinai and concentrated in defence of mainland Egypt.[375] Second, he set in motion extensive preparations for a 'popular war' to follow the inevitable Egyptian defeat. His guerrilla headquarters were to be established at Tanta in the Nile Delta.[376] There were plans for a network of 'safe houses' across Cairo.[377] Caches of small arms were hidden in the villages and secret radio stations were readied.[378] Heikal was asked to look after the 'information side'.[379] Old cells of *fidā'iyūn* who had fought the British in the Canal Zone were reactivated.[380] The struggle would be divided into a series of self-contained sectors, each with its own leader; secret communication routes were to be established. The Prime Minister's aide, Hamed Mahmoud, slept in his office in order to guard the sacks of five and ten pound notes that were to be distributed to finance this resistance.[381]

***

'*Sanaqātil wa lan nasallim!*' exhorted President Nasser, in a keynote speech broadcast on 1 November, even as his troops began the long withdrawal from Sinai. 'We shall fight and not surrender!' It would, he said, be a 'bitter war' – a 'total war'. And its soldiers would be the Egyptian people, who would fight 'side by side with their armed forces'.[382] In practical earnest of this, guns were already being distributed from the backs of trucks. The President had cheered up since the previous day; he was now 'even lively'.[383] By 2 November, Cairo Radio had been forced off the air, and the *Voice of Britain* had replaced it on the same wavelength. But the crowds still gathered around Al-Azhar mosque in the centre of the old city to listen to Nasser, where he promised to fight with them 'to the last drop of our blood'.[384] Later he expressed a similar sentiment – in somewhat less melodramatic terms – to the American Ambassador. Again, he seemed 'calm, relaxed and friendly,' if a little tired.[385]

His colleagues were less sanguine. That afternoon, General Amer lost his nerve and suggested a ceasefire. The alternative, he argued, was such widespread death and destruction that the regime would fall in any case. When Salah Salem arrived, he agreed, advising Nasser:

You have done everything you can. You have served the country to the best of your ability. But you have failed. There is just one more service you can do for the country. Sir Humphrey Trevelyan is still at the British Embassy. Go and give yourself up to him, for they only want you.

It was a minority opinion. The other Council members swiftly agreed that it would be better to die, and arranged to provide themselves with cyanide pills, just in case. 'Pull yourself together,' Nasser rebuked his old friend and military chief. 'Nobody is going to surrender or escape and everybody is going to fight.' Salem and Amer shamefacedly withdrew their remarks, and eventually they all agreed to battle on until Cairo fell, then go underground to continue the resistance, assassinating any politician prepared to serve in a collaborationist government.[386]

Nonetheless, it remained something of a comedown. Four years' worth of revolutionary achievements vanished in the blink of an eye, and they were all set to become conspirators again – only without the advantage of anonymity. Unsurprisingly, the tone of the discussions was sombre. Baghdadi went home that evening despite the air raids, 'in the hope that one of the pilots would make a mistake and my house would be hit'. At least if he died, he could avoid witnessing 'the impending disaster which I pictured to myself'. By 4 November, even Nasser admitted he was unable to sleep, weeping because 'he had apparently lost the state'. On a brief and quixotic night-time mission to the front line at Port Said, he was depressed by the many wrecked military vehicles, which looked like 'the remnants of a destroyed army'. 'I felt,' remembers Baghdadi, his chosen companion on this venture, 'that a broken man was in front of me'. On arrival, the news that the Anglo-French forces had just begun to land was conveyed to the President. He returned at once to the capital.[387]

The situation was certainly serious, but eyewitnesses have perhaps touched up the tragedy to emphasise the coming triumph. There remained some cause for optimism. 'I intend to stand back and wait for world opinion to save me,' Nasser had said in October, and he was now following global reaction to the events in his country extremely carefully.[388] So were the Egyptian newspapers, which hailed the vocal anti-colonialist protests in the UN General Assembly. They painted the interruptions and catcalls that greeted the British Prime Minister's statement in Parliament on 31 October as a 'Revolution in the House of Commons against Eden'.[389] On the very day of the Port Said landings, Nasser took heart from the news of massive anti-war demonstrations in Trafalgar Square. Consequently, according to Heikal, the plans for the Egyptian leadership to go underground were cancelled. A scornful Nasser felt that he had been saved by British folly in co-operating with Israel, vindicating his original judgement.[390]

***

With the United States, the case was quite otherwise. Throughout the war, Cairo continued to do everything possible to win over the Americans. 'Israel has invaded our land, with France and Britain,' Nasser warned his old revolutionary colleague Khaled Mohieddin, now editor of the Egyptian newspaper *Al-Masa'a*. 'But the US has a different position, against the use of force. So we must respect this and not criticise the US.'[391] Initial signs were hopeful. The USA had openly disagreed with Britain and France in the Security Council over the ultimatum. This emboldened Nasser to send a message to Eisenhower through Ambassador Hare, seeking 'United States support against Anglo-French aggression' – although he can hardly have been surprised by Hare's warning that military assistance was highly unlikely under these circumstances.[392]

The American President's own disapproval was public and explicit. He had not been consulted, and did not 'accept the use of force as a wise and proper instrument for the settlement of international disputes'.[393] This was even more than Egypt had hoped. Nasser admitted to Hare on 2 November that he had never really believed the Americans when they hinted that the European powers might attack without US approval. Now, however, 'he recognized he had been wrong. Our action had been clear-cut and doubt had been removed'.[394] Nasser apparently sent a secret message to Dulles, promising to oppose communism and reconsider the issue of peace with Israel.[395] On 3 November, speaking 'personally', Heikal told Hare that the government was willing to 'do anything' to end the war. They would accept a UN presence on Egyptian territory. They would reject Soviet arms. Nasser was said to be begging for a visit from the American Sixth Fleet. The USA, he averred, had won the Middle East without firing a shot.[396]

The warmth, however, was calculated. Ambassador Hare, quite rightly, was not sure that Nasser would deliver on these promises.[397] His professions of undying friendship were coupled with veiled threats, passed on by Ali Sabri, that Moscow might be called in.[398] Although the United States broke Eden's resolve with its refusal to support the plunging pound, and saved Egypt from occupation by negotiating the 6 November UN ceasefire, the regime did not believe such assistance was purely altruistic. Heikal records:

There was much discussion in Cairo about what game, exactly, the Americans were playing. Their hostility to the tripartite aggression was being made increasingly open and uncompromising, yet it was difficult to understand why Eisenhower had not simply picked up the telephone and ordered Eden to stop.[399]

The general perception was that the United States was trying to replace Britain as the regional power. 'We thanked them,' says Amin Howeidy. 'But everybody thought the Americans wanted to kill us by seizing our throats.'[400]

The process was not so calculated, and Cairo overestimated Washington's power over her allies, as became a pattern. But Eisenhower admitted that, while he felt a principle was at stake, 'I don't fancy helping the Egyptians'.[401] It is hardly surprising that the temporary alliance was never converted into renewed amity. Egypt saw herself as having received only her due, and made no concessions when finally vindicated. As early as 8 November, when the immediate danger had passed, Nasser began to cause difficulties over the composition of the United Nations Emergency Force (UNEF), which was to be stationed in the Sinai. (Certainly no Canadians, he stipulated, in spite of the fact that this particular compromise had been their idea in the first place. The uniforms were far too British, and they toasted the Queen.)[402] America had only done her duty, implied Ali Sabri:

> The USA from the start demanded a ceasefire and withdrawal of foreign forces from Egypt. This stand is gratifying, but we expect from the USA more material pressure on the aggressors. We also expect the USA to prohibit the export of oil to these countries, until they comply.[403]

Such high hopes could hardly fail to be disappointed. On 5 January 1957, Washington fulfilled all the darkest forebodings of the Egyptian regime with the 'Eisenhower Doctrine', which explicitly justified US involvement in the Middle East in order to balance Soviet influence. This was interpreted as absolute proof that Cairo had been right all along, and the Americans had only ever wanted to take over Britain's old colonial role in the Arab world. The brief Indian summer in US-Egyptian relations ended before it had truly begun. Nasser's resentment was compounded by the fact that he blamed the United States for a post-Suez settlement which he saw as fundamentally unjust, rewarding Israel for her aggression. From 1957, UNEF was stationed along the

Egyptian side of the border with Israel, as well as in the Gaza Strip and Sharm el-Sheikh, separating the erstwhile combatants, inhibiting guerrilla attacks and safeguarding Israeli access through the Straits of Tiran (claimed as Egyptian territorial waters) to the Gulf of Aqaba. The Soviet Union, by contrast, provided increasing assistance to Egypt, even funding the very Aswan High Dam project that had caused all the trouble in the first place.

***

In the aftermath of Suez, Nasser's anti-colonialist credentials were firmly established. He continued to be a powerful influence within the Non-Aligned Movement, and made a point of supporting popular struggles against imperialism everywhere, particularly in Africa, which he saw as one of the three regional 'circles' in which Egypt could play a catalytic role.[404] Most importantly, however, Nasser emerged as the inspiration of the Arab Revolution. 'Nasserism' combined anti-colonialism, Arab socialism and the ideal of Arab political union. The first was only enhanced by the Suez drama. The second was expressed through the nationalisation of industry and extensive land reform. But the final aspect was problematic. The strategic position of Israel, blocking Egyptian access to the Arab East, remained a nagging anomaly. This was compounded after 1957, when the military leaders of an increasingly unstable Syrian state abandoned the search for domestic compromise and begged to unite with Egypt under Nasser's rule. Nasser was initially reluctant, foreseeing all sorts of practical problems. When the Syrians accepted his stringent conditions, however, including the dissolution of their political parties, he had to choose between acquiescence and ideological retraction. The two countries combined to create the United Arab Republic (UAR) on 1 February 1958.

Nasser's influence in the Arab world was now at its height. The quasi-medieval Imamate of Yemen sought an incongruous federal association with the UAR in March 1958. Egypt's former ally, King Saud of Saudi Arabia, whom the Americans had hoped to support as an Islamic figurehead to rival Nasser in the Middle East, was manifestly outclassed. The Lebanese government, which had accepted the Eisenhower Doctrine, was destabilised by a series of insurrections blamed on Egyptian influence. Finding that national amalgamation was the flavour of the month, the Hashemite kingdoms of Iraq and Jordan had nervously announced their own nominal union. It was abolished without ceremony by a revolutionary *coup d'état* in Baghdad only five months later. The body of Nuri Pasha – Nasser's staunch old enemy, who had even then been preparing to oppose him in Lebanon – was torn apart in the streets, the woman's veil beneath which he had vainly attempted to conceal his identity ripped away by the mob.[405]

As his Arab leadership peaked in the late 1950s, so did Nasser's pre-eminence at home, which was largely founded on the massive popular appeal of his anti-colonialist foreign policy. Ultimately, the stability of the Cairo government depended on the President's charismatic legit-imacy, while his former Free Officer colleagues were cast into the shade. 'At the beginning we used to meet every day,' Kamal al-Din Hussein remembers. 'But after that we had fewer number of meetings, and then they were weekly, almost weekly meetings...'[406] Now they spoke of Nasser, in reverent tones, as 'the boss' (*al-ra'īs*). By the early 1960s, although the remaining revolutionaries and a few select newcomers retained some institutional importance as members of impressive-sounding bodies such as the Presidential Council and the Supreme Executive Committee (SEC) of the Arab Socialist Union, they were dominated by Nasser, and their many internecine disagreements meant that they rarely combined to defy him.[407] They remained more influential than the Cabinet, however, which tended to be sidelined in a crisis. Ministers served at the President's pleasure, and – certain estab-lished fiefs aside – Nasser moved them around fairly frequently, to keep them on their toes.

If the role of other institutions of government was minimal, that of the Egyptian populace *en masse* was practically non-existent. Student groups sometimes advocated particular policies, but their support tended to be focused around regime insiders who were probably deployed by the President for that very purpose – Ali Sabri and Khaled Mohieddin on the left; Zakaria Mohieddin and Abdel Latif Baghdadi on the right. The formal mechanisms by which ordinary Egyptians were supposed to participate in policy making were the National Assembly and, from 1962, the Arab Socialist Union (ASU). These were highly structured, top-down organisations managed by loyal sup-porters of the *status quo*. Nasser was particularly conscious of the power of the transistor, and Cairo Radio was a government mouthpiece. The *Voice of the Arabs* station, presented by Ahmed Said (who remains proud of the sobriquet 'Mr Hate' bestowed on him by British news-papers) was a key foreign policy tool, broadcasting the revolutionary opinions of the Cairo regime for 18 hours each day across the Arab world, while Egyptian Intelligence helpfully provided local impact assessments. It was, avers Said, 'the voice of Nasser and the voice of the Arab people at the same time'.[408]

Immediately after the revolution, press censorship had been imposed and lifted several times. Consolidating his power in the 1950s, Nasser personally revised the first editions of all daily papers. Newspaper editorships were given to former Free Officers and other loyal figures – who still risked imprisonment or exclusion if they published the wrong thing.[409] Anwar Sadat was editor of *Al-Gomhouriyya* from 1953, and the Amin brothers, founders of *Akhbar al-Yawm*, also worked closely with the regime until Mostafa Amin was arrested as a CIA agent in 1965. Like Mohammed Hassanein Heikal, the editor of *Al-Ahram* who co-operated even more closely with Nasser, Amin had sometimes been used as an unofficial channel of communication with Western governments.[410] All Egyptian newspapers were finally nationalised in 1960, after which journalists became, if possible, still more biddable.[411]

***

Nasser did sometimes seek opinions from a select few. His long-term Foreign Minister, Dr Mahmoud Fawzi, was a respected diplomat left over from monarchical times, although he tended to implement rather than influence policy. 'Nasser acts,' it was said, 'and Fawzi makes it legal'.[412] The journalist Heikal was another resource, although the real extent of his policy influence is disputed. 'I think it would be quite incorrect to regard Heikal's writings as the voice of Nasser,' argues former US Ambassador John Badeau, and Nasser's daughter Hoda agrees that his many subsequent books have magnified his role.[413] Nonetheless, by the 1960s, almost everyone read Heikal's Friday *Al-Ahram* editorial, 'To Be Frank', which interpreted current events. It was widely believed that Nasser used it to test public reaction to his new plans.[414]

In the final analysis, however, there was only one man in Egypt who had the potential to challenge Nasser in his heyday. Abdel Hakim Amer had been the President's oldest and most trusted friend among the Free Officers. One year apart at the Military Academy, they served together for three years in Sudan during the Second World War.[415] As young lieutenants, they shared a small flat, and Amer taught Nasser to smoke.[416] They fought together in the Palestine War of 1948 and talked over the problems of the Egyptian army 'as they lay on the camp beds under the stars in an orange grove at Isdud'.[417] They behaved as members of each others' families; they named their sons after each other; they visited and played chess together; Amer's mother reputedly bought underwear for Nasser when she bought it for her son.[418]

There are suggestions from former regime members that the closeness of this friendship was not politically healthy: it 'exceeded its limitations' and Nasser was 'emotionally weak' before his colleague.[419] Tharwat Okasha, who was in the same class as Amer at Military College, says it was 'wrong from the beginning'.[420] All agree that Amer was affable, brave, 'a fantastic human being', 'very human'.[421] Despite this (or because of it), he was simply not in Nasser's league as a soldier or as a conspirator. That very fact probably encouraged the habitually suspicious future President to trust him. Their 'complicated' relationship depended not only on old camaraderie, but also on Nasser's belief that he himself was the strongest influence on Amer, having formed his 'progressive ideas'.[422] Amer had a peculiar quality of straightforward naivety. One journalist recalls how he wept in front of his soldiers when they complained of missing their families, while Nasser used to say that Amer was incapable of telling a story. 'If you asked him what was the story of Joseph he would tell you "he was a boy who got lost and then was found".'[423] Even his later alleged opium addiction and abduction of a film star with whom he had fallen in love seem to have been treated as endearing foibles.[424]

Thus Amer was given command of the army in 1952 because of his closeness to Nasser – 'he is always the man on whom I rely'.[425] It was certainly not because of his military efficiency: he was a Major at the time and made no effort to rise to his new rank, tending to be 'overconfident' about his strategic judgment.[426] Like a petty village chief, he promoted his army commanders as he himself had been promoted – based on personal loyalty.[427] By the time of the Suez crisis, this attitude was already beginning to cause problems.[428] Nevertheless, Amer's power continued to expand in the late 1950s, and he was entrusted with additional civilian responsibilities. The most important of these was the new Syrian province. Following a certain amount of unrest after the creation of the UAR, Nasser's loyal deputy was sent to Damascus as an unofficial 'viceroy' in October 1959. However, the rush to apportion blame following the collapse of the union two years later caused the first open breach between the President and his newly created Marshal. That breach determined much of what was to come.[429]

4
Revolution or Something to Raise Our Morale: Intervention in Yemen

> *The Yemeni war as a matter of fact came at the time we were feeling that we [needed] a revolution or something to raise our morale.*[430] – Hamed Mahmoud, chef de cabinet to Prime Minister Ali Sabri

It was the greatest crisis never known. In March 1962, the Egyptian regime was secretly thrown into confusion when Nasser at last decided that enough was enough: a new Presidential Council should approve high-level army promotions.[431] 'We are not military officers now,' the President told Amer, 'we are politicians'.[432] This was an odd conclusion to draw from the fact that only six months previously the Marshal's heavy-handed administration had provoked a highly embarrassing *coup d'état* in Damascus. On 28 September 1961, Syria had seceded from the UAR, which now existed in name alone.[433] The secession was a great blow to Nasser's prestige, at a time when the Egyptian economy was also struggling. The friendship between Nasser and Amer suffered, and the President appears to have decided that the time had come to coax the Marshal into a position where he could do less damage.

Amer, however, was not to be coaxed, resigning in an emotional huff. Desperate to avoid an open confrontation, Nasser asked the other Council members to beg Amer to withdraw his resignation, effectively conceding the point. They disapproved. Hussein Shafei even wrote a letter to the President:

> Abdel Nasser is not able to take decisions against himself. And he thinks that he and Amer are one thing. But the truth is that Abdel Nasser is one matter and Abdel Hakim Amer is another matter... the injury on your hand will not disappear, and the wound that Amer inflicted on you will also never disappear.[434]

But Nasser disregarded this interesting analogy. All too aware of Amer's powerful patronage networks, he feared his old friend might rebel. After the 1967 defeat, the events of March 1962 would be depicted as 'a half *coup d'état*, after which Abdel Hakim Amer got hold of the army completely'.[435] Nasser ruefully revealed that, in a misguided attempt to assure Amer of his confidence, he had not supervised the military establishment for the last five years. 'I now consider this,' he confessed, with masterly understatement, 'to be a mistake on my part.'[436]

Seeking to deflect blame for the defeat, the President exaggerated. Nasser, although he had certainly been warned off Amer's turf, was still in charge. He had his own men in positions of power in the armed forces.[437] The Marshal, for his part, retained a personal loyalty to the President. Most sources agree that he sought only to consolidate his existing power within the country, and would never have attempted anything so 'drastic' as a coup – although his supporters, such as Shams Badran, may have been more ambitious.[438] The President was reluctant to move against Amer, or to contradict him in public, but this may have been as much due to the old friendship, which persisted in some form, as to fear of retaliation. The history of this unconventional feud is entangled with the Egyptian intervention in the Yemeni Civil War. Both engrossed the Cairo regime from 1962 to 1967; both constituted reactions to the Syrian secession; both were blamed for the army's poor performance in the 1967 War. Indeed, Nasser and Amer had a second major disagreement just one day after the Yemeni Free Officers' Revolution of 26 September 1962, which signalled the start of this long military confrontation that polarised the Arab world.[439]

***

Of course, inter-Arab squabbles did not begin with the Yemen conflict. The previous month had seen a disastrous Arab League meeting in Lebanon, where Saudi Arabia and Jordan sided with Syria over complaints about Egyptian interference in Syrian internal affairs. It ended in general uproar: the Egyptian delegation walked out, the police had to be called in and the Secretary-General burst into tears.[440] Egyptian-Saudi relations, in particular, had been deteriorating since the Suez Crisis, when King Saud had been offended that he was not given advance notice of the nationalisation – and disturbed by Nasser's growing regional popularity. From 1957, the two leaders were opposed in a series of plots, counter-plots and propaganda wars. After September 1961, the beleaguered Egyptian President made fiery speeches blaming the Damascus coup on global 'imperialism' and regional 'reaction' – naming Saudi Arabia and Jordan, at this time in close alliance, as instances of the latter. The clash between Egypt and 'reaction' came to be seen as a life-or-death struggle, and Heikal famously declared that Egypt 'as a revolution' would not observe the same territorial boundaries as Egypt 'as a state'.[441]

Following the secession, Nasser broke off diplomatic relations with King Saud, whom he accused of sending $2 million to the Syrian rebels. The story grew from there. Mahmoud Riad, later Egyptian Foreign Minister, claimed it was $7 million, but the conspirators pocketed the balance.[442] When Saud eventually came to Cairo as a refugee he reputedly named the sum as $12 million – which says something about Egyptian notions of Saudi economic management, if nothing else.[443] The King paid for the Syrian coup, wrote Heikal, 'with the utmost secrecy, hidden in the tunnels of his palaces and shrouded by the atmosphere of his harem full of the scent of incense, perfume, and poison'. When they informed him of the outcome, 'he rose and danced with his sword... Then he began asking every ten minutes: Have they put an end to Abdel Hakim Amer yet or not?'[444]

Saud came to be seen as a figure of fun, rather than a worthy adversary. In a reflection of his diminishing personal power, his brother and eventual supplanter, Prince Faisal, received the doubtful honour of being the addressee of an ongoing open letter roundly condemning his personal life and policies on the *Voice of the Arabs* 'Enemies of God' programme throughout much of 1962. The King himself was constantly accused of financial and moral corruption. 'If social justice were applied in Saudi Arabia,' asked Nasser sarcastically, 'what would King Saud spend on the concubines?'[445] The aim was revolution. 'The Saudi people will eliminate reaction and restore their rights,' Nasser predicted in mid-1962, helping them along with a rhetorical question. 'Do the funds deposited by King Saud in Swiss banks belong to him or do they belong to the people?'[446]

***

As the Arab world divided into two camps, the 'reactionary' regimes were increasingly depicted as having sold out to the Western powers. In July 1961, 'greedy British imperialism' was accused of provoking the Kuwait crisis as an excuse to return to the region.[447] (The Iraqi threat to Kuwait was highly embarrassing for Nasser, who had to support Kuwaiti independence whilst condemning the British intervention invited to protect it.) In September, Britain was also blamed for the Syrian secession. 'Suspicions of course existed,' Nasser warned the new Ambassador, Harold Beeley, and he had to ask himself 'whether they were merely suspicions or something more'.[448] Cairo continued vocally to oppose London's African policy. The UK was seen as the arch-conspirator amongst the enemies 'co-ordinating their steps' against the Egyptian regime and 'plotting to bring about Nasser's downfall'.[449]

The principal problem, however, remained the British military presence in Aden and Southern Arabia – 'linked with Britain by treaties in perpetuity concluded in the 19th century and valid until the earth is sucked dry and the crow flies away'.[450] Cairo was deeply concerned lest London's unification of these territories within the South Arabian Federation (SAF) should perpetuate her colonial influence. When the Governor of Aden, Charles Johnston, passed through Cairo Airport in November 1961 without making a statement, he was accused of being unable to face press questions on the iniquities of British imperialism. 'What would he tell these journalists about the federal union which Britain wants to establish there against the Arab people's will?' demanded *Voice of the Arabs*.[451] Minor revolutionaries from Aden were feted in Cairo; such small victories as the removal of the overly pro-British Principal of Aden Girls' College provoked sustained gloating across the airwaves.[452] In September 1962, the British finally forced through the agreement for Aden's accession to the SAF – just in time, since the Yemeni revolution, only days later, would certainly have thrown a serious spanner in the works.[453] Nasser seethed:

> The British are creating something they call the Arab South. Let them call it the English South so their talk will be intelligible. When they say the Arab South, however, we say that no Arab will ever accept the British-created Arab South.[454]

Britain's old allies from her Suez days were seen in Cairo as a diminishing threat, however. Relations with Gaullist France improved quietly but steadily as the decade advanced. Israel, of course, remained the ultimate enemy, but the presence of UNEF troops on the Sinai border defused that confrontation. Nasser was trying quite hard to keep the Arab-Israeli conflict 'in the ice-box', as he had agreed with the United States. The USA was not precisely a friend in the early 1960s. Neither, however, could she be unambiguously defined as an enemy – although she remained an ally of enemies: Britain, Saudi Arabia, Jordan, Iran and Israel. Large-scale US economic assistance – officially without strings, although balanced against certain assumptions – had begun in 1959 as a concrete expression of America's desire for good relations.[455]

When John F. Kennedy became President, he made a concerted effort to improve links with Nasser, sending the latter's old acquaintance John Badeau as the new Ambassador in July 1961, and engaging in a valued private correspondence.[456] Kennedy's letter expressing hopes of 'mutually beneficial cooperation' between the United States and the UAR – not to mention his hints of increased economic assistance and perhaps even movement on the Palestinian refugee problem – roused cautious enthusiasm in Cairo.[457] Nasser, whilst taking care to maintain his Arab nationalist orthodoxy, wrote a response in August 1961 that seemed to the Americans 'extraordinarily warm in tone, mild in language, forthcoming, and hopeful for the relations of the two countries in the future'.[458]

Rumours of CIA involvement in the Syrian secession caused a predictable wobble in the relationship. However, Nasser was placated when Badeau assured him that these tales were untrue, the US delayed recognising the new Damascus regime, and Kennedy approved a massive three-year food aid agreement.[459] There was serious discussion within the Kennedy Administration of an invitation for Nasser to visit Washington, while a series of high-level US officials stopped off in Cairo for a cosy chat with the Egyptian leader.[460] In June 1962, Kennedy received from his counterpart a missive of unprecedented gratitude, underlining the 'mutual understanding' between the two countries and expressing confidence that any differences could be kept 'within limits not to be exceeded'.[461] Even when the US decided to sell Israel surface-to-air missiles in early September 1962, Nasser made no public outcry.[462] In the end, it was the Yemen confrontation that would blight US-Egyptian relations in the 1960s.

***

Prior to the Syrian secession, President Nasser's relations with the Imam Ahmed of Yemen had been cordial, but afterwards, Egyptian criticisms of his absolutist rule increased. The Imam parried with a poem:

Taking property by forbidden means
On a pretext of 'nationalisation' or of 'justice'
Between those who have wealth and those with none,
Is a crime against Islamic law.[463]

This 64-line polemic against socialism, broadcast in December 1961, was construed as an indirect attack on Nasser, who responded vigorously. Cairo withdrew from the nominal federal union with Yemen, and her propaganda machine was fully unleashed against 'the reaction, ignorance and backward mentality of the Yemeni rulers'.[464] Indeed, the response was perhaps more vigorous than the occasion warranted. Nasser, who used to tell a joke about how God came down from heaven with the Archangel Gabriel to find Yemen, alone on this earth, exactly the same as the day he created it, may have been relieved to escape from the ideological difficulties posed by alliance with a feudal regime.[465] The Imam himself claimed the poem had been misunderstood, and a few days later was inspired to broadcast a second minor masterpiece, rebuking the Arabs for quarrelling among themselves.[466] Nasser's reaction is not recorded.

The birth of the YAR came on 26 September 1962, almost exactly nine months after this very public quarrel. But there is still considerable disagreement among historians regarding Egypt's role during the gestation period. Did she know about the revolution in advance; did she provide moral or actual support; was she the principal driving force? At one extreme, there are those who argue that the Egyptian regime sponsored the revolutionaries *because* they wanted a military presence in Yemen for strategic reasons. Others claim that all subsequent decisions became inevitable after Nasser committed himself to mere moral support for the Yemeni Free Officers, leading him into a trap from which he could not escape.

The official story is that Egypt did not know about the revolution in advance. 'The Yemen war came as a shock,' stated SEC member Abdel Latif Baghdadi.[467] Immediately after the coup, both Yemeni and Egyptian leaders were equally clear on this question. 'Thanks to God we staged our revolution ourselves,' announced the new YAR President, Colonel Abdullah Sallal, at a rally in Sana'a the following month – also attended by Egyptian Vice President Anwar Sadat.[468] 'Unity of aim, without any previous knowledge,' emphasised Heikal, 'made Abdel Nasser stand with Al-Sallal and his popular revolution'.[469] And Nasser himself agreed:

> We had to back the Yemeni revolution, even without knowing who was behind it... We did not know the names of the leaders of the revolution, because the Government had not yet been announced then.[470]

Various external commentators have followed a similar line. Ambassador Badeau emphasises that the Egyptians knew so little about the locality at the time of the coup that 'Nasser sent Sami Sharaf privately to ask if the US Embassy had any information on Yemen that would be helpful to them'. (Sharaf confirms this incident, although he implies his real purpose was to probe the American attitude to the revolution.)[471] Egyptian influence was strong in Yemen, and Egyptian military and technical personnel who had once been stationed there maintained local contacts. On the other hand, it is true that pro-Nasser rhetoric was not always evidence of manipulation by the Egyptian regime. 'I can control whom I choose, but I cannot control who chooses me,' Heikal quotes Nasser as telling King Saud 'rather wistfully' – although perhaps disingenuously, given the habitual involvement of Egyptian agents in insurrections elsewhere in the Arab world at that time.[472]

The difficulty is that all sorts of people were plotting in Yemen that year. Several attempts were made to assassinate the elderly Imam Ahmed. There are tales of a secret revolutionary committee; of internecine succession struggles; of a palace cleaning woman recruited to place a bomb under the Imam's bed. When the neighbouring Sharif of Beihan first heard of the September coup, he concluded that it had been undertaken by some anti-Egyptian contacts of his own.[473] But 86 of the 400 Yemeni army officers were conspiring in the pro-Egyptian camp. Colonel Sallal, who was also in contact with dissatisfied leaders of the Hashid tribal federation, is said to have rejected Cairo's initial proposals for a *coup d'état*. The revolution was eventually instigated by a younger and more radical set of officers, led by Lieutenant Ali Abdel Moghny, who was killed in the fighting. Sallal was brought in as a belated figurehead, *à la* Naguib.[474]

In the student riots of early September 1962, pictures of Nasser were displayed, and Cairo Radio publicised and intensified the unrest.[475] Following the infamous poem, Nasser had begun to support the Yemeni Free Movement (YFM) in Egypt, which had previously not been permitted to act openly against the Imam. Dissidents were given access to the highly effective Cairo propaganda machine.[476] The *Voice of the Arabs* broadcast helpful suggestions for the wording of a republican constitution. A new series called 'The Secrets of the Yemen' began in July 1962, presented by Abdel Rahman Baydani, 'the Yemen revolutionary'.[477] Baydani accused Imam Ahmed of rapaciousness, injustice and drug addiction. The Imam's son, Crown Prince Badr, was condemned as having 'no principles', and when he succeeded his father in September 1962, the tone remained unyielding:

> Free sons, the sins of the past are still those of the present. Even the people who served the departed Imam are the same that serve the new Imam... The people will break all bonds and shackles and will impose themselves for the building of the future of Yemen.[478]

***

Beyond this moral support, however, the Egyptian regime was at least informed in advance of the Yemeni revolutionaries' plans, promising to provide support after the coup had been accomplished.[479] There is disagreement over whether Nasser was also aware of the timing of the coup, but, on balance, it seems probable. Although Cairene sources tend to be cagier, former Yemeni revolutionaries are unanimous on this point. Some versions name specific Yemeni emissaries to Cairo, who were in contact with Baydani and Sadat. Others emphasise the role of the Egyptian *chargé* in Sana'a, Mohammed Abdel Wahed, portrayed as manipulating several separate sets of plotters and Crown Prince Badr himself.[480]

Abdel Rahman Baydani tells a splendidly detailed story suggesting that the Egyptians actually instigated the revolution. He claims to have been in regular contact with Sadat and Nasser on the one hand; and the Yemeni revolutionaries on the other, using the codes of the Egyptian Embassy in Sana'a for secure communications. Six shipments of weapons, he asserts, were sent to the conspirators in Yemen, transported in large suitcases on British Airways passenger planes via Aden. (On one occasion the bearer had a nervous moment when the British Governor was on board and the plane was met by police at Aden airport.) Baydani states that his final radio announcement, on 26 September 1962, contained secret code words referring to a well-known Yemeni story, which signalled the start of the revolution: 'Friday is Friday, the sermon is the sermon.' Nasser and Sadat not only knew he was sending the signal, but Sadat waited for him outside in a car. After the revolution had been announced, Baydani adds, he had a quick meeting with Nasser, who provided him with a secretary so they could keep in direct contact, and kissed and congratulated him: 'Yes, your people did it.' Then he was flown straight to Sana'a in a special plane with extra fuel tanks and no seats, which had been standing by since July, awaiting the revolution.[481]

Baydani was dismissed by Robert Stookey of the US Legation in 1962 as an 'incorrigible publicity hound' prone to distort facts, and subsequent commentators have been little kinder.[482] However, he includes much circumstantial detail, and certain aspects of his story are confirmed by Egyptian insiders. The well-informed journalist, Youssef Sherif, agrees that the Sana'a Embassy was used for communications before the revolution; General Hadidi, who was then in charge of Military Intelligence, admits that he was contacted by the Yemeni Free Officers through Baydani and gave them a few small arms in June or July 1962; Ahmed Said, manager of *Voice of the Arabs*, believes Baydani sent the signal for the revolution.[483] Amin Howeidy of General Intelligence remembers an occasion in early 1962:

> We expected that something would happen in Yemen... There was a person who was called Abdel Rahman Baydani. He was there. Sadat told me, 'Amin, Baydani expects change in the Yemen. We will support them, and you are the man who will be responsible for this assistance.'... I heard him, and I had no confidence in Abdel Rahman. So I left.[484]

'We are now concentrating on dealing with the young Yemeni officers we trained in Sana'a and are in direct contact with them,' an Egyptian Colonel revealed over dinner to the exiled Mohsen Alaini, soon to become – albeit briefly – the first Foreign Minister of the YAR. 'We expect that a revolution will occur soon,' he added.[485] The Egyptians undoubtedly had substantial control over the Yemeni revolutionaries. The YFM was forced to accept Baydani, Sadat's protégé, who had never been involved with them and whom they did not trust, as their leader and spokesman. The most respected Yemeni dissident, Ahmed Mohammed Nu'man, who did not immediately express his full support for the revolution, was forcibly detained in Cairo.[486] Baydani himself was imposed on Sallal as his Prime Minister by Nasser, who wanted a reliable pro-Egyptian near the seat of power. The names of most other new ministers were also sent from Cairo.[487]

However, the only possible piece of concrete evidence that Egypt masterminded the coup depends on the claim that the arrival of Egyptian military assistance in Sana'a was so prompt that it must have been arranged in advance. The charge that Egyptian helicopters arrived within 24 hours (and must therefore have been hidden in the Embassy or on ships off the coast) rests on the highly partial testimony of the Imam Badr.[488] The journalist Edgar O'Ballance states that the Egyptian paratroopers who were to form Sallal's personal bodyguard began arriving by air on 28 September, which is prompt but not impossible.[489] The key question therefore concerns the arrival of the first Egyptian military transports, which were sighted at the Yemeni port of Hodeidah very soon after the revolution. One Saudi commentator gives the date as 1 October, in which case the ships must have been loaded in advance and almost certainly 'would have to have embarked from Egypt *before* the coup, clearly suggesting Nasser's foreknowledge and predetermined intent to intervene'.[490]

The first official news report of the arrival of an Egyptian vessel, said to be carrying only medical supplies and food, was not until 6 October.[491] However, a contemporary British Embassy observer felt 'tolerably certain', based on enquiries made in Suez, 'that UAR shock troops, probably of battalion strength, embarked on *S.S. Sudan* and *S.S. Taludi*, and that both ships sailed on 3rd October'.[492] Others agree that the *Sudan* arrived on 5 October, although estimates of the number of troops on board range from 100 to 'several thousand'.[493] However, Salah Nasr says that the first ship did not even depart until 5 October, eight days after the revolution, while Baghdadi claims that Nasser waited 15 days before sending one detachment on a ship.[494] These later, obviously exaggerated estimates, together with Heikal's disingenuous attempt to give Egypt credit for miraculously fast preparation in his *Al-Ahram* editorial of 16 November, may imply that the Egyptians did have something to hide.[495] In any case, the general argument that Nasser knew about the coup in advance, was aware of its approximate timing, and supported it with both overt propaganda and covert assistance remains highly convincing.

***

Less than two hours after the first reports of the revolution, the Egyptian government broadcast its opposition to 'any foreign interference in the affairs of Yemen'.[496] The initial Expeditionary Force was dispatched shortly thereafter, and a substantial body of troops had arrived in Sana'a well before the formal announcement on 10 October that Egypt would 'stand with all its powers by the side of Yemen to resist any aggression'.[497] The decision to launch 'Operation 9000' was Nasser's, although he later seemed disinclined to take responsibility.[498] 'He brought us into this,' he told the Saudi monarch querulously, pointing the finger at his eventual successor Anwar Sadat.[499] Sadat did play a key role in influencing Nasser's policy.[500] 'He has the file,' the President informed Mohsen Alaini, insisting Sadat attend a Yemen-related meeting – and later, when things began to go wrong, Alaini quotes Nasser as exclaiming: 'I want to hang him!'[501] Indeed, Sadat never denied his own part. 'I was the first to support it,' he wrote later of the Yemeni request for assistance. 'I convinced the Council of the necessity for supporting the Yemeni Revolution, and we did so.'[502]

Sadat stands accused by many former colleagues of 'deluding' Nasser by giving him false information, which the President used as a basis for his decision to intervene.[503] He told him that the venture would not require many Egyptian soldiers, perhaps as few as 100, and only a couple of planes.[504] Sadat himself is not usually blamed for deliberate deceit, merely for telling Nasser what he wanted to hear, for inefficiency, or for excessive dependence upon his brother-in-law Abdel Rahman Baydani, an unlikely Svengali.[505] Baydani, detractors suggest, made misleading claims about the degree of Egyptian assistance that would be needed, the level of support the revolution had in Yemen and the apparent death of the Imam Badr. Because Sadat 'did not like to read,' remembers Foreign Minister Mahmoud Riad, Baydani 'was able to control his mind'.[506]

However, Sadat is not the only member of Nasser's elite who is blamed for under-estimating the difficulties of intervention in Yemen. The President also felt that he had been deceived by poor military intelligence, and the over-confidence of Marshal Amer, who told him: 'With my life, Mr. President, I will get Yemen subdued for you in two weeks.'[507] Heikal asserts that, as Sadat was in charge of the Egyptian political effort in Yemen, his patron Amer was responsible for the military side.[508] Alaini concurs that Nasser once insisted to him that the Yemen issue could only be discussed in the presence of both Amer and Sadat.[509] In the end, however, the army's eagerness to intervene was merely positive reinforcement, pushing the President in the direction he wanted to go. 'The man who gave his decision was Nasser,' Amin Howeidy concludes firmly. 'Amer didn't object. Sadat was enthusiastic. But the decision was taken by Nasser.'[510]

***

'Principles and nothing else induced us to go to Yemen,' Nasser later felt the need to explain. What else could it have been? 'In Yemen there is no oil, no water, nothing. It used to have coffee in the old days, now it does not have any.'[511] Former insiders agree that idealistic motives inspired them to protect a revolution explicitly identifying itself with their own.[512] The Imam's medieval regime was distasteful to the modern revolutionary mind. However, this does not imply that Nasser's decision was necessarily disinterested. Given his role as the leader of Arab nationalism, supporting new-born revolutions was what he was supposed to do. 'One, he assisted every revolution in the Arab world,' explains Howeidy. 'This is the first thing.'[513] A contemporary Egyptian joke related how, after seeing the film 'Mutiny on the Bounty', Nasser at once cabled his Foreign Ministry:

> Contact the mutineers on the *Bounty* immediately. Tell them we support their cause and any attack on them will be considered an attack on the UAR![514]

Nasser's prestige was at stake. The collapse of the Yemeni revolution would have been a major defeat for the Egyptian President, in that he would have failed to live up to his own image.[515] The Arab revolution had suffered one defeat with the Syrian secession. There was need of a 'distraction' to divert attention from other problems – 'a victory in the Arab theatre', specifies one former aide; 'a revolution or something to raise our morale,' adds another.[516] The reason Nasser's prestige was affected by the success or failure of the Yemeni revolution was, however, ultimately strategic. It would be seen as a victory or defeat in a broader, ongoing struggle against his enemies. There were clear geopolitical advantages to the presence of a strongly pro-Egyptian regime in Sana'a. It might enable Egypt to escape from economic encirclement, pressuring the Saudis, the British in Aden, and even the United States.[517] In particular, access to the Bab al-Mandab strait could give Egypt control over both ends of the Red Sea, turning it into an 'Arab Lake' and enabling Nasser to deny Israel access to the Iranian oil that reached her through Eilat.[518]

It has been argued that oil also constituted a more direct incentive for the Egyptian intervention. 'No one from Cairo to Kuwait had any illusions about Nasser's goal,' wrote Sir Kennedy Trevaskis, the Colonial Office's staunchest representative in the SAF. 'It was not the Yemen. It was the oil, over which we in Aden stood guard.'[519] Naturally, Egyptians deny this, although Mahmoud Riad's argument that Egypt was rich enough not to need the money is hardly borne out by the economic realities.[520] It is, at least, safe to conclude with Heikal that the Yemen War was part of a wider conflict made much more sensitive by its proximity to the Gulf oil reserves.[521] But the problem remains of reconciling two extreme points of view. On the one hand,

Saudi and British sources suggest that Nasser was planning to use Yemen as a foothold from which to take over the entire Arabian Peninsula. On the other, his former associates emphasise that his primary motivation was simply to safeguard the internal changes in Yemen.

In fact, the internal changes in Yemen were a key part of Nasser's campaign against the Saudis and the British. Thus his military intervention in Yemen is best understood in the context of his revolutionary struggle. The Yemeni coup offered Nasser a unique chance to bring direct pressure to bear on Britain's last major outpost in the Arab world, through cross-border contacts with the insurgents in Aden and the Protectorates. 'They are concerned about oil and their colonies in the Arabian Peninsula,' sneered the Egyptian President. 'They know that imperialism is bound to die, that Aden is bound to be liberated, that the South is bound to be delivered from imperialism.'[522] The UK was certainly perceived as a dangerous enemy of the nascent YAR. Sadat predicted that she would manipulate the situation to further her own aggressive interests, and the newspapers echoed this.[523] However, the Egyptian elite did not believe the British reaction would be strong or concerted enough to affect its own plans for Yemen.[524] 'The British lion has turned into a wolf following his defeat on the shores of Suez and in the Arabian Peninsula,' wrote Heikal, adding lyrically:

> Who knows what fate the British obstinacy in the face of history will bring to the wolf in the south of the Arabian Peninsula? Perhaps, the wolf which was a lion may turn into a cat lost in the barren part of the Arabian Desert.[525]

However, although Nasser was naturally glad to gain a strategic advantage against the British in the Gulf, at the outset it was their support for Saudi Arabia and the royalist tribes that made them a significant enemy. The Saudis were seen as the primary threat.[526] Sadat later told a subordinate:

> If we did not go to the Yemen the result would be the revolution would collapse and Saudi Arabia would rule the Arabian Peninsula and then Egypt, so we have to support the Yemen Revolution.[527]

The Saudi regime was threatened after the revolution from both Cairo and Sana'a. Vast quantities of hostile propaganda were broadcast. The exiled 'Committee of Free Princes' was calling for reform on *Voice of the Arabs*; and King Saud was explicitly informed that he was the next target.[528] Arms, which it was vainly hoped would be discovered by the opposition forces, were dropped on the Saudi north coast.[529] In November, there were even Egyptian air attacks on the disputed border towns of Najran and Qizan. Saudi dissidents were in regular contact with members of the Egyptian regime.[530] 'Our attack on the Saudi regime,' explained Nasser brightly, 'means that we are supporting the aspirations of the Arabs in the Arabian Peninsula'.[531] Nevertheless, most Egyptians agree they had no intention of actually invading Saudi Arabia. Cairo, although covertly and overtly encouraging revolution in Aden and Riyadh, as it had in Sana'a, was not preparing a military assault. The Egyptian presence in Yemen facilitated such subversive activities, but it was not such an important prerequisite that it can be sufficiently explained by the desire to continue them. The case of Yemen itself showed that revolution could be adequately incited from an even greater geographical distance.

***

Nasser had always claimed that the Egyptian troops were sent in response to immediate external aggression against the new Yemeni Republic. 'It turned out that King Saud would not remain silent,' he proclaimed at Port Said that December, to an appreciative audience who jeered at the very mention of that monarch. 'Of course,' he added, 'it also appeared that those *khawājāt* (foreign gentlemen), the English, who are sitting in the south – in Aden and the Protectorates – were frightened and would not remain quiet.' After all, the President explained with some complacency, 'the appearance of the revolution in the Arabian Peninsula disturbs imperialism, reaction, the English and King Saud, the enemies of progress, the servants of imperialism, King Hussein...' Nasser identified the defections of Saudi pilots asked to fly supplies to the Yemeni royalists, which began on 2 October 1962, as the trigger for his realisation that Saudi Arabia was actively attacking the YAR, goading him to send Egyptian troops.[532] However, it is not clear that this story holds up when set against the known facts.

First, it seems probable that Nasser sent military support earlier. The journalist Edgar O'Ballance remembers seeing at least 3000 Egyptian soldiers camped round Yemen's major cities by the beginning of October, 'with armoured vehicles in conspicuous evidence and scores of aircraft flying noisily overhead'.[533] Second, the Saudi and British roles at this stage seem to have been minimal. Prince Hassan, the brother of the deceased Imam Ahmed and apparently his heir, since Badr was believed dead, was in New York at the time of the coup. He immediately requested aid from the British Colonial Secretary, Duncan Sandys, who was discouraging.[534] Hassan's son was received in Aden on 1 October, and Sir Kennedy Trevaskis, on his way home for consultation, 'fixed up a small present of £7,500... and also some ammunition'. Only on 5 October did Sandys decide 'to give all reasonable support to Hassan in so far as this can be done without undue risk of open involvement,' allowing him up to £50,000 and 5000 rifles. Trevaskis then met the SIS Chief to discuss covert ways and means, as a result of which two radio operators were sent to the royalists.[535] By the time any of this assistance could have arrived, substantial Egyptian forces were already firmly entrenched in Sana'a.[536]

The Saudis, for their part, certainly received Prince Hassan on 29 September, and by 1 October gave him some money and weapons, augmented over the next fortnight. The Jordanians soon followed suit, while a royalist radio station began to operate from Saudi territory. However, this was not as yet a major commitment.[537] By early November, the royalists were avowedly being trained by Jordanian technicians, who came and went into Yemen, but no Saudis crossed the border (their army being, in any case, unreliable).[538] The idea of large-scale military intervention from Saudi Arabia at this time was 'simply laughable'.[539] Indeed, Cairo Radio did not start reporting attacks by Saudi infiltrators against the YAR until 7 October, while Nasser himself later dated the beginning of the trouble to 15 full days after the revolution.[540]

However, although Nasser intervened pre-emptively, it is possible that he was responding to the *general* threat he saw the Saudis as posing to the new Republic. He later claimed that King Saud started sending arms and massing his army on the border from 27 September.[541] This would be a matter easily susceptible to misinterpretation, since such a move could have been either offensive or defensive – complicated by the fact that the new YAR government was reviving the historic Yemeni claim to the territories around Najran. The mere arrival of Prince Hassan in Saudi Arabia may have cemented Nasser's conviction that the Saudis would not stay out.[542] In the early stages, therefore, he was probably reacting to perceived Saudi hostility and *intention* to interfere, rather than to any significant moves against the Yemeni revolution.

This interpretation initially seems incompatible with the common contention that Nasser did not expect a proxy war in Yemen, and believed that it would be sufficient for Egypt to send a symbolic force – 'we never thought it would lead to what it did'.[543] The evidence for this contention is convincing. General Murtagi, later commander of the Expeditionary Force, says that Egypt originally sent only a symbolic detachment of paratroopers, and the Director of General Intelligence, Salah Nasr, agrees.[544] Heikal depicts Nasser as convinced, based on military reports, that one such regiment and a wing of fighter-bombers would be able to secure the coup.[545] Marshal Amer apparently estimated in private talks that the Egyptian forces would only need to stay for a few weeks.[546] It might be argued that if Nasser was genuinely surprised by the subsequent escalation, he cannot have seen Saudi Arabia as determined to intervene in Yemen.

***

However, the situation was never so simple. There were two elements to the Egyptian miscalculation. First, they did not expect significant internal opposition to the new Republic. 'Yemeni tribes should not bother us,' proclaimed Anwar Sadat breezily to the new YAR Foreign Minister, Mohsen Alaini. 'Don't they know yet that we are about to send our storm troopers over there? Those are the troops we train to even eat serpents.'[547] Egyptians had little knowledge of the geography, people or culture of Yemen. Because the Shafeis in the south, who largely accepted the coup, controlled the major towns, Cairo assumed this equated to universal support, disregarding the Zeidi tribes of the northern mountains. Their ideological predisposition was to believe that revolution against a corrupt and oppressive tyranny *would* be met with universal support. They had a fixed image of the Yemenis tribes as backward and incapable of holding their own in modern warfare without external intervention. Immediately after the revolution, Cairo Radio blamed the Saudis and Jordanians for attacks on the new Republic – 'together with some reactionary royalist remnants mobilised and armed by Saud'.[548] The Egyptians felt that revolutionary right was on their side. Once the benighted tribes had been exposed to their benevolent influence, they would surely come round.

Moreover, Cairo's main sources of information were the Yemeni revolutionaries themselves, who had an interest in portraying themselves as more popular than in fact they were. In particular, it has been claimed that they deceived Egypt by concealing the fact that the Imam Badr had escaped. Otherwise, Mahmoud Riad argues, 'Egypt would not have intervened in Yemen because al-Badr was an open-minded

Imam'.[549] It does seem probable that the republican leaders must have suspected the possibility that Badr had escaped their somewhat chaotic coup almost at once – although they did not publicly accept it until he gave an international press conference (attended by, among others, Kim Philby) in a cave on 10 November. The first royalist statements that Badr was alive began on 9 October, and even journalists in Sana'a were made suspicious by the lack of a body, the state of the palace, and the inconsistencies in republican stories regarding this death.[550] It may also be the case that these suspicions were not passed on to Egypt.

However, there is no evidence that this particular information would have changed Egyptian choices. As Crown Prince, Badr had certainly flirted with the idea of Arabism. 'The Imam is of the opinion that Al Badr will throw the Yemen to the bosom of the Egyptians,' wrote the anonymous author of an intelligence report that came into the hands of the British authorities in Aden before Ahmed's death.[551] 'The moment the old man is dead,' predicted the Sharif of Beihan in 1961, 'Badr will be on the telephone to Cairo and we will have Nasser as a neighbour'.[552] Badr himself later confessed to a British contact that in 1958–9 he was 'conniving secretly with Egyptian officials to bring about the early demise of his father's reign'.[553] However, Heikal implies Nasser did not have such a high opinion of Badr, since one particular occasion when the Crown Prince was taken to visit Cairo Zoo:

> All went well until he discovered a Qat tree that nobody else had recognised and he climbed into the tree, sat on a branch, and chewed Qat. When this was reported to Nasser, he wondered no more about Badr's capabilities.[554]

Badr was subjected to Egyptian propaganda as vicious as that against his father, and he was not so popular in Yemen that it made a difference whether he or Hassan was the heir. Cairo's misunderstanding of the Yemeni internal situation was more important.

Nasser's second miscalculation related to his image of Saudi Arabia. The Saudis were seen as extremely hostile to Egypt, the YAR, and revolutions in general. Therefore, they had a powerful motive for intervention against the new Yemeni regime. They were also seen as strong enough to threaten it in the absence of external support. But they were *not* seen as capable of surviving a direct confrontation with Nasser. Chatting with the US Ambassador, Egyptian Vice President Anwar Sadat 'lightly dismissed' the efficacy of any counter-revolutionary action.[555] It was expected that the Saudis would concentrate their inferior armed forces internally to control the opposition, rather than moving them to the border.[556] The monarchy's internal stability seemed doubtful, especially if the Yemeni revolt proved infectious. 'Goodbye, Your Majesty,' wrote Heikal to Saud, prophesying an armed uprising in his own country.[557] The point of Nasser's symbolic intervention was to show that Egypt was prepared to send military support to the Yemeni revolution – and thus, it was hoped, to avoid the necessity of so doing. But Saudi Arabia's real power had always lain not in arms nor in legitimacy, but in money. Nasser did not yet realise what an important factor that could become when combined with the unexpected recalcitrance of the royalist tribes.

5
A Very Big Forest: Lions and Tigers and Bears

We were in a very big forest and the beasts all over the world were very dangerous, outside and inside.[558] – Hussein Shafei, Vice President and SEC member

The British lion has turned into a wolf following his defeat on the shores of Suez and in the Arabian Peninsula.[559] – Mohammed Hassanein Heikal

As we've said, Nasser has tiger by the tail.[560] – Robert Komer of the NSC

Nasser has the bear by the tail and the fool can't let go.[561] – Komer

'We sent a battalion to Yemen,' Nasser needled his colleague Anwar Sadat, whom he tended to blame for the entire enterprise, 'and reinforced it with two divisions.'[562] Within a year, the number of Egyptian troops in Yemen soared to unanticipated levels. It was a slippery slope. As Egypt became more and more deeply committed, the political costs of withdrawal rose. The original 'symbolic' force of 2000 men had quadrupled by mid-November 1962.[563] Marshal Amer arrived in January 1963 and remained until March, increasing the troop contingent to 20,000 and directing a successful offensive. Small detachments came home to be welcomed as victorious heroes – and quietly replaced by others.[564] By the first anniversary of the revolution, the Egyptian Expeditionary Force in Yemen numbered about 30,000 (nearly one third of Nasser's entire army), and had been re-organised for a long-term occupational role, holding key towns and lines of communication.[565]

On this basis, some suggest that Nasser's apparent co-operation with the US search for a settlement was merely an expedient pose. US recognition of the new Yemeni republican regime in December 1962 was negotiated with relatively little trouble, as both parties were anxious to avoid confrontation.[566] In return for this recognition, Nasser assured President Kennedy that Yemen would not be used as a base to attack Saudi Arabia or Aden. The Egyptian regime also issued an agreed statement that it was ready 'to begin gradually to withdraw its forces'. However, in contravention of the British Prime Minister's urgent advice to Kennedy, no timetable was agreed. Although the US seems to have understood the statement as an absolute commitment to withdraw, Nasser later emphasised that it was strictly conditional upon Riyadh ceasing assistance to the Yemeni royalists.[567]

Moreover, on the very day of the statement, Cairo Radio announced that the prevailing opinion at the High Command was that there was 'a new round coming up in Yemen'.[568] Within a fortnight, the very idea of withdrawal was painted as an anti-Arab plot:

> The imperialist mind and the reactionary mind thought up a new plan, demanding the withdrawal of the UAR forces from Yemen. Why? So that armed aggression against Yemen might continue.[569]

Nasser deliberately worsened the confrontation, claims the former Yemeni Foreign Minister, Mohsen Alaini. He sought any excuse to augment the Egyptian military presence in Yemen, wantonly antagonising both Britain and Saudi Arabia, and cunningly sabotaging the UN mediation efforts in 1963 by neglecting to ask for sufficiently stringent guarantees.[570]

***

Others argue that the gradual military increase was more or less accidental. Nasser had a 'tiger by the tail' and was unable to back down, forcing him to protect his existing investment (both of prestige and of more tangible resources) at higher and higher cost. 'We started the battle and we had no way to return back,' remembers Nasser's former aide, Hamed Mahmoud; 'we had to continue'.[571] There is a certain amount of evidence that Nasser was indeed hoping to pull out in 1963. In January, he was said to have 'drawn up a plan for withdrawal within 60 days'.[572] He continued his friendly correspondence with Kennedy, repeatedly promising restraint.[573] In gratitude for all her mediation efforts, he presented the United States with a large antique temple.[574] He even signed a disengagement agreement with Saudi Arabia, which would eventually result in the belated dispatch of a force of UN peacekeepers.

Pro-Egyptian coups in Iraq and Syria temporarily made Nasser's position in the Arab arena much easier – indeed, in March, the three governments discussed the possibility of military unity. 'At least we will be reassured; if we go to Yemen or anywhere we can feel reassured,' Marshal Amer noted in its favour. The Syrian leaders were keen to jump on the bandwagon. 'Obviously, 30,000 soldiers from the Egyptian army, from you, go to Yemen – why should we not take part?' one asked, with gratifying enthusiasm. 'Because you were objecting,' answered Amer, with more truth than tact. The Syrians were unabashed. 'Sir, regarding Yemen, with God's will we shall join you. The unified command will be established.' It was left to the Egyptian President to avert this somewhat alarming prospect. 'No,' stated Nasser firmly, 'the Yemeni war is over.'[575]

This conversation hints at a difference in perspective between Nasser and Amer, who appears to have been thinking in terms of a continuing Egyptian presence in the Arabian Peninsula. 'You must always be ready to replace your brothers in Yemen,' the Marshal told troops practising incongruous mountain fighting techniques in Sinai that November.[576] Hussein Shafei claims that Amer saw the conflict as an opportunity to increase his own influence.[577] The ever-eloquent Baydani paints a vivid picture of Nasser as desperate to withdraw, featuring Amer as a Soviet instrument and the villain of the piece. 'I am in a corner in Yemen,' the despairing Egyptian President apparently told the new Yemeni Prime Minister in January 1963, burying his head in his hands. 'You are in one here in Egypt,' returned Baydani, who claims that the overbearing Amer wanted to stay in Yemen to please the USSR and regain the reputation he had lost in Syria.[578] Unfortunately, this version of events is largely unsupported. The Soviets may have had an interest in the Egyptian presence in Yemen, but there are no other indications that they dictated it; indeed, Mourad Ghalib, former Egyptian Ambassador to Moscow, expressly denies that they influenced Cairo's policy.[579]

Although Amer naturally had substantial control over military decisions, he did discuss them with Nasser, and both were keen for the Yemeni revolution to be preserved. It was a fine balance. The Marshal continually pressed the President to make additional resources available – but he avoided broader policy issues. Nasser sometimes cited the desires and demands of the army as a factor limiting his freedom of action in discussions with US representatives – but this was also a negotiating strategy.[580] The fact that his military chief helped to determine military policy can hardly absolve the President of responsibility. In reality, although the army was an important influence, and Nasser was sensitive to its demands, the two men had only minor disagreements on this topic.[581]

***

Nasser felt he had pressing reasons to maintain the flow of troops to Yemen. These reasons were founded in his changing perceptions of his enemies, especially Britain and Saudi Arabia. Nasser tried and failed to limit the British response by promising that he had no designs on Aden and offering a deal whereby the new Yemeni regime would drop its territorial claims in return for diplomatic recognition.[582] President Sallal guaranteed that the Republic would 'leave our brethren in the south to determine for themselves their own destinies'.[583] Although the Foreign Office was inclined to accept this offer, the Colonial Office disagreed and the Prime Minister, Harold Macmillan, temporised.[584] Initially, he merely hoped for a short delay to placate the South Arabian Federation rulers. 'Sharif Husein will have hysterics whenever we decide to recognise,' predicted Charles Johnston, the Governor of Aden, 'and is likely then to demand immediate independence for the Federation or Beihan or both.'[585] Thus Cabinet approved recognition of the YAR 'in principle' on 23 October, and Macmillan expected to have to follow through by the end of the month.[586] That day, however, there was an Egyptian air raid on Beihan, Britain's ally. The Federation rulers panicked, relations deteriorated, and by November, Sallal was calling on 'the sons of the south' to rise against the British oppressor.[587] The UK government deferred recognition once again, although it was still seen as ultimately inevitable until the YAR broke diplomatic ties of its own accord, in February 1963. Macmillan formally told the Cabinet that he 'regretted this result'. But he wrote more cheerfully in his diary. 'The Yemen problem (like so many) has settled itself!'[588]

By this time, however, Nasser was deeply suspicious. Egyptian attention was initially focused on the British backbench MP and reporter, Colonel Neil 'Billy' McLean. One of Nasser's top advisors, Hassan Sabri Al-Kholi, thought he was 'organising a tribal war in the Yemen'. The British Embassy in Cairo concluded: 'I fear the Egyptians regard McLean's trips to Yemen with genuine suspicion – it goes deeper than propaganda – and believe that we are "pulling a Lawrence" on them.' The suspicion *was* exaggerated, but perhaps not by far. 'Sabri's main theme is a bit too true,' scribbled the FO's Brian Pridham on a report of this conversation.[589] McLean's first 'unofficial' visit in late October 1962 was inspired by Macmillan's son-in-law, the Aviation Minister, Julian Amery, following a consultation with King Hussein of Jordan at Claridge's.[590] The Colonel's mandate was to investigate and deliver an informed report to the Prime Minister, and he relayed private messages from Saud and Badr to Macmillan – who diplomatically declined to see him in person.[591] Later, McLean did co-ordinate British assistance to the Imam; although it is unlikely that serious operations commenced before March 1963.[592]

McLean travelled from Aden with the assistance of the Sharif of Beihan, to whom he wrote a note reporting his safe arrival in Yemen 'thanks to god and your excellent arrangements'.[593] This missive ended up among the private papers of Sir Kennedy Trevaskis, a Colonial Office man who was to succeed Johnston as Governor in July 1963 – although he was an influential personage long before that.[594] Trevaskis was strongly in favour of helping the royalists, sending repeated futile pleas (including carefully budgeted operational plans) to be permitted to 'resort to extraordinary and covert action to eliminate the threat from Yemen'.[595] Although some aid was eventually provided to the royalists through Beihan, it was not on the scale the hard-liners wished.[596] The truth was that the UK decided against forcibly preventing the Sharif of Beihan from assisting the royalists, rather than persuading him to do so. It was impossible to keep out members of the Yemeni Royal Family, Johnston argued, since 'if they should come as fugitives Arab tradition would not allow the Emir to deny them refuge. Nor is it reasonable that we should press him to do this'.[597] There would be a 'Shariffian explosion looming up', a subordinate warned Trevaskis, if Beihan's ruler were not permitted to purchase material in his own name to help 'the relatives and tribes supporting the rightful Imam's son who is a personal friend of his'.[598] Even then, it was not until December 1963 that the British Cabinet (under the new Prime Minister, Sir Alec Douglas-Home) grudgingly concluded that 'it might improve our relationship with the rulers in the Aden Federation if we ceased trying to prevent them from supplying arms to the Royalists'.[599]

Nevertheless, Nasser's fixed belief in the hostility of the British led him to blame them from the outset for the recurring friction along the YAR-SAF border. 'We know that there is an imperialist agent in Bayhan,' he stated darkly in January 1963, 'and also other agents who carry out British imperialism's plan'.[600] There was an atmosphere of pervasive distrust. 'Confidence in British intentions is a tender plant here,' Beeley, the British Ambassador to Cairo, wrote in February. He felt that Nasser had never forgiven the UK's colonial misdemeanours, approaching her 'rather like a police officer giving a reformed criminal the benefit of the doubt while more than half expecting to detect symptoms of recidivism'.[601] These feelings were reciprocated. 'For Nasser read Hitler and it's all very familiar,' scribbled Macmillan on Beeley's telegram advocating the development of a good working relationship.[602] But the Egyptian President would have reversed the analogy:

> Of course the English are unhappy, because we stick in their throat. The English want to colonise the world – colonise the Arab world. They want to agree with the Saudis to strike at Yemen and we should have nothing to do with it.[603]

Images of Saudi Arabia were therefore also crucial. Prince Faisal had returned from New York to take over effective power from his weaker brother Saud in late October 1962. The change of leadership, together with developments on the ground in Yemen, including the arrival of a squadron of Jordanian fighter planes on 8 November, seems to have convinced Cairo that the affluent monarchy was not entirely helpless.[604] Faisal decided to continue and even increase aid to the Yemeni royalists; he sacked those Cabinet ministers suggesting recognition of the YAR; and on 6 November he severed diplomatic relations with Egypt.[605] By December, Cairo Radio was attacking Faisal as 'no better than his brother'.[606] Faisal was once pro-Nasser,' reported Robert Komer of the US National Security Council (NSC), 'but now hates and fears him'.[607] The Yemen conflict became a personal duel between the two rulers.

'Saud and Faisal were the first to begin the aggression,' stated Nasser firmly in early 1963, 'and Saud and Faisal are the ones who are continuing the aggression'.[608] In order to justify the Egyptian Expeditionary Force in the eyes of the world, the President certainly had a strong ulterior motive to depict Saudi Arabia as hostile. However, two private letters of December 1962, written to Marshal Amer in Sana'a, suggest that his doubts about Saudi intentions were genuine, and he truly believed they were committed to opposing him. He argued that developments on the Saudi-Yemeni border showed 'that Saudi Arabia will not commit itself to the Kennedy letter on disengagement, because they are storing arms and ammunition and sending in infiltrators and paying money'.[609] Nasser continually complained of Faisal's 'bad faith'.[610] Saudi Arabia was depicted as a crucial link in an imperialist conspiracy against the new Yemeni regime:

> Evidence gathered recently proves that King Husayn and King Saud have allowed British imperialism to prepare the plan for aggression against the Yemeni revolution, and that the two kings, together with al-Badr, depended on aid offered to them by the USA from behind the scenes.[611]

In short, then, Nasser was genuinely eager to leave Yemen, *provided that* to do so would not endanger the new Republic. However, in reality there was no chance that he could ever believe this condition to be fulfilled, given the aid provided by the Saudis and British to the royalists, the difficulty of entirely stopping such aid when private individuals had motives to continue it, and the impossibility of verifying whether or not it had in fact ceased. The problem was that Nasser's distrust of 'reactionary' and 'imperialist' motives was also genuine, rather than being a mere excuse for expansion. How could he trust the word of the Saudis, rivals in an ideological battle for the Arab world, or of the British, his old imperialist foe? (Their own reasons for distrusting Nasser's word were equally powerful, exacerbating the problem.) The Egyptian military, meanwhile, seems to have been confident that it could swiftly defeat the undisciplined Yemeni tribes – with just a few more men. Nasser repeatedly consented, unwilling to alienate the army or risk the loss of prestige if the YAR should fall.

***

The Yemeni Civil War became Nasser's 'Vietnam'. The Egyptian military presence continued to increase steadily, rising to 50,000 troops by the end of 1964 and peaking at about 70,000 the following year.[612] The Egyptian economy struggled under the burden, and the simultaneous loss of international goodwill, particularly from the US, made it ever harder to procure aid to make up the shortfall. Many ordinary Egyptians came to oppose the Yemen involvement. The military consequences were also serious. At least 10,000 Egyptian soldiers and officers were killed.[613] The commitment of a major proportion of the Egyptian army in Yemen would contribute to the defeat of June 1967. Morale and discipline were sapped by the corruption of Amer's clique and the constant stresses of guerrilla warfare.[614] Soldiers who had expected to spend a few weeks in Yemen, with a warm welcome from the locals, discovered that they would probably have their noses and ears cut off if captured by the tribes.[615]

'We wrote to the President and told him that the Yemen was not benefiting us,' remembers General Murtagi. SEC members Baghdadi and Kamal al-Din Hussein also begged him to draw back, to no avail.[616] 'Withdrawal is impossible,' Nasser told the reluctant leader of the Expeditionary Force, General Anwar Qadi:

> It would mean the disintegration of the revolution in Yemen... This is more a political operation than a military one... I consider it to be a counter-response to the separation from Syria. We cannot leave Yemen.[617]

The conflict had turned into a debilitating and unpopular war of attrition against the royalists, the Saudis and the British.

British covert intervention in the Yemeni Civil War was a highly secret initiative, spearheaded by a small group of establishment figures including Amery (sometimes informally called the 'Minister for Yemen'), McLean and Trevaskis. Operations began in April 1963, when they set up a London office recruiting mercenaries – several of whom were former SAS members – to assist the royalist tribes.[618] They worked on a small scale, remembers David Smiley:

> At the height of the mercenary effort, when I was commanding them, they never numbered more than 48, of whom 30 were French or Belgian and 18 British... none of the mercenaries actually fought in the war; their job was to advise the commanders, train their troops and provide communications and medical services.[619]

By 1964, however, this operation was taking place in the context of a much broader deterioration in Anglo-Egyptian relations. Douglas-Home's widely-reported throwaway comment in Ottawa in February 1964 that he wished the US had not intervened to stop the Suez offensive was certainly unhelpful in this respect.[620] But the key flashpoint was the high-profile raid on the Yemeni Harib fort by British jets on 28 March 1964. This attack itself followed a series of republican raids on Beihan, apparently directed against royalist forces gathered there. Nevertheless, the Harib incident was roundly condemned in the UN. Nasser saw it as a hostile escalation rather than a simple retaliation, as

Beeley, who opposed the raid, along with most of the Foreign Office and in stark contrast to Trevaskis and his Colonial Office colleagues, had predicted only days earlier:

> The Egyptians have been warned more than once of the risks of further intrusion; I am sure they have interpreted these warnings to mean that their aircraft might be attacked (and <u>not</u> that retaliatory action might be taken across the frontier).[621]

Nasser struck back at the end of April 1964, on his sole visit to Yemen. He called for a holy war 'to crush British imperialism' and free Aden from 'the most gruesome forms of cruelty, terror and torture'.[622] Egypt already supported Southern revolutionary groups such as the National Liberation Front (NLF), but after the President's summons to arms, Cairo comprehensively backed action against British interests, sponsoring and supplying dissidents.[623] Based in the Yemeni town of Taiz, Egyptian Intelligence dispatched camel-trains of agents – including a couple of journalists who lived to tell the tale – over the border to foment resistance and deliver weapons. Cunningly, they sent British arms left in the Canal Zone Base, hoping to eliminate evidence of their direct involvement.[624] Moreover, remembers Foreign Minister Riad, 'all the anti-British South Yemeni groups were headquartered in and operating from Cairo and were receiving Egypt's financial and military support'.[625] As a result, from May 1964 the UK did approve certain retaliatory measures from the SAF – although this approval would be largely revoked after Harold Wilson's Labour government came to power in October.[626] The bulk of British covert assistance to the royalists seems to have been a response to, rather than a cause of, Nasser's 'declaration of war'.

Relations therefore continued to deteriorate. In May, Nasser, after publicly denouncing the British habit of 'sucking the blood of the Arabs', told the US Ambassador that Egypt had evidence of UK support for the Yemeni royalists.[627] He was probably referring to the five captured letters between participants in the mercenary operation published in *Al-Ahram* that month, although he had various sources of information. Cairo offered rewards for the seizure of named mercenary leaders, and one Briton even received a message 'saying that if he cared to come to Egypt he would have a free holiday in government premises for seven years'.[628] By June, the British Chiefs of Staff were noting reports 'that the number of Egyptian intelligence officers in the Yemen has increased and that the Egyptians are providing increasing material aid not only for dissidents but also for terrorism'.[629] Nasser admitted as much to Beeley when he paid a farewell call, describing the Harib incident 'as an attempt to humiliate the UAR and as a major turning point' that moved Aden up on his agenda. He emphasised 'that it had always been within his capacity to harm us in Aden, and that after Harib there was no reason why he should not do so'.[630] That July, in a vituperative speech threatening to attack the British in fifty places and eliminate their interests everywhere, Nasser still referred back to the same grievance:

> The English, of course, are vexed because we are in Yemen. Let them die in their vexation... We shall break the legs of anyone who will try to commit aggression against Yemen. We have avenged the Harib raid.[631]

***

Egyptian suspicion of British intentions in Yemen had originally been compounded by the fact that the UK was seen as the Arab monarchies' unconditional ally and arms-supplier. It now became clear this distrust had deeper roots. From late 1963, Egypt had tried to improve relations with the other Arabs, even the inveterate 'reactionaries'. In January 1964, Cairo hosted the first Arab summit, in response to the smouldering dispute with Israel over the division of water from the Jordan River. That spring, Amer and Sadat visited Riyadh, and diplomatic relations between Egypt and Saudi Arabia were renewed. In July, as the Egyptian Expeditionary Force gained ground in a major summer offensive, King Hussein of Jordan bowed out of the Yemen conflict altogether: he recognised the YAR and stopped helping the royalists. However, these tentative *rapprochements* actually worsened Anglo-Egyptian relations. After the second Arab summit at Alexandria in September, Cairo Radio rejoiced that the final resolutions mandated collective action against the British in the Arab South as well as against Israel, placing 'Britain's threat on the level of the Zionist threat'.[632]

At the same summit, Egypt and Saudi Arabia made their first serious attempt to settle the Yemen problem. The Alexandria Agreement of September 1964 instigated talks between Yemeni royalists and republicans, resulting in a brief ceasefire and plans for a National Congress that never happened. Nasser saw it as 'a golden opportunity to escape from the trap of Yemen,' remembers his Intelligence Chief.[633] When Faisal finally deposed his brother Saud that November, he did reduce financial aid to the Imam's forces. 'In my conversations with King Faisal, I felt there was goodwill on both sides,' Nasser told his people the following month. 'King Faisal wants, and we here in the UAR want, relations between us and the Kingdom of Saudi Arabia to be strengthened.'[634] Nevertheless, vicious anti-Saudi propaganda continued on the clandestine Egyptian radio station, *Voice of the Arab Nation*.[635] Heikal wrote some strongly hostile editorials (although emphasising they represented his 'personal opinion only') on the very eve of the Alexandria meeting, and another series the following spring accused Faisal of selling out Palestine for the sake of Western arms. There were 'misunderstandings' with Riyadh, Nasser complained to the US Embassy in April 1965, signalling difficulties to come; three days later, Faisal in turn claimed not to understand Nasser's aim in denying that a withdrawal had been agreed, 'for at Alexandria he had said he wanted some way out'.[636]

The Alexandria Agreement broke down due to squabbles among the various Yemeni factions, but Nasser was perhaps not displeased. Tensions between the Egyptians and their Yemeni protégés were on the increase. When Saad el-Din Shazly joined the Expeditionary Force, his distrust of the locals – who might, for all he knew, have been bribed by the Saudis – led him to move his headquarters from the city to the desert.[637] Cairo was deeply suspicious of the northern tribes, who periodically rearranged their loyalties to receive benefits from both sides.[638] They 'prolonged the war in order to satisfy their own greed', complained Foreign Minister Riad.[639] Amer raged against everyone 'who tries to play a double game and obtain money from us and from others, who pretends to be a republican during the day and turns royalist in the evening.'[640] (King Faisal was more sanguine about the situation. 'We know our people there,' he commented wryly. 'They are the Royalists. If they can get something from the other side that is up to them.')[641]

However, there were worse Yemeni traitors in Egyptian eyes. Cairo maintained a 'close tutelage' over the YAR government, even – in an ironic echo of British colonial administration in Egypt – providing each government department with an Egyptian advisor who was actually in charge.[642] Egypt was forced to 'run the whole show', Nasser wearily informed the former Canadian Prime Minister.[643] Many Yemeni politicians resented their displacement, concluding that the real war was between Nasser and Faisal. It just happened to be taking place on Yemeni soil. Thus a dissident group of republicans emerged. Led by the new Yemeni Prime Minister, Ahmed Mohammed Nu'man, they became known as the 'Third Force', and their independent attempts to reach a *modus vivendi* with Riyadh caused Nasser to cut off financial support, threatening an immediate and unilateral withdrawal.

When the Nu'man government came to Cairo to discuss a compromise in May 1965, Nasser at first seemed in full – if dismissive – agreement, complaining that Egypt was bearing an unexpectedly heavy burden. 'We do not have any interests in staying in Yemen.' Some people were talking about Egyptian colonialism in Yemen – but who, he asked somewhat rudely, would ever want to colonise you? The mood changed, however, as Marshal Amer joined the meeting. When Amer stated that Cairo could not accept a solution independently negotiated by the Yemenis, Nasser agreed. 'You people think that we are embroiled in Yemen! Not at all! It is you who are embroiled!' he exclaimed, adding ominously: 'I am telling you quite frankly that I already have many plans, ready and set out for implementation.'[644] In the end, for their efforts to build bridges with the enemy, Yemeni apostates were more condemned in Cairo than the royalists themselves. 'I don't really care who is in charge there,' Nasser told US Ambassador Lucius Battle – with an air of deep disillusion – in November 1965, 'as long as the Hamid ad-Din family is not involved... There was no real revolution in Yemen. It was only a plot. But I just found that out lately.' Then they both laughed uproariously.[645]

***

Nasser's pique at the Sana'a government's perceived disloyalty led him to make a second attempt to cut a deal with the Saudis, in the Jeddah Agreement of August 1965. The Yemeni royalists had been conspicuously successful that spring, while Egyptian forces were in a bad way. In July, Nasser began to utter noisy threats against Saudi Arabia. Cairo later claimed that a massive military assault was scheduled for 7 September until Nasser called it off at the last minute, overriding military advice in a highly statesmanlike manner.[646] Under the circumstances, however, this seems unlikely. The President was probably feigning belligerence in order to achieve a ceasefire. For in August, he suddenly announced that he was ready to go anywhere and make every effort for peace – and set off for the Saudi port of Jeddah.[647] The President was 'cheerful' as he passed through the Red Sea district *en route*, according to the local governor, his former aide, Hamed Mahmoud. He seemed sincere and confident of a successful peace.[648]

At Jeddah, Nasser and Faisal agreed that Egypt should evacuate within ten months; that Saudi military assistance should end; and that a conference should take place in November, through which the Yemenis might determine their own destiny. (This was embarrassing for the republicans, who claimed they were already so doing.) There may also have been a secret clause excluding both President Sallal and the Imam Badr from any future role.[649] This time, the conference did happen, but it soon broke down. Nasser is frequently blamed for the failure. According to Saudi sources, who write off the entire episode as a cynical and obscure attempt to blackmail the Soviet Union, Cairo informed the Yemeni leaders that they would be 'buried alive' if they compromised.[650] However, discontented republicans take the opposite tack, complaining that Egypt betrayed them by advocating concessions. Cairo denied a previous promise to the Yemeni delegation that the Saudis would agree to exclude the Imam's family – the 'Hamid al-Din' – from power, claims Alaini. When the Yemeni leaders flew over to complain to Nasser personally, they were first told they could meet Amer, then downgraded to Defence Minister Shams Badran – who shouted at them – and finally imprisoned in cells.[651]

Despite periodic squabbles, Egyptian regime members regularly (if distrustfully) expressed a desire for better relations with Saudi Arabia to US diplomats. 'Egypt still seems sincere in trying to pull out of Yemen,' Komer wrote to President Johnson at the end of the year, 'although that's going slowly because of bickering among the Yemenis themselves.'[652] Even the Saudis at the time thought Nasser 'courageous' and 'determined'. They were sure he had 'matters firmly in hand' as regards the reintegration of 50,000 soldiers into the shaky Egyptian economy: he was probably going to teach them handicrafts.[653] When US Ambassador Lucius Battle asked Nasser about the Jeddah Agreement's chances in late November, 'he replied that three or four days ago he had been pessimistic but things looked somewhat better'. There was 'every evidence' that Faisal too wanted a settlement – although Nasser added that the Saudis were confusing things by asking for understandings not in the basic text. The Egyptian leader plaintively sought US help to keep things from going wrong.[654]

In the end, however, every circumstance conspired to prevent Egypt's withdrawal from Yemen. If she retreated from a position of weakness, she would be doubly exposed to her enemies. Not only would the besieging hordes of reactionaries, imperialists and Ba'athists count it as a major victory; but also, even if the Yemeni Republic did not actually fall – and it is worth noting that it survived the eventual Egyptian with-drawal from a position of unprecedented weakness following the 1967 defeat – the untrustworthy leadership could be bought by the British and Saudis. On the other hand, the Egyptian military leaders were most reluctant to withdraw from a position of strength. Successes against the royalist forces only encouraged them to follow up their advantage. Amer and his faction enthusiastically supported the Yemen adventure, continually demanding additional resources to maintain their ascend-ancy. Financially and politically, army officers tended to do rather well out of the war. They received additional allowances and could purchase black market consumer goods, as well as increasing their relative impor-tance within the regime.[655] The army would have great problems accepting withdrawal from Yemen, Nasser told Ambassador Battle in 1966. 'If we bring it back, I can control it,' he said, with a certain lack of conviction, 'but it will not be easy.'[656]

This does not mean that Nasser was under duress. In fact, the Pres-ident tended to act as arbiter among competing Egyptian factions on the Yemen issue. While the military establishment dug in its heels, the Egyptian 'political' set believed they could pull out without the fall of the Republic; indeed, Heikal, one of the leading lights of this group, had argued from the outset that it would be wiser to send a force of pan-Arab volunteers, *à la* Spanish Civil War.[657] In a revealing episode, Makram Mohamed Ahmed, then *Al-Ahram's* Sana'a correspondent, was caught up in this struggle, spending three weeks imprisoned by the military in Yemen for publishing 'sensitive military information' – despite the fact that Heikal, as editor, cleared such matters with the President. When Heikal found out, he spoke to Nasser, who spoke to Amer, and Ahmed was freed, but forced to return to Egypt, illustrating the delicacy of the internal power balance.[658] The President himself seems to have been more concerned about YAR connivance with his enemies than about the prospect of withdrawal *per se*. Meanwhile, citing the concerns of the military in conversations with the US Ambassador was an effective strategy protecting him from negotiating pressure.

***

Whether or not his previous search for a withdrawal mechanism had been as committed as he made out to the Americans, on 22 March 1966, Nasser announced a dramatic change in his official position, unveiling the 'Long Breath' strategy. The number of Egyptian troops in

Yemen would be reduced from 70,000 to 40,000, concentrated around urban focal points in the southern coastal plains. 'We are an able people and a strong people and a patient people,' the President exhorted his nation. Due to the disappointing failure of the Jeddah Agreement, 'we are revising our plans so that we may stay in the Yemen if necessary for five years or longer'.[659] And 'if anyone interferes,' he later clarified, 'we will break his neck'.[660] Amer was even more generous with his forces' time. 'We shall remain there for 20 years despite imperialism,' he confirmed; 'and if we get tired they will get 24 times as tired'.[661]

From this time onward, although Egyptian leaders still paid grudging lip-service to the idea of peace, it became increasingly obvious that they did not intend to withdraw from Yemen. There was 'no better than even chance' of a settlement in the next two years, concluded the CIA in May 1966.[662] Angered by continuing royalist-republican contacts, in July Nasser sent former President Sallal, who had been detained in Cairo for a year, back to Sana'a to take control. The senior delegation – comprising most of the Yemeni government – that went to Cairo to protest was imprisoned.[663] *Al-Ahram* put it all down to a comprehensive plot to overthrow the Yemeni Republic – fronted by Nu'man, funded by Faisal, organised by the CIA, and timed to coincide with a Jordanian invasion of Syria.[664] The low-key Kuwait Agreement negotiated with Saudi Arabia that August never had much prospect of implementation, largely due to the Egyptians' explicit statement that under no circumstances would they remove their troops. In the absence of support from Cairo, Washington Ambassador Mostafa Kamel's efforts to persuade the Americans to renew food aid and encourage further Kuwaiti mediation developed a desperate tone. 'Who knows who brought us to Yemen,' he asked dramatically but fruitlessly in January 1967, presumably referring to the USSR, 'and who knows who will bring us into other situations if you leave us?'[665]

Egypt's change of strategy had two immediate causes: the British announcement that they would withdraw completely from Aden by 1968 and King Faisal's call for an Islamic Conference. The 'Long Breath' moves allowed Nasser to wait out the UK, and the southward redeployment of his forces assisted his increased focus on subversion in Aden. There were deeper reasons for his violent reaction, however. Distrust of the British convinced him that they had plans to reorganise the Arabian Peninsula before they left; distrust of the Saudis sparked the fear that they would try to move into the vacuum left by Britain, and made the Islamic Conference seem more sinister than perhaps it was. Finally, Nasser's belief in a broader conspiracy among his enemies, also including the United States, made the coincidence of all these developments seem positively diabolical.

***

King Faisal first called for an Islamic Conference during a series of official visits to local fellow-monarchs at the end of 1965. Nasser saw this as a serious new attempt to isolate him in the Arab world.[666] Egyptian distrust of Saudi Arabia immediately became more marked, and the desire for improved relations less so. Faisal was playing a 'mysterious and evasive game,' remarked one of Nasser's senior advisors in January 1966.[667] He 'kept saying he wanted a settlement in Yemen, but his acts were beginning to point to another conclusion, and it was the acts that counted, not the words,' Sadat complained.[668] The simultaneous £125 million Anglo-American arms deal with Saudi Arabia was cited by Heikal as clear proof of conspiracy. 'The problem of this Islamic Alliance has ceased to exist; in fact it was never worthy of battle,' he wrote contemptuously: 'it is remote from God and his Prophet, but close to Johnson and Wilson'.[669]

Nasser's response was violent. His 'Long Breath' speech threatened to attack 'the bases of arms and aggression' in Saudi Arabia itself.[670] 'We have given up,' he confirmed to Ambassador Battle the following month. 'King Feisal believed when I entered into the Jeddah agreement that it was a move from weakness but it was not. It was a move to avoid a clash between the United Arab Republic and Saudi Arabia. That clash now is before us.' He refused even to send a representative to Riyadh:

> The Jeddah agreement is finished. There is no agreement. As I told you last time, we are consolidating our troops and will withdraw in large numbers, perhaps even up to half of them, but we can stay in Yemen for ten years. We are not weak. This does not cost us as much as Feisal thinks it does.[671]

The fear that the Saudis believed Egypt to be *incapable* of remaining in Yemen is particularly marked. Due to a more general atmosphere of threat, Egypt interpreted Faisal's anodyne and ineffective concept of a conference among Islamic countries as a successor to the Baghdad Pact and a blatant move against the Arab revolution. Such a provocation could only be taken to confirm the perception that the King thought

Nasser's wrath of negligible account. The Egyptians were determined to prove him wrong.

The President was constantly threatening to 'occupy' and 'punish' the Saudi bases of aggression.[672] Heikal helpfully took up his pen and started a new series of open letters directed against Faisal. Zakaria Mohieddin complained to the US that the Saudi and Jordanian kings believed the time had come 'to work openly and otherwise to cripple if not destroy' Nasser – and Yemen was the primary theatre of confrontation.[673] The Saudi regime was once more depicted as under threat. 'Revolution is on the verge of breaking out in the capitals of those who concocted plots against the Yemeni revolution,' announced Nasser at the end of 1966, adding meaningfully: 'King Faisal knows better than I do what is happening in his own country.'[674] (The Saudis believed Nasser knew only too well, blaming the Egyptian Embassy in Jeddah for 'planting a number of bombs within the *hajj* ceremonial areas', and the Egyptian Expeditionary Force in Yemen for sending a local stooge to carry out sabotage in Riyadh.)[675]

The enmity between the two countries had never been so explicit. By the end of January 1967, the Egyptians were once again – more or less openly – bombing Saudi border towns.[676] In April, Nasser tried to set up a Liberation Front for Saudi Arabia, and transported the deposed King Saud, who had been permitted to settle in Egypt and make inflammatory radio broadcasts, to Sana'a, where he declared himself the rightful Saudi monarch.[677] The embattled Faisal was not seen as an equal adversary. He was merely the junior partner in a Western conspiracy against Egypt, as Nasser explained:

> Saudi Arabia concluded a very expensive arms deal with the United States and Britain... A part of the Saudi army, under the command of an American military mission, has become fully versed in plans to defend the Middle East while another part of this army, under the command of a British military mission, has become fully versed in plans to dominate the Arab South.[678]

***

The British Defence White Paper of 22 February 1966 had promised that the British would withdraw entirely from Aden by the end of 1968, abandoning their military base and, critically, signing no treaty with the SAF government. The ruling sheikhs were 'deeply and bitterly resentful' of a decision that essentially left them at the mercy of the

mounting revolutionary forces in Aden.[679] Nasser, however, was gal-
vanised into an immediate change of policy. 'Our troops in Yemen will
not be withdrawn,' he revealed, 'until the Yemeni revolution is capable
of defending itself against the plots of imperialism and of reaction'.[680]
The President later had some trouble explaining this phraseology to
the US Ambassador, resorting to the schoolboy excuse of inadequate
time to prepare his notes. He gave 'what he described as an explanation and which contained some elements of apology but which was in
fact neither. He appeared to regret the speech,' Battle noted tartly, 'as I
suspect he does many of his speeches'. Nasser's assurance that he had
not changed his position on Yemen in response to the British
announcement was emphatic but ultimately unconvincing.[681]

London's revelation was seen as a signal to attack rather than a
peace-offering. British officials had recognised this as a possibility.
'I am of course very conscious of the risk,' one diplomat noted to
another in mid-February, 'that Nasser may feel that henceforth the
prime objective of his policy must be to get us out of the Gulf and that
to this end he will wish to see our departure from South Arabia accompanied by maximum confusion.' The Americans were asked to use their
increasingly dubious influence with Nasser to avert this scenario – to
no avail.[682] 'Don't you know that the White Paper declared Britain
would leave in 1968?' Foreign Minister Riad incredulously asked
Mohsen Alaini, when the latter wondered aloud whether this was
really the best time to attack Aden. 'So why don't we let them leave?'
queried Alaini. 'Since they are leaving,' Riad explained, turning the
argument neatly and cynically on its head, 'we may as well fight'.[683]
The President's goals were explicit:

> the British are of course embittered because they will leave Aden
> and they will leave the Arab South and they will leave the Gulf and
> they will not be able to remain in the Arab world and we are after
> them until we cleanse it of them.[684]

It is often suggested that Nasser saw the British announcement as an
easy opportunity for expansion. Egypt is 'playing a double game in
Yemen,' opined suspicious US diplomats in Taiz, who believed Nasser
was unable to resist the temptation to move into the power vacuum in
Southern Arabia that would inevitably follow the UK's ignominious
exodus.[685] Egyptian covert operations in the SAF increased following
the White Paper, in an initiative pointedly dubbed 'Operation Saladin'.
From Taiz, Egyptian Intelligence systematically armed and trained dis-

sidents to infiltrate the Federation, working with local Nasserist groups.[686] Amer and his coterie made tactless statements rejoicing that the withdrawal might allow Egypt to close the Red Sea to Israeli ships from the far end.[687]

Nevertheless, Nasser's incredulous reaction to Ambassador Battle's accusation – 'You cannot believe we would ever put troops in Aden!' – has the ring of truth.[688] Given the weight of the burden Egypt already bore, it is unlikely that Nasser planned to extend the Egyptian military occupation of Yemen southward. He hoped instead to bring about an anarchic situation whereby his local supporters could take over as soon as the British left, enhancing his own regional status. Nasser had forced the bickering southern revolutionaries – themselves supported by different Egyptian factions – to merge in Cairo in January 1966, forming the Front for the Liberation of South Yemen (FLOSY). The coalition was uneasy, eventually collapsing when the radical NLF re-emerged as the focus of resistance.[689] Initially, however, Egyptian tactics appeared to be succeeding. 'The only politicians who counted in Aden were in FLOSY and fighting us,' remembers the last High Commissioner, Nasser's old adversary Sir Humphrey Trevelyan.[690]

The UK was on the defensive in Southern Arabia, but this very fact made her seem more dangerous than ever.[691] Nasser condemned Nu'man as 'a strong favourite of the English' – like all others who rejected the Yemeni revolution. 'They go to Aden,' he complained, 'where they are honoured and given money and welcomed...'[692] Cairo was particularly worried that Britain might attempt to rearrange the Arabian Peninsula on her way out, permanently shifting the balance of power in the Arab world. 'Before quitting, the British want to leave their agents, and thus rule indirectly,' Nasser warned in February 1967. 'It was reported today that the agents will seek an alliance with Saudi Arabia.'[693] However, Riyadh and London were no longer the only threats. 'Britain has been transformed into a US colony,' announced Nasser, 'to a degree which does not allow it even to express views on any international question before choosing words and obtaining Washington's permission'.[694] As the United Kingdom was increasingly seen as subservient in the 1960s, distrust of the British could not but increase distrust of the Americans. Similarly, as Saudi Arabia continued to supply the Yemeni royalists with US arms, the boundaries of hostility and neutrality seemed less clear-cut. Nasser's ultimate fear was that he might be facing a concerted conspiracy among all of his enemies – including the USA.

6
Different Names for the Same Thing: Imperialism, Zionism and Reaction

The conspiracy has disclosed the well-known fact that imperialism, Zionism and reaction are only different names for the same thing – the alliance which is hostile to us, our Arab nation and its principles and objectives.[695] – Gamal Abdel Nasser

How did the United States – which had so obligingly recognised the Yemeni Republic and provided Egypt with much-needed food aid under President Kennedy in the early 1960s – manage to redefine itself within a few years as Nasser's Public Enemy Number One? US-Egyptian relations had begun to degenerate by 1964. Kennedy's assassination was depicted in Cairo as a Jewish plot, and Nasser perceived his successor, Lyndon Johnson, as substantially less well-disposed toward the Arab world.[696] The two countries disagreed on a multitude of global issues, from Yemen to Vietnam. There was one controversy in early 1964, when, under Egyptian pressure, King Idris of Libya announced that he would not renew his air base agreement with the Americans, leading to 'one of the stormiest meetings' Badeau ever had with Nasser.[697] The US Secretary of State, Dean Rusk, identified Nasser's support of African 'wars of liberation' in general – and of the Congolese insurgency in particular – as the core of the problem between the two countries.[698] The Egyptian press was increasingly critical of Washington's Congo policy, and when the US flew in Belgian paratroopers to rescue a group of Western hostages in November 1964, a furious mob attacked the US Information Agency Library in Cairo. US diplomats felt that the Egyptian authorities did too little to avert this assault at the time, and failed to apologise adequately afterwards. They were hardly propitiated when a plane belonging to a personal friend of President Johnson was shot down by the Egyptian air force the following month. As a result, the new Ambassador Lucius Battle apparently spoke rather shortly to the Egyptian Minister of Supply.[699]

Unfortunately, his remarks and conduct were misreported to Nasser on the train to Port Said, where he was due to give his annual 'Victory Day' speech, by none other than Ali Sabri. Jaded perhaps by the spectacular failure of his weapons-buying trip to Washington in 1953, Nasser's one-time US Embassy liaison had become the most pro-Soviet member of his regime – the figurehead of the left. But he remained high in the President's esteem; indeed, he was 'very often Nasser's alter ego'.[700] The Egyptian leader was furious with Battle, and his address expressed graphic contempt for American opinions. (Later, he claimed to have been carried away by his feelings, although he may also have been rather conscious of the Soviet Deputy Prime Minister listening politely in the front row.)[701] 'Whoever does not like our behaviour,' Nasser publicly informed the 'glum and sulky' US Ambassador, 'can go and drink up the sea'. If the Mediterranean were insufficient, they could drink the Red Sea too. And if anyone dared say one word of criticism to Egypt, Nasser added viciously, 'we will cut his tongue off'.[702]

The President later tried to patch things up, activating a long-unused secret channel 'to express his desire to avoid further deterioration' in relations.[703] But the US remained resentful; in March 1965 it was 'perforce re-examining its relationship' with Egypt.[704] That autumn, Nasser again attempted to propitiate Washington, by naming a new 'austerity' Cabinet under Prime Minister Zakaria Mohieddin, seen as a prominent right-winger. He was 'embarrassingly friendly' to Battle, who reported, with massive condescension: 'Obviously he wishes desperately get back in good graces with us and will I believe try in his own way to do his part.'[705] It did not last. By 1967, two internal irritants had convinced the Cairo regime that a confrontation with the United States was inevitable.

***

First, the poor state of the economy in the 1960s meant that Egypt was increasingly dependent on American food aid. US wheat shipments made up more than a third of Egyptian net supply in 1961, and more than half the following year.[706] As a result, wrote Ambassador Badeau, Egypt had become 'nervous about anything which might suggest a sudden shift in American policy and scrutinizes carefully and suspiciously every American statement, fearing the worst'.[707] In Washington, both senators and journalists were apt to adopt an aggrieved tone on the subject of aid to Egypt whenever they objected to Cairo's policies. In November 1963, the Gruening Amendment to the Foreign Assistance Act banned US aid to any country engaged in aggressive military action against the United States or her allies. The congressional sponsors of this amendment implied that it referred principally to the Egyptian confrontation with Saudi Arabia in Yemen. Nasser complained bitterly. Although Kennedy publicly condemned the Amendment, Johnson's attitude was more ambiguous. Despite State Department denials, the legislature at least seemed intent on using food aid as a blunt and humiliating instrument to control Egyptian foreign policy.[708]

There was, of course, a tacit understanding in Cairo that US aid was provided on a *quid pro quo* basis. However, in theatres such as Yemen and Congo, Nasser was not prepared to trade his foreign policy autonomy for economic development – and he was even less willing to risk the *appearance* of so doing. Unfortunately, Johnson and many of the more vocal Members of Congress were of another mind, expecting immediate, tangible returns to their investment. A little gratitude, they felt, would be appropriate.[709] These diametrically opposed expectations spiralled out of control during 1966. That January, President Johnson offered only a much reduced food aid agreement of $55 million.[710] Following a perceptible hardening of Nasser's public attitude, even this level of support was allowed to lapse. 'He has almost dared us publicly not to renew our agreement,' Special Assistant Eugene Rostow wrote in a bemused memorandum to Johnson that June. 'We are not quite sure what he is up to. Our guess is that he is worried about his political base.'[711]

Nasser, however, saw United States actions as intrinsically aggressive. 'They know what they are doing to us, and they know how to please us if they want,' he declared to an aide, refusing a private approach from Battle asking him to moderate his rhetoric in July.[712] 'If you are our friend why have you done this?' Nasser demanded indignantly of unofficial envoy Robert Anderson. 'Do you want riots in the streets?'[713] By the time the departing Ambassador Battle paid his farewell calls on Egyptian luminaries in early 1967, the President was emphasising that although Egypt 'did not want American wheat', it would respond to any attack and could no doubt damage the US and her allies. The President was 'more emotional than I have ever seen him', reported Battle, and at times his eyes glazed over.[714] Anwar Sadat, then Speaker of the National Assembly, was even blunter, condemning the current US Administration as worse than that of Dulles, in that it 'dangled hope of aid and never gave answer' while, he suspected, engaging 'in unfortunate behind scenes actions' with Egypt's enemies.[715]

Nasser knew that the US spoke with many voices, including the White House, the State Department, the CIA, the Pentagon and Congress – not to mention the Press, to which he remained inordinately sensitive. But he tended to overestimate the potential for central control. Even under Kennedy, 'there were times when he thought that the chaos was deliberate,' according to Heikal; 'that one arm of United States government would pursue a friendly policy calculated to act as a cover while another arm worked against Egypt's interests'.[716] Later, the authoritarian Egyptian leader could not grasp that congressional criticism might occur without tacit presidential approval. 'Johnson can do whatever he wants to do,' he would exclaim to Battle, pounding his fist on the table.[717] Nasser was *aware* of internal constraints on US foreign policy, Ambassador Kamel confidentially explained in 1965, but 'he does not understand them'. Believing the American President to be capable of fully controlling domestic pressures, he suspected his reluctance to provide additional wheat was a plot to 'embarrass and overthrow him'. Were he assured of this, Kamel warned, 'he would react violently and irrationally regardless of consequences'. It was a fateful prophecy.[718]

***

To add injury to insult, Nasser was firmly convinced that the CIA was conspiring against him. It is not impossible that he was correct. Very little documentation on the Agency's Middle Eastern activities during this period has been declassified, and the sources that do exist are anecdotal. There are suggestions that the CIA turned against the Cairo regime in the early 1960s, despite President Kennedy's drive for compromise.[719] CIA station chiefs based in Arab countries, fearing that the Egyptian involvement in Yemen heralded a Soviet advance in Arabia, allegedly met for a two-day conference in Beirut in November 1962 'to plot the Agency's defeat of Nasser'.[720] At the height of the honeymoon with Kennedy, Nasser complained to Ambassador Badeau that the CIA was tailing him too closely. Badeau put a stop to it, later stating that he was *almost* sure the CIA was not then involved in a dirty tricks campaign against Nasser.[721]

In July 1965, however, Nasser told Chou En Lai, Sukarno and others that he was convinced that the US had begun a counter-offensive in the Third World and the CIA was seeking to topple him.[722] At the same time, the Egyptian publisher Mostafa Amin – previously used by Nasser himself as a private channel to the US – was arrested and the American he was lunching with detained, amid charges of a CIA-sponsored coup linked to the banned Muslim Brotherhood.[723] The US officially dismissed the whole affair as a set-up, although telegrams reveal occasional hints from Cairo Embassy diplomats that the CIA was indeed involved.[724] The incident was used by Egyptian officials for some time to justify charges that the US was plotting against them.[725] Nasser complained in October 1966 that he 'had indisputable evidence that within the last several months agents of the CIA had entered into a conspiracy with Egyptians aimed at his assassination and violent overthrow of his government'. He was speaking to James Birdsall, an otherwise unremarkable New York lawyer whom Nasser summoned from Europe and repeatedly used as a private messenger to Johnson – although nobody knows quite why. When Ambassador Battle followed up on this complaint, the Egyptian President seemed 'flustered' and backtracked – citing only the Mostafa Amin incident.[726]

Much suspicion was focused on the CIA's alleged activities in Yemen. Former Nasserist insiders still claim with great conviction that the Agency actively supported the Imam, particularly towards the end of the conflict, recruiting mercenaries (or bringing them up from Congo) to train the royalists.[727] Nasser himself even accused US Intelligence of catching two discharged Egyptian airmen in Germany and sending them to Saudi Arabia to pretend they had defected from the Expeditionary Force.[728] However, it was not until an incident in April 1967 that Egyptian suspicions became fully explicit. Two USAID employees were arrested and accused of attempting to destroy the city of Taiz through a bazooka attack on an ammunition dump. This was certainly nonsense. 'We shall be announcing tomorrow that these charges are without foundation – which they are,' Rostow informed President Johnson.[729] There was 'no espionage and nothing sinister going on,' CIA Director Richard Helms told the Secretary of State, adding: 'it is quite clearly a political move against the United States'.[730]

Equally certainly, however, there was a CIA connection. US documents concerning this incident have an unusual number of sections that remain classified. 'Our main loss,' Rostow briefed Johnson on 10 May, 'will be some CIA material the Egyptians filched from one of the safes left behind when our people were dragged off'.[731] These documents, an Egyptian general alleges, revealed that most US personnel in Taiz were CIA agents, detailing their planned activities across the region.[732] In fact, the Taiz network was long-established, delivering intelligence on points including the Egyptian use of poison gas in Yemen, which was a major bone of contention in the UN at this time.[733] Egyptian Military Intelligence, supported by Yemeni counterparts, seems to have fabricated this specific incident as part of a move by anti-American factions to sabotage Washington-Sana'a relations.[734] Nasser may not have authorised it personally, however. Rostow suggested that although he used the fracas 'for its full propaganda and intelligence advantage,' it was created by Egyptian mishandling on a local level, then interpreted by Nasser according to his well-known habit of seeing the CIA's sinister hand behind everything.[735]

Egypt had indeed come to perceive the United States as the director of a covert and underhand global conspiracy against radical Third World regimes. It was 'a large-scale imperialist campaign', suggested Cairo Radio, 'based on a comprehensive plan which is being directed from that centre of present world imperialist influence, Washington'. US motivation for such underhand plotting was said to be that it considered itself 'colonialism's sole heir' – and that it sought to distract attention from Israel.[736] The image appears to have held sway at the highest levels. 'No amount of logic,' Hal Saunders of the NSC marvelled in a March 1967 telegram from Cairo, was sufficient to persuade the Egyptians that not all US actions in the region were directed against them:

It amazing what shreds of evidence they have woven together to prove this to themselves. These not just debating points. Every official I talked to from Foreign Minister on down obviously sincerely believes this. Main thread this fabric of illogic seems be philosophy those not helping them must be against them. [sic][737]

***

Saunders grasped the essence of the problem. The USA had painstakingly improved relations with Egypt whilst continuing support for Israel by agreeing to keep the Arab-Israeli dispute 'in the ice-box'. The Egyptian elite had long been aware of the equally firm American commitments to 'imperialist' Britain and 'reactionary' Saudi Arabia. Unfortunately, the Yemen War, which brought these into sharp relief, resisted all attempts at refrigeration. Given the strains of increased conflict within the region, America's ambiguous position as the well-disposed ally of Egypt's enemies ultimately proved unsustainable. 'We try by every means to preserve good relations,' Nasser had asserted to the National Assembly in November 1964. 'We have no direct problems with the USA, never.'[738] But the indirect problems were soon to become overwhelming.

US support for King Faisal was a key problem. Shortly after the Yemeni revolution, in the period of acute tension between Egypt and the Saudis, American military advisors and planes were stationed in Dhahran. They had strict orders not to engage the Egyptians without personal reference to Kennedy, who still saw himself as an impartial moderator between the two sides.[739] In late 1965, the US drew up detailed military contingency plans for intervention in the case of a full-scale Egyptian attack on Saudi Arabia. These were for use 'only in the most extreme contingency' – all other options were preferable first.[740] However, Cairo did not always appreciate this. 'Once,' remembers Badeau, 'when things were really bad in Yemen, I was afraid that some of the Egyptian planes that were helping the Yemenis would fly up into Saudi territory and run afoul of some of our ambushes there. I went to Sadat to warn them, and he bridled.' Sadat accused the hapless Ambassador of giving him an ultimatum.[741]

In Egypt, the United States came to be seen as attacking Nasser by means of Saudi Arabia. Ambassador Kamel reported as early as August 1964 the growing belief 'that the US was contributing to the difficulties in Yemen through Saudi Arabia and Iran'.[742] Within two years this had progressed to the conviction that Washington was actively encouraging Faisal's intransigence in order to bring down Nasser's regime.[743] It was 'well known', remembers General Hadidi, then heading Military Intelligence, that the US backed Saudi Arabia in Yemen, even sending volunteers to support the insurgents.[744] Many Egyptian insiders still assert today that the conflict was called 'Komer's War' because Robert Komer of the US National Security Council masterminded it, whereas in fact the phrase became current in Washington only because the White House rather than the State Department was tasked with the delicate decision-making on this issue.[745] 'America and Britain want to pass on their influence in the South to Saudi Arabia,' Marshal Amer told army officers in May 1966, 'so that actual control will remain in the hands of America'.[746] A couple of days later, Sadat complained to Ambassador Battle that Faisal 'could not act as belligerent or confident as he does without US support.'[747]

In 1966, Nasser rejected further co-operation with the Arab 'reactionaries'. The Arab summits, he said, had merely 'confirmed previous experiments with reaction, namely, that it is, wittingly or unwittingly, a party to the imperialist-Israeli collusion'.[748] The conservative rulers of the putative 'Islamic Alliance' – Hussein in Jordan, Faisal in Saudi Arabia, Bourguiba in Tunisia and the Iranian Shah – re-emerged as rhetorical targets. Nasser continued to attack King Faisal with laborious sarcasm:

He wants the people to say to him: You are the prince of the believers, your beard is long, and you take our money; we agree that you grow your beard and take our money, because Islam says so.[749]

In 1967, King Hussein came in for particular vituperation: as a CIA traitor; the 'stooge' of imperialism; the Jews' 'foster-child and favourite'; the 'male whore' of Jordan.[750]

***

By May 1967, therefore, on the eve of the Six Day War, the enemy from Nasser's point of view was threefold. 'Imperialism' was represented by the USA and her 'lackey' Britain. They led 'the West', an inchoate, deceitful and hypocritical entity that despised and ignored the Arabs, disregarding their legitimate aspirations and rights. The West was viewed as the staunch political ally and arms supplier of its own creation, 'Zionist' Israel, formulaically described as the 'imperialist base in the heart of the Arab homeland'. Since the 'Arab reactionaries' were also supported by imperialism, they and Israel 'cannot by any means be two conflicting sides but must be two co-operating sides, even if that co-operation is through a middle-man'. There was no question of who was in charge, however. Imperialism was 'the origin and the source of planning'; the others were 'only satellites spinning in the US orbit and following its steps'.[751] Therefore:

> with subservient regimes in Saudi Arabia and Jordan collaborating and co-operating with imperialist forces, and with imperialism an ally of Israel which is its bridgehead, imperialism wants to split the Arab world.[752]

The Egyptian President had come to believe that 'the co-ordinated, hostile movements against our nation' could only be explained by a 'wider conspiracy' between imperialism, Zionism and reaction – 'only different names for the same thing'.[753] 'The battle we are fighting is not an easy one,' declared Nasser; 'it is a major battle led by America, the greatest power in the world'.[754] The Egyptian ruler saw the USA as his ultimate opponent, out to destroy both him and his revolution. He identified a worldwide imperialist onslaught against progressive regimes behind the replacement of Nkrumah in Ghana and Sukarno in Indonesia by right-wing, pro-Western figures, and the interventions in the Dominican Republic, the Congo and Vietnam.[755] He suggested that the United States had created Israel and fostered the Islamic Alliance in order to control the Arab world, and that the CIA was planning his own assassination for the same purpose. In fact, although Nasser was intensely disliked in certain US government circles by the mid-1960s, it seems improbable that there was a concerted plot against him. Richard Helms has stated that 'the CIA had a good relationship with Egyptian intelligence during the months leading up to the '67 war and in the period thereafter'.[756] This is confirmed from the opposite side by Nasser's confidential aide Sami Sharaf.[757] However, the idea became so fixed in his mind that American denials were useless.[758]

The state-controlled media echoed Nasser's insistence that the US was the primary enemy and conspirator. In early 1967, Heikal wrote a series of 11 *Al-Ahram* editorials on the conflict between Egypt and America. He charged that the US had developed a 'sinister dangerous complex', consisting of 'economic and psychological warfare, the hatching of plots and assassinations, and a basic and fundamental reliance on secret activities'. This, he stated, had brought deteriorating US-Egyptian relations 'to the brink of the abyss' in a 'violent clash' that would 'heighten in intensity and drag on'.[759] Even at the height of the confrontation with Israel that May, the *Voice of the Arabs* would retain its priorities. 'We challenge you, Israel,' it announced, before changing its mind. 'No, in fact, we do not address the challenge to you, Israel, because you are unworthy of our challenge. But we challenge you, America.'[760]

There was never any fear that the US would launch a conventional military attack on Egypt. The Vietnam imbroglio was causing so much embarrassment that she seemed unlikely to involve herself in yet another regional conflict. But most of the Egyptian elite acknowledged that she would be militarily capable of imposing her will if provoked – after all, her armed forces were vastly superior to those of all of the Arab states combined. 'If I started considering how strong America is and how strong I am,' admitted Nasser publicly, 'even before I started my calculations I should come to the conclusion that America has air, land and sea superiority over us'.[761] Although many of his speeches emphasise his readiness to confront America, it is clear that he had no real illusions in this regard. Conversely, the Minister of War, Shams Badran, once likened the US Sixth Fleet to 'a can of sardines', claiming: 'we have a weapon that can deal it a lethal blow'. His hearers concluded he had received Soviet arms or assurances on his recent visit to Moscow, although it is possible, given the incongruity of the boast, that he did not mean it seriously.[762] There is, at least, no evidence that other members of the military establishment shared his confidence.

***

The mounting rhetorical confrontation with the United States had the unfortunate side-effect of exacerbating tensions with Egypt's Jewish neighbour. In a perilous perceptual shift, Israel came to be seen as increasingly aggressive, while estimations of her military capability remained ambiguous. For some years, it had been getting harder to keep the Israel issue 'in the ice-box'. In the mid-1960s, Nasser intended that the Arab summit conferences should stave off the necessity of direct confrontation with Israel, while preventing radicals from criticising Egyptian inaction. Although the January 1964 Cairo summit proposed joint Arab action to counter Israeli plans for diversion of the Jordan waters, it was generally agreed that no direct confrontation was yet feasible. Plans were instead drawn up for the creation of a United Arab Command (UAC), seen as a necessary first step. However, although this body existed on paper, most Arab governments – including Egypt – were unwilling to provide money and resources. Others, led by Jordan, objected to the presence of foreign troops on their territory. Consequently, the joint military development was largely unsuccessful.

Instead, certain states encouraged the activities of Palestinian guerrillas, as an alternative to the conventional war with Israel they were not yet ready to wage. In September 1964, the Alexandria summit saw the establishment of the Palestine Liberation Organisation (PLO). The PLO, under Ahmed Shukeiry, was sponsored largely by the Egyptians, who hoped to channel radical Palestinian aspirations in order to dilute confrontation with Israel. Syria supported the rival *Fateh* organisation, which began commando raids in 1965. Both organisations, however, had the effect, unintended by their creators, of challenging the inaction of Arab governments. Moreover, both became increasingly activist, provoking Israeli reprisals.[763] Nasser publicly abandoned the principle of Arab summitry in July 1966, following the dramatic deterioration of relations with the monarchies. A dangerous increase in inter-Arab competition and propaganda followed, with a high degree of polarisation between conservatives and radicals. Given this atmosphere of competition, the increased number of Arab-Israeli border incursions is hardly surprising.

In Nasser's public speeches and private conversations of 1967, Israel's intentions are consistently portrayed as hostile, threatening, deceitful and aggressive. She was viewed as fundamentally expansionist: 'the fundamental enemy who is a manifestation of perpetual aggression'.[764]

She was, however, subordinate to external forces: the international Zionist movement, Western imperialism and the United States. 'Today, Israel is America,' Nasser announced.[765] This was a constant theme. The Palestine question was difficult because: 'It is the question of Israel backed by, or more clearly, it is the question of America.'[766] Few insiders questioned the extent of this subordination, although Heikal once made a tentative beginning:

> For the sake of simplification we sometimes say that Israel is nothing but an imperialist tool... But such a statement is only part of the truth... In most manifestations of its existence, Israel is a tool. But at the same time, it is a party by virtue of the Zionist racist plans, and in addition to the imperialist designs and ambitions, it has its own designs and ambitions as well.[767]

***

The Egyptian defence establishment believed by May 1967 that it could defeat Israel. Leaders said so, in private and in public. At his trial for conspiracy the following year, Defence Minister Shams Badran testified:

> We were confident that our army was ready and that Israel could not attack because intelligence estimates pointed to the fact that we were superior in armoured weapons, artillery and air power. It was calculated that Israel would not walk into an open grave.[768]

A year before, Marshal Amer had told the army: 'We are capable of defeating Israel at any time, for we are superior to it in arms and morale'.[769] Now, asked by Nasser whether the forces were ready for war, Amer pointed graphically to his neck, exclaiming: 'On my own head be it, boss! Everything's in tiptop shape.'[770] In early June 1967, he told the Foreign Minister: 'If Israel actually carried out any military action against us I could, with only one third of our forces, reach Beersheba.'[771]

On the whole, Amer's subordinates seem to have shared his opinion. 'The commanders thought that they would need only one fourth of their army to deal with Israel,' recalls Mohammed Riad of the Foreign Ministry. They were all, he adds, 'very nice fellows who put their friends in high positions. Unfortunately, they were not competent.'[772] The British war hero, Field Marshal Montgomery, visiting the Egyptian armed forces on 12 May, gave a blunt warning that they would lose a war with Israel, to which General Murtagi replied complacently that they had the latest Russian equipment.[773] Murtagi expressed a similar opinion to a domestic audience, reporting from Sinai that 'our forces are fully prepared to take the battle outside the UAR borders'.[774] A constant barrage of internal propaganda convinced most military officers that their capabilities were superior to those of the Israelis.[775]

This was a major misperception. An impoverished Egypt had been rapidly falling behind in the arms race since 1965. The CIA advised President Johnson in May that the Israeli military was qualitatively superior to the combined Arab forces, predicting: 'Israel could almost certainly attain air superiority over the Sinai Peninsula in 24 hours after taking the initiative or in two or three days if the UAR struck first'.[776] However, the politicised Egyptian intelligence apparatus, focusing on quantity of weapons and soldiers rather than quality, seriously underestimated relative Israeli strength. Indeed, Arab tacticians in general agreed that Israel would be unable to fight a long war, and that there would be 'a crushing military advantage once Arab military operations against Israel are conducted according to a single, co-ordinated plan'.[777] Consequently, public opinion inside Egypt was certain that Israel was weak, divided and afraid to fight without outside support. This was the belief that had long been promulgated by Heikal in *Al-Ahram*:

> Imperialism has built up an image of Israel as a ferocious power which no Arab could challenge. But this is a myth, because the UAR can eliminate Israel single-handed. The problem is the forces protecting Israel and their military presence, above all the American Sixth Fleet in the Mediterranean.[778]

It was also a theme emphasised in Nasser's speeches of May 1967, which portrayed Israel as militarily boastful, deluded by false past successes and ripe for destruction by the Arab nation.

***

Did he believe it? It is possible, as many insiders suggest, that since Nasser had limited access to the armed forces, Amer was able to deceive him with regard to Egypt's relative strength. Nasser thought that 'the Egyptian army was ready for any type of attack that the Israelis might attempt,' asserts Mohammed Riad. His mistake was to place too much trust in his commanders.[779] Meeting the UN Secretary-General in late May, Nasser informed him that his military chiefs had given assurances they were ready.[780] 'Nasser did not take Israel seriously,' recalls one Egyptian diplomat.[781] Other regime members were similarly convinced. When Sadat heard of the Israeli attack on 5 June, he merely thought: 'Well, they'll be taught a lesson they won't forget'.[782] Likewise, Salah Bassiouny of the Foreign Ministry, hearing a military friend predict disaster, was shocked and incredulous.[783]

The alternative possibility is that Nasser knew Israel to be stronger than Egypt, but was bluffing and did not really expect to fight. The well-informed Zakaria Mohieddin confirms that Nasser still had ways of knowing what was going on in the armed forces and knew that they were inferior in quality.[784] Miles Copeland likewise alleges:

> Nasser told me himself of a conversation with Field Marshal Amer, only a week before the war started, when he berated Amer for being 'ten years behind the times' and for the Egyptian army's not being capable of defeating a lot of Yemeni hopheads, let alone a modern well-trained army like the Israelis.[785]

This perception should have been reinforced by the March 1967 UAC report, which emphasised the poor defensive capability of Arab states. Indeed, Nasser had often expressed his awareness that the time was not yet ripe to fight Israel, and that 'the way back to Palestine is hard and long'.[786] 'We do not now possess a joint plan for the liberation of Palestine,' he allegedly told King Faisal in September 1965, 'and we do not possess the means to achieve that aim supposing that we had a plan. So my estimation is that the struggle between us and Israel is a hundred-year problem...'[787]

The key to this apparent contradiction is that Nasser's belief in Israeli strength was based upon two assumptions: that the Arabs were divided and that Israel was supported by powerful external forces. 'We could annihilate Israel in twelve days,' he told a Beirut publication in March 1967, 'were the Arabs to form a united front'.[788] Israel when isolated from the aid of global imperialism was consistently portrayed as weak. It was generally believed that she had only survived the Suez conflict with the help of Britain and France. The United States had now taken the place of the European powers as Israel's protector. Thus Nasser's image of Israeli capability should be described less in terms of objective strength or weakness, and more in terms of dependency. 'Israel could not live for one day,' he proclaimed, 'without US economic and military aid.'[789] This fundamental belief was to be expressed, during the shocked early hours of 5 June 1967, in a widespread conviction that the USA must be fighting on the Israeli side. They were doing far too well to be managing on their own.

7
You Are Welcome, We Are Ready
For War: 1967

Under no circumstances will we allow the Israeli flag to pass through the Gulf of Aqaba. The Jews threaten war. We tell them, you are welcome, we are ready for war.[790] – Gamal Abdel Nasser

The aftershocks of the 'Six Day War' of June 1967 reverberate into the present day. Known optimistically in the Arab world as '*al-naksa*' ('the setback'), it created new *de facto* borders that define the politics of the modern Middle East. It is credited with responsibility for developments ranging from the demise of Arab nationalism to the rise of militant Islam. Egyptians had still believed that Israel was 'the real enemy', even as they sent their army to the Arabian Peninsula.[791] Now, their instinct seemed justified. In Yemen, according to conservative estimates, Egypt lost 10,000 men in five years. In June 1967, she lost the same number in as many days, and forfeited the Sinai Peninsula besides – not to mention more intangible assets, such as regional and global credibility.[792]

President Nasser's intentions present the most enduring mystery of this controversial conflict. Did he plan a war? Did he expect one? Or did he simply blunder into it through a process of uncontrolled escalation? Ashraf Ghorbal, Egyptian envoy to Washington in the immediate aftermath, favours the third option: 'Nasser went to the brink but wanted everyone to stop him. When he was not stopped the results for Egypt were disastrous.'[793] But the truth seems to have been more complicated. Nasser made war neither by accident nor by design. He took a set of actions primarily aimed at reaping political gains, but he was well aware that they carried a high risk of precipitating military hostilities.

The crisis of May 1967 blew up very quickly. In retrospect, it is poss-ible to identify the various trends that coalesced to produce a highly volatile regional situation. The dispute between Israel and her Arab neighbours over the equitable division of waters from the Jordan River had been simmering throughout the decade, occasionally being brought to the boil by one diversion plan or another. The series of Arab summits that had begun in response to this dispute not only failed to contain it, but also contributed to the formation of Palestinian guer-rilla organisations that had carried out a series of attacks on Israel across the Syrian and Jordanian borders. Israeli reprisals followed, cul-minating in a devastating raid on the Jordanian village of Samu in November 1966, which raised regional tensions to a new height.[794] Israel was perceived as increasingly threatening in the Arab world, due not only to the many retaliatory raids, but also to the development of a nuclear reactor at Dimona and extensive arms purchases from the United States.

Equally, however, Tel Aviv felt itself to be under threat. A highly radical regime, controlled by Salah Jadid and Hafez al-Asad, had taken power in Syria in February 1966. The new government was domestically weak, barely surviving attempted coups in September and the following February. In consequence, it was impelled to seek popularity through a militant attitude toward Israel and more overt sponsorship of Palestinian paramilitaries, apparently envisaging an Algerian-style revolutionary war against the Zionist interloper. Strongly socialist and anti-Western, the new Syrian regime received substantial support from the Soviet Union, which promoted the Egypt-Syria Defence Agreement of November 1966. Nasser appears to have hoped that this treaty would enhance his control over the spiralling militancy of his competitor. In fact, it increased the risk that Egypt would be faced with a stark choice between war with Israel and severe Arab censure. This became clear in April 1967, when Syrians fired on an Israeli tractor attempting to cultivate land in a de-militarised zone and the Israel Defence Force (IDF) responded. The clash culminated in an air battle on 7 April, when Israeli planes shot down 6 MiGs over Syrian territory and performed a triumphant overflight of Damascus. The Egyptian government's refusal to intervene to help Syria, on the grounds that this was merely a local action, provoked gloating censure from the conservative Arab states.

Such border incidents continued, on a smaller scale, into late April and early May, further destabilising the precarious balance that consti-tuted the 'Arab-Israeli Question'. Even at this juncture, however, few observers had any expectation of an immediate war. In mid-April, the US intelligence community remained sanguine. 'Although periods of increased tension in the Arab-Israeli dispute will occur from time to time,' it predicted placidly, 'both sides appear to appreciate that large-scale military action involves considerable risk and no assurance of leading to a solution. In any event, the chances are good that the threat of great power intervention will prevent an attempt by either side to resolve the problem by military force.'[795]

It has been suggested that the Cairo regime alone was not surprised by the crisis, having plotted the whole course of events (except the defeat, naturally) in advance. Some foreign diplomats believed at the time that the Egyptians had a plan. They saw small indications of fore-thought and organisation, noting the speed of the movement into Sinai and the atmosphere of overwhelming confidence.[796] An intriguing hint that might confirm this possibility has been dropped by Gamal Naguib, then *chef de cabinet* to Nasser's personal foreign affairs advisor Mahmoud Fawzi, who recalls that discussions of the legal ramifications of closing the Gulf of Aqaba to Israel 'started in April – they wanted to read the file and so on'.[797] Most Egyptian accounts, however, emphasise that in fact there was a high degree of confusion and improvisation. On 22 May Nasser asserted that Egypt had no plan prior to 13 May; while four days later he implied the opposite. 'Recently we felt we are strong enough, that if we were to enter a battle with Israel, with God's help, we could triumph,' he informed the nation. 'On this basis, we decided to take actual steps.'[798] It is probable that he was merely taking credit for the inevitable. Although Cairo certainly had contingency plans for this sort of situation, the specific occasion came as a surprise.[799]

***

The first intimation to an unsuspecting world that the Arab-Israeli problem was poised to fall once again out of the ice-box came on 14 May. In response to a report that Israeli troops were massing on the Syrian border, the Egyptian armed forces were ordered to mobilise on full alert. Troops were sent to Sinai, while the Chief of Staff, General Mohammed Fawzi, travelled to Damascus to investigate the alleged Israeli threat and assure the Syrian regime of Egyptian support.[800] Reports of Israeli troop concentrations had often been received – and ignored – before, but this one was more convincing, including circumstantial detail on the nature and location of the putative 13 brigades.

Moreover, the Egyptians noted, there were fewer troops and less heavy equipment than usual in the Israeli Independence Day parade in Jerusalem on 15 May. This gesture, intended to reduce provocation, went sadly awry. It could *only* mean that they must be busy elsewhere, US chargé David Nes was informed by an Egyptian official.[801] Finally, the intelligence was received from several sources, including Syria, Lebanon and, most importantly, the USSR, which accorded it particular emphasis. The Soviet Ambassador gave the Egyptian Foreign Ministry a detailed report; the Soviet Deputy Foreign Minister passed similarly specific information to Anwar Sadat (in transit via Moscow airport); and the story was also relayed directly from Soviet to Egyptian Intelligence.[802]

When Sadat arrived home from Moscow, late on 13 May, he and Marshal Amer went to Nasser's house, where the decision was made to mobilise troops in the Sinai.[803] The next morning, Amer met General Fawzi, Defence Minister Shams Badran and the heads of the various divisions of the armed forces, in order to formulate operational plans. The move was sudden – to the extent that the Chief of General Intelligence, Salah Nasr, was not even informed. He turned up to give a lecture as planned at the Military Academy, only to discover that it had been cancelled so the officers could return to their units. 'I have no information about that,' remarked Nasr, when the Academy Commander, General Hadidi, told him of the reputed Israeli troop concentrations.[804]

The aim at this stage appears to have been to deter Israel rather than to start a war.[805] There was nothing covert about the ostentatious march through Cairo of the Egyptian detachments.[806] Nasser himself later claimed that he estimated the likelihood of war at only 20 per cent at this time.[807] Amer reassured Chief of Operations Anwar Qadi 'that this was no more than a "demonstration" in response to Israeli threats against Syria'.[808] He ordered General Fawzi to implement an existing defensive plan, codenamed 'Conqueror'. Fawzi was told that the aim was 'to make this mobilization and deployment of troops like we did in 1960'.[809] (The reference was to the 'Rotem' crisis, when Nasser had sent 50,000 troops into Sinai in reaction to an Israeli strike against a Syrian village, but withdrew a couple of days later, having successfully made his point.[810]) In May 1967, therefore, Nes reported to his superiors that he was certain the Egyptians were only reacting to their fears and had 'no aggressive intent'.[811]

On the other hand, the report of Israeli troop concentrations alone cannot explain the Egyptian decision to mobilise. It was very soon contradicted. General Fawzi found no evidence of abnormal Israeli movements on his visit to Syria; indeed, he was told that the report itself was merely based on verbal threats and the experience of past raids. Fawzi informed Amer of this on 15 May.[812] Tel Aviv repeatedly denied – through the USA, the USSR and a secret channel formerly used by Mossad – that unusual numbers of troops were present on the border.[813] Washington confirmed this – but Cairo remained sceptical. The Foreign Minister later told UN Secretary-General U Thant:

> Strangely, after we had decided to move against Israel, US Chargé told us that there were no concentrations but would not give us any guarantees. We were back in a similar situation as existed in 1956 when the US Ambassador gave us similar information, and yet we were attacked.[814]

The denials were not received until the Egyptian troops had begun to move into Sinai, when withdrawal would have meant a loss of face. 'Everything had got escalated,' Badran later remembered, 'and we can't just turn the key and get all the troops back as if nothing happened'.[815] Nevertheless, this does not account for the sheer scale of the continuing military build-up. Surviving insiders continue to profess ignorance of the reason for the ongoing mobilisation. 'Nobody knows,' General Hadidi says simply.[816]

***

In fact, phantom Israeli troop concentrations were relatively unimportant. The critical factor was the Egyptian regime's firm preconception that Israel was limitlessly aggressive, which caused contrary evidence to be discounted. Egyptian General Intelligence believed that stable US-Israel relations and increasing US-Egypt tension 'could push Israel to undertake a military action against Syria to embarrass the Egyptian leadership in the Arab world', according to the diplomat Salah Bassiouny, while:

> During the three months preceding the June War, the assessments of the Egyptian Foreign Ministry were consistent in warning of an increased threat of war by Israel on the Syrian and Jordanian fronts.[817]

Indeed, the Soviet report may never have been taken literally. It represented a political rather than a military reality. Since Israel could mobilise within hours, the lack of troop concentrations was not in itself significant. The perception that Israel intended to attack Syria had recently been reinforced by Israeli decision-makers' reported threats. An 11 May press briefing by General Yitzhak Rabin had been misquoted and misinterpreted as a threat to occupy Damascus and overthrow the Syrian regime. Prime Minister Levi Eshkol also threatened Arab rulers with drastic measures: 'We do not recognise the limitations they endeavour to impose on our acts of response... If they try to sow unrest on our border – unrest will come to theirs.'[818] When even international observers speculated that an Israeli attack might be forthcoming, Nasser and the Egyptian media naturally took such words as evidence of aggressive intentions toward Syria.[819]

However, even an Israeli threat to Syria was not necessarily a sufficient reason for action. Syria was no longer part of the United Arab Republic, as it had been when Nasser mobilised in 1960. The Egyptian-Syrian Defence Agreement, concluded in late 1966, did not mandate a response to normal raids, just as none had been made the previous month when six Syrian planes were shot down in a major dogfight. The problem was that such statements by Israeli leaders and widespread reports of troop movements attacked Nasser's prestige. They showed that he was unable to protect Syria, laying him open to deeper criticism from the Arab conservatives. 'Every day there was an attack against Egypt from Jordan and Saudi Arabia,' recalls Information Minister Mohammed Fayek. They accused Cairo of hiding behind the United Nations Emergency Force (UNEF) stationed on the Sinai border.[820]

The threat to Nasser's prestige seemed part of a US conspiracy. The Egyptian government, Nes concluded, 'had talked itself' into believing in a US-Israeli plot to create an incident resulting in the stationing of UNEF along the Syrian border with Israel also.[821] The Egyptian Foreign Ministry credited the reports of Israeli troop movements because Israel seemed to have reached the level at which she could find 'strategic alliance' with the USA.[822] On 12 May, Heikal had published the final article in his series about the clash between Egypt and America, entitled 'The Cobweb Broken'. He depicted the United States as at last prepared to deal the *coup de grâce*. In this atmosphere of danger, the heavy emphasis laid by the USSR on the warning of troop movements seemed like an opportunity not to be missed. It implied an invitation for Egypt to confront her enemies with Soviet support, without which the US was unassailable. Such support seemed particularly valuable since it could not, the Egyptians feared, be taken for granted, given the threatening possibility of superpower détente.[823]

***

Nasser's next move was to get rid of UNEF. 'For the sake of complete security of all UN troops which install Observation Posts along our borders,' General Fawzi wrote in a letter to Major General Indar Jit Rikhye, the UNEF commander, on 16 May, 'I request that you issue your orders to withdraw all these troops immediately'. Rikhye had no authority to comply, and referred the matter to Thant, who made it clear that UNEF could be expelled but would not stand aside to allow the resumption of hostilities. Foreign Minister Mahmoud Riad then sent a second letter with a more comprehensive formal request 'to terminate the existence of UNEF on the soil of the UAR and in the Gaza Strip'.[824] Fawzi failed to realise the significance at the time, but Riad claims to have understood the likelihood of a military confrontation immediately upon reading the first letter.[825] Rikhye thought it would make war inevitable, especially when cheerfully told by his Egyptian liaison: 'We have arrived at this decision after much deliberation and are prepared for anything. If there is war, we shall next meet at Tel Aviv.'[826]

Nasser, who also acknowledged that this request increased the chances of war, certainly ordered both letters.[827] He planned the first on the morning of 14 May, in consultation with his foreign affairs advisor, Mahmoud Fawzi. He then apparently delegated the task to Amer, who gave instructions to General Mohammed Fawzi. However, when Nasser saw the English version of the missive, he was concerned about the wording. Wanting to clarify that UNEF could remain in Sharm el-Sheikh and the Gaza Strip, Nasser asked the Marshal to change 'withdraw' to 'redeploy' and remove 'all' before 'these troops'. That, Amer replied, was impossible. The letter was already being delivered.[828] Therefore it seems that, two days later, Nasser ordered Foreign Minister Riad to request the full withdrawal reluctantly, to preserve his dignity. 'Nasser had no alternative solution but to request the withdrawal of the force from all its positions,' writes Heikal.[829]

Nonetheless, once the lines had been drawn, Nasser rejoiced with the Egyptian people at the expulsion of UNEF, which he saw as infringing on Egyptian national sovereignty.[830] He had no intention of seeking a graceful way to back down, advising Thant not to send an appeal that would certainly be refused.[831] Although a full withdrawal at this juncture raised political problems for which the regime was not ready, it had been one of Nasser's long-term goals. Amer, conversely, may have planned the complete termination of UNEF from the outset. He had suggested it twice previously, telegraphing Nasser from Pakistan with a recommendation to that effect as early as December 1966. On another occasion, standing with the President to watch an infantry brigade setting out from Suez to Yemen, he suggested that they send it to Sharm el-Sheikh instead. Both times, Nasser refused.[832]

On 16 May 1967, however, Amer decided the time had come. General Noufal, then assistant to the Chief of Operations, telephoned him that afternoon to ask if a force should be sent to take over Sharm el-Sheikh, as well as the less significant border posts. After a delay of two hours, Amer called back to say that it should. When the consequent danger of war was pointed out to him, the Marshal reconsidered, deciding it would be better *not* to send troops to Sharm el-Sheikh. But later he changed his mind again. Noufal was ordered to dispatch the forces after all, sending paratroopers instead of the planned Fourth Brigade, so that they might arrive by 18 May at the latest.[833]

Consequently, Rikhye was asked that night to withdraw from Sharm el-Sheikh also, even though it was not mentioned in Fawzi's letter. He prevaricated, but on 18 May a group of Egyptian officers duly arrived by helicopter to take over the camp, demanding a reply within 15 minutes.[834] Since Amer seems to have been aware that the occupation of Sharm el-Sheikh would force the closure of the nearby Tiran Straits, provoking Israel, this implies that he may already have intended war in mid-May.[835]

Nasser, by contrast, was seeking primarily to increase the political gains from his previous move. Although UNEF consisted of only 3,378 men and could not in practice prevent aggression from either side, its symbolic importance made the concentration of Egyptian troops in Sinai less credible as a deterrent against an Israeli attack on Syria.[836] While Amer and his military supporters perceived Israel as the primary enemy, and her military inferiority as the key factor determining action, Nasser's calculations were more complex, since his emphasis on the hostility of the United States caused him to pay greater attention to the global situation. Unlike the Marshal, who never seriously considered the option of partial UNEF withdrawal, Nasser was probably not committed to the occupation of Sharm el-Sheikh until Thant on 17 May refused to evacuate only the border posts.[837]

Nevertheless, he must have approved it thereafter. Rikhye, in his discussions of the handover, communicated largely with General Fawzi, who was avowedly Nasser's man. At 2pm on 17 May, Fawzi definitely confirmed that UNEF had to withdraw from Sharm el-Sheikh within 48 hours. When Rikhye, hoping to delay the removal until Thant arrived in Cairo to mediate, asked for three extra days, it was Fawzi who refused, but granted him until 22 May as an act of co-operation.[838] This particular day was almost certainly chosen because Nasser planned then to announce the closure of the Tiran Straits, which depended on an Egyptian military presence in Sharm el-Sheikh. It was therefore probably Nasser who gave the order.[839] He knew the implications. 'Taking over Sharm el-Sheikh meant confrontation with Israel,' the President proclaimed soon after. 'It also meant that we were ready to enter a general war with Israel.'[840]

***

In retrospect, however, it was the next Egyptian decision – to close the Gulf of Aqaba to Israel by controlling passage through the Tiran Straits, thus blockading the Israeli port of Eilat – that was to prove the most fateful. (Former Ambassador Battle, who had reported after his departure in March that Egypt was in a dreadful condition and Nasser would do something drastic, remained bemused by such an irrevocable move, speculating 'whether Nasser either has more Soviet support than we know about, or had gone slightly insane'.[841]) The decision was made on the morning of 22 May by a meeting of the Supreme Executive Committee (SEC), chaired by Nasser. A vote was taken, but only Prime Minister Sidqi Suleiman voted against closure, citing economic concerns.[842] On this basis, Heikal argues that the choice was not made autocratically, but by consensus, after 'responsible study' – although this is disputed by various diplomats, who note that the Foreign Ministry was never even asked for its opinion.[843]

That evening, Nasser made a speech affirming 'our rights and our sovereignty' over these waters. 'Under no circumstances,' he emphasised firmly, 'will we allow the Israeli flag to pass through the Gulf of Aqaba'.[844] On 23 May, Cairo Radio added that the President had banned 'the passage of strategic materials through the Gulf to Israel even on non-Israeli ships'. It was also (falsely) announced that the Tiran Straits had been mined in order to enforce the blockade. Although Brigadier Abdel Moneim Khalil, who had arrived in Sharm al-Sheikh with his 4000 paratroopers three days earlier, did receive orders from Cairo to impose a blockade on 22 May, no mines were to be laid, as there was no appropriate equipment. Israeli merchant ships should receive warning shots across the bows and stern, but he was to allow passage to all naval vessels or merchant convoys with a naval escort – 'even Israeli ones'.[845]

Did the President believe he was inviting war? Israeli leaders had long reiterated that they would view the closure of the Gulf of Aqaba as a *casus belli*, as the law professors Nasser consulted informed him.[846] 'Interference, by armed forces, with ships of Israel flag exercising free and innocent passage in the Gulf of Aqaba and through the Straits of Tiran,' Golda Meir proclaimed to the UN General Assembly as early as March 1957, 'will be regarded by Israel as an attack entitling it to exercise its inherent right of self-defence under Article 51 of the United Nations Charter.' Although few Israeli vessels had passed through recently, Cairo Radio's gloss on Nasser's announcement threatened Israeli oil importation from Iran, access to Africa and Asia and, most importantly, deterrent capacity. There was the obvious precedent of 1956, when such a blockade had been a crucial motivation for the Israeli attack. Officers in the Egyptian armed forces learned during training that Israel had laid down certain 'red lines', to cross which meant to declare war. One of these was the closure of the Tiran Straits.[847]

'Israel used to say in the past, and even just before Egypt took its decision to close the Gulf of Aqaba, that the existence of a single soldier in Sharm el-Sheikh would mean war,' Heikal wrote in his editorial of 2 June.[848] Three days prior to the announcement, the Israeli Foreign Minister Abba Eban had warned the Soviet Ambassador: 'there will be no war if the Egyptians do not attack and do not interfere with Israel's right of navigation'.[849] It seems certain, therefore, that Nasser and Riad were being disingenuous when they told Thant on 24 May that the Gulf of Aqaba was not really important to Israel.[850] According to two of those present at the 22 May meeting, Sadat and Shafei, Nasser said even then that the blockade would make war 100 per cent certain, although he himself claimed in a later self-justificatory speech that his actual estimate at that time was 50 per cent or 80 per cent.[851] On the other hand, it is interesting that the pilots who were the original audience for Nasser's 22 May speech were apparently disappointed. They thought he was trying to tell them that US-related considerations would prevent war. Amer had to reassure them: 'don't worry children, we're going to fight'.[852]

***

The main motivation for the blockade was the criticism of Egypt by the other Arab states, especially Jordan. 'Will Egypt restore its batteries and guns to close its territorial waters in the Tiran Strait to the enemy?'

Amman Radio had asked pointedly on 19 May. 'Logic, wisdom and nationalism make it incumbent on Egypt to do so.'[853] Extravagant domestic propaganda had also raised high expectations.[854] The losses of Suez rankled, and there was a deep desire to wipe them out, both because they endangered the myth that Israel had not been the victor and because they were seen as unjust. 'Israel will not profit from that aggression any more,' Riad told Thant firmly.[855]

Some observers believed that Nasser never wanted to close the Gulf of Aqaba, but was forced to it by the occupation of Sharm el-Sheikh, which was in turn necessitated by the termination of UNEF. As Amer protested at the meeting on 22 May, Egyptian troops could not simply sit in Sharm el-Sheikh and watch the Israeli flag go past.[856] Why indeed, asks General Hadidi, 'would we send troops to Sharm el-Sheikh if not to close the Gulf of Aqaba?'[857] In fact, however, the closure did not follow inevitably from the occupation. Even after UNEF had been asked to leave, the possibility of a blockade was hardly mentioned in the Egyptian press until it became reality. Both Egyptian and Israeli sources assert that Amer told a group of officers in Sinai on 20 May that the Straits would not be closed, which, even if he was lying, must have seemed plausible to his audience. At his trial, Badran stated Amer had told him dismissing UNEF need not mean closing the Gulf.[858] Moreover, to the extent that it was a significant factor, the link between occupying Sharm el-Sheikh and closing the Tiran Straits was recognised all along.[859] Nasser did not seem to feel trapped by the course of events. Thant, visiting Cairo, was puzzled by the President's air of blissful confidence.

Why, then, did Nasser decide to risk war by blockading the Tiran Straits? The weak and apparently irresolute Israeli response to his previous provocations was one reason. Eshkol sent secret messages urging de-escalation, while publicly asserting Israel's peaceful intentions, calling for international mediation and avoiding criticism of Egypt.[860] This reinforced the existing image of Egyptian military superiority. If Israel wanted to avoid war, it was presumably because she thought she would lose. If she relied on the international community, she must be too weak to stand alone. Nasser was therefore encouraged to believe Israel might not fight, especially if the US urged a peaceful solution.[861]

If Israel did fight, however, the Egyptian President still thought he could win in the long run. Nasser would not have abandoned his control of the timing of any hostilities, argued Nes, were he not 'fairly confident of victory'.[862] The other Arab states were seeking Egyptian leadership. The Soviets would assist him in the UN Security Council.[863]

'Nasser may be convinced,' concluded the CIA, 'that his armed forces are sufficiently strong to be able successfully to hold off an Israeli attack at least for long enough to get great power intervention.'[864] Amer continually assured him that his army was more than ready.[865] 'We were 100 per cent sure that Israel would not dare to attack or take a first step or the initiative for a first strike,' Badran declared at his trial. 'Any action by Israel would mean a suicidal operation because it was certain to be defeated.'[866]

***

Over the next fortnight, the Egyptian leaders had three options. They could launch a first strike against Israel. They could continue to escalate the situation, forcing Israel either to attack first or to back down. Finally, they could seek a compromise. In the end, they seem to have chosen the second alternative. However, there are indications that the first was under consideration and was rejected. 'Number one, the Egyptians were planning an attack on Israel,' US Defence Secretary Robert McNamara has since stated. 'Number two, we knew it; the Israelis knew it, the British knew it. Number three, we were convinced that the Israelis could repel the attack.'[867]

However, contemporary US documents uniformly confirm what McNamara himself told Eban on 26 May: 'that three separate intelligence groups had looked into the matter in the last twenty-four hours and that our judgment was that Egyptian deployments made were defensive'.[868] Egyptian military plans later captured by the Israeli army have been dismissed as 'nothing more than the kind of operational orders that any military staff prepares for possible operations'.[869] Egyptian commanders deny there were ever any offensive orders beyond normal contingency scenarios: their only aim was to defend their borders.[870] This was the impression of many contemporary observers. Visiting Cairo, the Jordanian Chief of Staff concluded that the Egyptians had no meaningful attack plans and were 'playing a political game rather than preparing for war'.[871] Egyptian front-line troops were 'under strict orders not to start anything', US diplomat Richard Parker was told on 20 May.[872] In fact, the troops moving into the Sinai were themselves unsure whether their goal was offensive or defensive. Despite the intense military activity, 'no orders were issued for any military operation,' Qadi recalled. 'This led to some confusion as to the purpose of these preparations.'[873] Nasser added to the chaos by his constant interference in military affairs, while Amer was surprised to learn from his deputy 'that his forces were not trained for offensive action'.[874]

Nonetheless, the military command had been urging a first strike, as Nasser openly informed Thant and Badran later admitted at his trial.[875] In fact, they went even further. The unfortunate Egyptian commanders were inflicted with 'four plans in 20 days' during the 1967 crisis.[876] Replacing the established, defensive 'Conqueror' plan as the troops moved into Sinai, Marshal Amer apparently introduced the offensive Operation 'Lion', which mandated an attack on Eilat and part of the Negev.[877] After the closure of the Tiran Straits, he broadened his objectives to include the entire Negev, with Operations 'Dawn' and 'Dusk', the orders for which were to be issued directly from Amer's own house.[878] On 20 May, Saad el-Din Shazly, commander of a Special Forces unit in Sinai, was given an offensive mission plan involving an advance through Israel.[879] The *Voice of the Arabs* radio station was ordered to 'heat it up' in preparation for war. Five days later, Marshal Amer told the presenter Ahmed Said that an Egyptian first strike was imminent, and they needed to be prepared to relocate if their transmitters were targeted.[880] On 25 May, therefore, everything was in train for an attack at daybreak on 27 May.[881]

However, at a meeting in military headquarters on 25 May, Amer failed to convince Nasser of the case for a first strike, necessitating a change of plan.[882] Even then, the Marshal did not comply immediately with the President's order. It was only one hour before the planned offensive on 27 May that Said's army liaison officer told him the attack had been aborted after a US request to the Soviets; while Shazly, on the front line, was not informed of the shift to a defensive posture until about 1 June.[883] While Nasser reiterated that Egypt would not strike first, tanks and planes in the Sinai were fully fuelled and not concealed, as if they were going to attack, implying that 'the political decision did not match with the military one'.[884] At last, however, the President prevailed, and 'the situation was turned from attacking to defence' – which Badran blames for all the confusion.[885]

The relationship between Nasser and Amer was at this time extremely sensitive. Their March 1962 quarrel had been patched up. By 1967, the President and the Marshal, who was also First Vice President, seemed as close as they had ever been. The year before, Nasser had put Amer in charge of the 'Committee for the Eradication of the Remnants of Feudalism', overseeing a new phase of land redistribution. Amer's daughter married Nasser's younger brother. His protégé Shams Badran was appointed Minister of Defence.[886] It has been alleged that Nasser was effectively superseded before the Six Day War. Sadat quotes him as complaining in February 1967 that he could not 'continue to be President, to hold such a serious responsibility, while it is Amer who actually rules the country and does precisely what he wants'.[887] These claims must be treated with extreme caution, given the rapidity with which the Marshal was made a scapegoat in the wake of the disaster. 'Nasser was obliged to give the army rope to regain the reins,' notes Vice President Hussein Shafei, rather cryptically. 'He paid a great price.'[888] Amer's top commanders emphasise that the President made the final policy decisions, and this is borne out by the subsequent course of events.[889]

Amer and his faction do seem to have made their attack plans independently, not revealing them to Nasser until the 25 May meeting, which was followed by a private showdown between the two leaders.[890] Fawzi's plausible testimony on this point agrees with the account of Ambassador Bassiouny, who recalls that Nasser and Amer were 'not on speaking terms' on 26 May. When the Washington Embassy reported that Dean Rusk had information Egypt was going to start the war, the Marshal:

> wrote on the cable, 'Shams, it seems there is a leak.' According to an assistant in the Secretariat of the Presidency, Nasser commented on the behaviour of 'Amr in these words: 'Why is 'Amr upset? Does he think that we shall start the war?'[891]

Some alternative accounts suggest that Nasser himself considered the first strike option until early on 27 May, when he was hauled out of bed at 3am by the Soviet ambassador and warned not to precipitate a confrontation.[892] Michael Oren even claims that Nasser was fully aware of Operation 'Dawn' from the outset, but preferred to overlook it, cancelling it at the last moment only because he took the Soviet warning to prove that Israel had compromised Egyptian military secrets.[893] However, although Nasser gave Amer much latitude, it seems unlikely that he was prepared to allow him to start a war without taking at least a passing interest, and other evidence suggests that he never had any intention of attacking first.

All of Nasser's plans depended on the assumption that the Israelis would make the initial move. An Egyptian first strike was politically impossible; it would, he believed, give the United States and Israel the very pretext they sought.[894] International opinion would be alienated, the Soviets might withdraw their support and the USA could enter the war on Israel's side. 'Would you like us to begin and lose the whole world?' Nasser demanded, when he met with the military commanders on 2 June. He asked the air force commander, Sidqi Mahmoud, to estimate his losses following the anticipated Israeli first strike. Nasser's aide Sami Sharaf claims the President was told he would lose only 10–20 per cent of the air force – an acceptable result.[895] The opposing faction remembers differently.[896] According to Badran:

> Sidqi just said 'Sir,' he said it in English, 'it will be crippling to me'... Abdel Hakim Amer looked at Sidqi and said, 'Sidqi, do you accept the first attack or do you want to fight the United States?'

By this time, therefore, even Amer had accepted the political parameters within which Nasser was working. Badran himself tried to persuade Amer to allow a small first strike in order to provoke a war, but the Marshal unwillingly refused. 'I wish but I can't do that,' he replied. 'I am obliged with a policy and it's the policy that the President does and I can't do anything about it.'[897]

***

However, if Egypt now had no intention of attacking first, neither did it make any great effort to defuse tensions with Israel. There were some minor concessions. In addition to the reiterated promise not to fire the first shot, Nasser agreed with Thant to accept a two-week moratorium on action in the Strait if Israel did the same, and to refer the issue of passage to the International Court of Justice. He also sent an extremely indirect message to Johnson (via the businessman James Birdsall), emphasising 'that this matter would soon be terminated without any fighting' and begging him to take no action.[898] By 2 June, the British Foreign Office noted some 'signs that the Egyptians were already tending to modify the application of their blockade'.[899] The following day, an agreement was reached that Vice President Zakaria Mohieddin should go to Washington, reviving Egyptian hopes that the superpowers might compel Israel to accept the new *status quo*. Tasked on 3 June with preparing passports for the mission, the diplomat Gamal Naguib was optimistic.[900] There was a military relaxation, as staff officers 'were ordered to de-escalate and to get back to our offices'.[901]

Nevertheless, Nasser's small concessions do not suggest that he was making a concerted effort to avoid war. The appearance of reasonableness kept the international community from turning against him, while every delay was to his advantage. Egypt needed time to complete her military preparations and co-ordinate with the other Arabs; conversely, Israel could not afford to sustain total mobilisation for long. Moreover, Nasser continued to raise the stakes with highly belligerent rhetoric. 'You are welcome, we are ready for war,' he announced to the Jews on 22 May.[902] 'The rights of the people of Palestine must be restored,' he declared the following week, threatening the very foundations of Israel, with whom Egypt would 'accept no basis for coexistence'.[903] By 4 June, his tone was triumphant. 'We are, with God's help, advancing along the road towards our rights and the rights of the people of Palestine, and God willing, we shall be victorious.'[904]

Nasser had also crossed another of Israel's 'red lines' on 30 May, when he signed a Joint Defence Agreement with Jordan. King Hussein's Chief of Staff had been sent to Cairo nine days earlier to inform the nominal United Arab Command that Jordan was ready to do her part. He was rebuffed, on the grounds that the Egyptian military would not share its plans with traitors. Meanwhile, the Egyptian President continued to excoriate the 'reactionary' monarchies.[905] By 26 May, however, he had begun to express the wish for 'one united front around Israel'.[906] Two days later, with his domestic situation growing increasingly precarious as the Arab masses rallied around Nasser, Hussein arranged a secret meeting with the Egyptian Ambassador, asking permission to visit Cairo. Late on 29 May he received the reply that he should come as soon as he could.

Hussein flew to Egypt first thing the next morning, piloting his own plane. Barely pausing for a couple of uneasy jokes with Nasser about the gun he was carrying, and without even reading the text in full, the desperate king signed an agreement handing over operational command of the Jordanian armed forces to an Egyptian general, Abdel Moneim Riad, who arrived in Amman on 1 June.[907] He had his brief reward. Egypt's new ally Jordan, Nasser conceded publicly, was 'full of confidence, power and pride'.[908] However, the treaty had the effect of increasing the risk of war still further. Egypt had effectively encircled Israel, and was taking military control of its most vulnerable border. Indeed, Shimon Peres stated that the meeting of the two Arab leaders at Cairo Airport was the key factor in Israel's decision to fight: 'This was an historic and crucial kiss... we were now surrounded by a sort of banana filled with Russian weapons.'[909]

***

Nasser himself still seems to have been in two minds about whether he expected war. On the one hand, Nasser's confidant Heikal proclaimed the inevitability of an armed clash with Israel, recommending that Egypt should wait to receive the first blow, since Israel must either strike against the blockade or do nothing and collapse from within. 'No matter what happens – and this is not an attempt to get ahead of events – Israel is definitely heading towards final collapse from within or without.'[910] On the other, Heikal later stated that this was not then Nasser's own opinion, arguing that the President planned to 'make intense political efforts to prevent the outbreak of military operations' and believed that 'the probability of the outbreak of military operations would reduce with time'.[911] At a press conference on 28 May, Nasser said that he expected an Israeli attack 'daily'.[912] But two days later, King Hussein received the impression that Nasser did not want war, did not believe it would happen and thought there was a way out, perhaps through international intervention.[913]

There is general agreement that on 2 June, following an Israeli cabinet reshuffle in which the 'hawks' overcame Eshkol, Nasser concluded war was certain, telling the military leadership that he expected an attack on the air force on Monday 5 June.[914] He made the same prediction to his aides. 'Mind you, Dayan appointed as Defence Minister, means war in maximum 72 hours.'[915] The next day, Ali Sabri relayed Nasser's warning to the provincial governors whose territories bordered Israel, asking them to undertake defensive measures. (He did not inform them of the exact date, however. Hamed Mahmoud, the Governor of Suez, was out of his office doing pistol practice with the Chief of Police when the Israelis attacked on Monday morning.)[916] Nasser may have been drawing on information from King Hussein and ambassadors in Brussels and Moscow, as well as the estimations of the military attaché in Turkey and the Information Minister, Mohammed Fayek, who was alerted by the intransigence of Israeli broadcasts in Hebrew as well as those in Arabic.[917]

It is strange, therefore, that Egyptian forces were demonstrably taken by surprise when Nasser's prediction proved accurate. Amer and his senior officers were in an aeroplane on their way to the Sinai front on the morning of 5 June, not only rendering them vulnerable and out of touch, but also forcing the air defence systems to cease operation.[918] The military command did not take Nasser's warning seriously, or pass it on to the lower ranks. Shams Badran thought the President was merely repeating the speculation of an American journalist.[919] Nasser, who had been so badly caught out in 1956, 'had no transparent soul that would enable him to foresee the future,' Amer scoffed.[920] Amer's own information from Military Intelligence – which had long served particular factional interests and bought into the myth of Egyptian military superiority – did not lead him to expect war so soon. Indeed, by 28 May his analysts are said to have predicted only a limited attack on Sharm el-Sheikh aimed at opening the Gulf of Aqaba. They consistently ruled out any chance of a full-scale Israeli attack.[921]

In any case, by 3 June, new doubts seem to have arisen in Nasser's own mind, as he claimed in one interview that conflict was imminent and in another that the crisis had already passed.[922] The President was basically unsure whether there would be war. He changed his mind frequently, but not his policies, because, in one sense, the question was unimportant. If war did break out, he believed that 'the Egyptian armed forces would be capable of entering a prolonged defensive battle', creating global pressure for an early ceasefire.[923] Nasser thought he could 'repeat what happened in '56,' recalls Mohammed Fayek, and other sources emphasise the importance of the same analogy – with the difference that, this time, Britain and France would not be there to rescue Israel.[924] If there were no war, however, Nasser would have achieved a great symbolic triumph for Arabism and regained sovereignty over the Tiran Straits. He expected a political victory in either case.

***

Nasser's confidence was therefore founded not only on his belief, acquired from Amer, that the Arabs were militarily capable of holding their own against Israel, but also on his estimation of the international situation. His beliefs about the Soviet stance are crucial to explaining his perception of the degree of threat from the United States. However, his views on this point are often misinterpreted. In late May, Shams Badran headed a delegation on a mission to Moscow to discuss the crisis and seek additional arms. Badran was rude to the Soviet leaders, lying about having mined the Tiran Straits and speaking 'nonsense' about Egyptian readiness to confront the USA, remembers the Egyptian Ambassador to Moscow. In the discussions, Soviet premier Kosygin constantly pressed for Egypt to reduce tension and withdraw her forces. When Badran predicted that his country would attract global support, Kosygin asked: 'Are you sure of what you are saying? Who will come?' – implying that the Soviet Union, at least, would not.[925]

Escorting Badran to the airport, however, the Soviet Defence Minister, Marshal Gretchko, slapped him on the back and expressed his support in hearty terms: 'Keep on, keep up, we are with you.' Badran (who denies everything) is alleged to have taken this empty compliment at face value, giving Nasser the false impression, when he returned on 26 May, that the USSR would provide Egypt with military support if Israel attacked.[926] He may indeed have influenced Nasser's speech of that evening, which seemed to anticipate Soviet assistance. However, the President was immediately given the true picture by Deputy Foreign Minister Feki, sent with the Moscow delegation by Sami Sharaf for that very purpose.[927] 'Be careful,' Feki is said to have warned, 'don't jump into war.'[928] Two days later, Nasser was clearly conscious that the US would counter any Soviet intervention, perhaps resulting in world nuclear war. 'If war breaks out between Israel alone and us alone,' he predicted at a press conference, 'I think that it will be restricted to this area'.[929]

The Egyptian President was relying on the USSR, but not to fight Israel. That battle, he thought the Arabs could win alone. Moscow's role, as Nasser saw it, was simply to deter the Americans from intervening in support of their regional protégé. He seemed confident, King Hussein told a US representative the day after his Cairo visit, that if the United States took 'aggressive action', the Soviet Union would provide 'the required support'.[930] The USSR did make some tentative moves in this direction, stationing additional naval units in the eastern Mediterranean. Since the two superpowers had been in touch at the highest levels since 22 May, to avoid misunderstanding, this action itself seemed to suggest a lowered Soviet estimate of the probability of US intervention.[931]

Nasser's judgement that the Soviet Union would deter US involvement simultaneously made it seem less likely that Israel, viewed primarily as an American instrument, would act independently. This was partly because she was not perceived to be strong enough; partly because Nasser assumed she would follow US orders. Hussein also reported that the Egyptian President 'believed the United States had the power to prevent Israel from going to war'.[932] The USA was clearly emphasising a diplomatic approach. Following her initial support for the vain British attempt to organise a flotilla of UN members' ships to break the blockade (the 'Red Sea Regatta'), an exchange of visits between the Egyptian and American Vice Presidents was negotiated. Cairo believed the USA was also endorsing Thant's moratorium – and pressuring Israel to comply.[933] The US diplomat David Korn remembers:

As the crisis wore on, some in Washington were heard to say that the Egyptian blockade was, after all, perhaps not so much of a catastrophe as had first been thought. Ships under Israeli flag hardly ever called at Eilat anyway.[934]

***

Indications of the American search for a peaceful solution, if they could be taken at face value, must also be indications of the fact that Israel would not strike first. This basic assumption was at the root of the many Arab conspiracy theories prevalent after the defeat. However, Nasser had an established image of the US as deeply hostile towards him personally. Therefore, he did not take such signs at face value, and did not rule out the possibility of war. When he received Johnson's letter of 23 May, expressing friendly intentions and condemning all aggression, he doubted its sincerity.[935] This suspicion was reinforced by indications from the American side, such as US Ambassador Richard Nolte's estimate that the chances of an Israeli attack were about fifty-fifty and the report that Johnson had told his aides: 'Israel will hit them'.[936] However, so deeply ingrained were the images of American hostility and Israeli dependency that these were seen as signs of US hypocrisy rather than genuine inability to dictate to the Jewish state.

The extent to which such images really were distorted remains a contentious question. Allegations that the whole war was 'a CIA operation, designed to get Nasser' seem wholly unsubstantiated.[937] But did US officials such as Defence Secretary Robert McNamara really give a 'green light' to Mossad chief Meir Amit, as some historians suggest?[938] McNamara himself claims President Johnson went 'to the limit' trying to persuade Tel Aviv 'not to pre-empt'.[939] In fact, however, the Western powers were in a difficult position by early June. By holding Israel back they were taking responsibility for a crisis that appeared increasingly difficult to resolve. Although Nasser certainly did over-estimate US control over Israeli foreign policy, there may, on the American side, have been some mixed signals and a desire not to enquire too closely into Israeli plans.[940] The former diplomat Richard Parker concludes:

> American opposition to an Israeli first strike was not as unequivocal as it could have been, and Johnson's performance after the fighting started showed a clear and lasting bias in favour of Israel... but there was no deliberate US attempt to mislead them in the period leading up to the war. Rather, a serious effort was made to restrain all the parties and prevent a resort to arms.[941]

As the crisis mounted, however, every new piece of information was interpreted by the Egyptian elite as confirmation of Israeli weakness. When the United States counselled restraint, it was seen as an attempt to protect Israel from Arab wrath – and therefore as further evidence of her need for protection. Israel's initial response to the Tiran blockade had been relatively mild. Prime Minister Eshkol spoke in the Knesset of his readiness to participate in a peace effort, repeatedly calling for international support and action. Although he also emphasised the strength of the IDF and – in coded terms – Israel's willingness eventually to use force, his poor delivery confirmed the impression of irresolution.[942] Egyptian generals dismissed indications of an Israeli attack as 'only display'.[943] When Amer sent a reconnaissance flight over Beersheba, he 'laughingly' announced the panicked Israeli response to Nasser over lunch.[944] Similarly, Sidqi Mahmoud told the Jordanian delegation that Egyptian squadrons had been flying into Israeli air space unchallenged for the last few days and that 'this indicated that Israel's fear of the Egyptian air force was sufficient to prevent them from challenging it'.[945] King Hussein, with rather different preconceptions, interpreted such forbearance as Israeli intelligence gathering.[946]

Israeli military inferiority had become an article of faith in Cairo. Nasser 'appears sincerely to believe Egyptians can beat Israelis if we do not intervene,' Nolte reported on 27 May, 'and his estimate is shared by every official Egyptian we have talked to'. Foreign observers were amazed by the confidence of the ruling elite.[947] At the end of the month, Nasser told Robert Anderson that he had to accept the risk of an Israeli first strike, 'that elaborate plans had been made for retaliation, and that he was confident of the outcome of a conflict between Arabs and Israelis'. 'He kept reassuring me,' Anderson added, 'that he was not going to start a war but that he was not responsible for all groups and that he would intervene in any actual conflict begun.'[948] The Cairo regime had blinded itself. Egyptians preserved their deeply ingrained images of Israel and America simply by ignoring or reinterpreting all contrary evidence. Only a sufficiently dramatic and discontinuous event could undermine such images. At dawn on 5 June 1967, one took place. The Six Day War broke out.

8
One Continuous Nightmare: The Aftermath of Defeat

> *I felt intensely, indescribably bitter... I felt so vulnerable that I sent my family away from Cairo and kept my gun beside me to use at the final moment and to the last bullet.*[949] – Gamal Abdel Nasser

Israel at last launched her attack on Egypt on the morning of Monday 5 June. Most of the Egyptian air force was destroyed within a few hours, before the planes could leave the ruined runways. Ignoring existing plans, Marshal Amer ordered an immediate retreat from the Sinai Peninsula, which rapidly became a shambolic rout. Jordanian forces, under Egyptian command, had responded to the outbreak of war with an attack on Israel, provoking a crushing response. On 7 June, Israeli troops took Sharm el-Sheikh, the Gaza Strip and East Jerusalem. By the following day, the entire West Bank and the oil-rich Sinai had been occupied. The stunned Egyptian government agreed to a ceasefire late that evening. In the initial phase of the war, taken by surprise, Syria did little but fire across the border. When the other Arab states had been defeated, Damascus also requested a ceasefire. A few hours later, however, at dawn on 9 June, Israel advanced, quickly seizing the Golan Heights. The Soviets told the United States that they would intervene, and this warning was passed on to the Israeli Prime Minister, who ignored it. The USA moved up the Sixth Fleet to deter the USSR, and a genuine superpower confrontation seemed possible. At length, a final ceasefire was negotiated on the evening of 10 June.

No one in Egypt had expected such a disaster. Nasser later described the immediate aftermath of the war as 'one continuous nightmare'.[950] Initially, he was overcome by the shock. 'We were in a state of confusion, uncertainty and doubt,' he recalled. 'We did not know, but we feared what the Israelis were going to do.'[951] One Egyptian diplomat remembers seeing the President walking in his garden just before the ceasefire, stooped over like a broken man.[952] On 9 June, Nasser publicly resigned his office. 'His face was pale,' remembers Amin Howeidy, who saw him shortly afterwards. 'His eyes were wide open and staring straight ahead.'[953] Even now, he failed to comprehend the full scale of the defeat, assuming events would follow the Suez pattern. He talked of settling various issues 'after the withdrawal'.[954] 'We have to be aware that Nasser is still in a state of shock and cannot understand many things,' Tito told Soviet bloc leaders on 11 July. 'I don't know if it is possible to talk yet with him.'[955] Some suggest Nasser was never the same – that he became 'a different man'; that 'there was a deep scar on his soul'; that he died that day.[956] 'His hair quickly turned white,' recounts Agriculture Minister Sayyid Mar'i, 'the spark disappeared from his eyes and he was full of bitterness. He tried to conceal his wounds, but to no avail.'[957]

The whole debâcle had a devastating effect on Egyptian morale. There was an immediate regime crisis, in the course of which both Amer's protégé, Shams Badran, and the darling of the West, Zakaria Mohieddin, were named as possible successors to the Presidency.[958] 'They'll put me on trial,' Nasser told his Minister of Information, Mohammed Fayek, shortly before his resignation broadcast, 'and hang me in the middle of Cairo.'[959] In fact, Nasser's dignified speech taking full responsibility for the 'setback' provoked a massive popular response. The Egyptian mob begged him to stay and save them. Most sources accept that the demonstrations of passionate support were genuine, if based on incomplete information – although there are also claims that Ali Sabri trucked the protesting crowds in from the provinces.[960] There was a major clash between Nasser and Zakaria Mohieddin over the issue of the President's abortive resignation, and Mohieddin was eased out by March 1968.[961] By that time, Badran had already been imprisoned for involvement in an alleged coup headed by Marshal Amer.

Immediately after the ceasefire, the remnants of a dangerously discontented army were confined to barracks. Amer, who was blamed for the defeat, refused to retire gracefully, and his effective patronage structure meant that he retained substantial support among the military.[962] Nasser and his supporters moved swiftly to undermine the Marshal. Amer is now portrayed as a deluded fool, who expected to retain command of the armed forces after his spectacular failure, promised to defeat Israel in six months, and attempted a *coup d'état* when he realised that his resignation – unlike that of the President –

was to be treated as permanent. He was placed under house arrest in August, when Nasser sent an intermediary to offer him a comfortable exile in Europe. The messenger was their former Free Officer colleague Tharwat Okasha, who had been exiled himself in the 1950s, and could recommend the cultural delights of France and Switzerland with genuine enthusiasm.[963] The Marshal nonetheless refused, apparently committing suicide soon afterwards. Nasser seemed devastated. He never visited his country house again, overcome by memories of Amer there.[964] In the early days, he was unable to eat or work because, he said, the face of Abdel Hakim, the one old friend he had trusted, was always before his eyes.[965]

There is no reason to believe his grief was not genuine. But whether it was mixed with guilt – whether Nasser had tacitly allowed or encouraged the suicide; or seemed, like Henry II, to ask his over-eager subordinates, 'Who will rid me of this turbulent priest?' - is now Impossible to determine. In any case, this Banquo's ghost did not prevent Nasser from taking the opportunity to consolidate control over the army. Amer's supporters were dismissed or imprisoned. Defence Minister Shams Badran, Head of General Intelligence Salah Nasr, and Interior Minister Fathi Radwan were arrested that autumn on suspicion of subversion.[966] The Egyptian military establishment possessed a special status as the founding power of the regime, and Amer's strength had been grounded in its fundamental legitimacy as much as its influence was based on his special access to the President.[967] This legitimacy, however, had been severely damaged by the comprehensive defeat in June 1967. Popular respect for the army plummeted, and soldiers were mocked in the streets. A joke current in Egypt at that time recounts:

> A young lieutenant in a hurry ran after one of Cairo's crowded buses and just managed to get in when he was flung into the lap of an old woman who held him by the shoulder and said tenderly: 'Hi sonny, still running?[968]

Nasser made Mohammed Fawzi Supreme Commander of the Armed Forces and Abdel Moneim Riad his Chief of Staff, with a serious reform agenda.[969] Neither general had any inclination to dispute the President's absolute control of policy. His personal focus on the armed forces now 'absorbed all of Nasser's time and attention'.[970]

***

In other respects, however, Nasser's position within the regime had become less secure. Even as he gracefully acquiesced to popular demand, withdrawing his resignation, the President had to emphasise that his return to office was conditional and limited. 'I have decided to remain in my place and to stay where the people want me to stay until the end of the period in which we can remove all traces of aggression.'[971] Later, he promised to pass on the flag to another generation once he had wiped out the stain of defeat.[972] 'Nasser's method of conducting affairs of state also changed at this time,' remembers Abdel Magid Farid, the General Secretary of the ASU. 'He became more inclined to consult those around him, even summoning senior army officers and influential government officials who had long since retired.'[973]

Escalating unrest and student riots in February 1968 forced the government to promise greater freedom in the '30 March Programme'.[974] The ASU was reorganised to become slightly more representative. A National Congress chosen by lower-level party members voted for the Central Committee, which elected the 11-member Supreme Executive Committee (SEC). Although SEC involvement in decision-making did increase, it was automatically chaired by Nasser and consisted entirely of regime insiders, including Ali Sabri, Hussein Shafei, Mahmoud Fawzi and Anwar Sadat.[975] Sadat, as one of the last original Free Officers, drew closer to Nasser at this time, acting for him after his first heart attack and being appointed Vice President – although perhaps only because nobody saw him as a threat – in December 1969.[976] The necessity for increased Soviet assistance to rebuild the armed forces enhanced the power of the left-wing figurehead, Ali Sabri. He dominated *Al-Gomhouriyya* newspaper, and many of the new SEC members, such as Labib Shuqair and Dia al-Din Dawud, were his clients.[977] On the right, even Heikal's *Al-Ahram* became less whole-hearted in its endorsement of government policy.[978]

Although not all domestic discontent demanded a hard-line policy vis-à-vis Israel, growing support for the *fidā'iyūn* presented a major difficulty for Nasser. He was facing very serious internal problems with elements which would 'welcome a return of hostilities', the President told Anderson in May 1968.[979] Meanwhile, the economic situation continued to deteriorate. Even before the war, Egypt had been saddled with an unserviceable foreign debt estimated at $2 billion.[980] Now she had lost her major sources of revenue ($400–500 million per year from the Suez Canal, the Sinai oil fields and tourism). The loss was only partially made good by Arab aid. Although after the Khartoum Conference

Kuwait, Libya and Saudi Arabia provided up to $250 million per year, Farid states that Egypt received only $95 million – which, asserts Heikal, was all spent on defensive engineering works in less than six months.[981] Moreover, receipt of the subsidy depended on Egypt's continuation of the fight against Israel.

***

The international environment was also irrevocably changed by the Six Day War. 'Since June 1967,' wrote Malcolm Kerr simply, 'Arab politics have ceased to be fun'.[982] In the atmosphere of acute crisis following the crushing Arab defeat, friendships and enmities became starker. Nasser 'tried to promote more harmonious relations' with the Arab monarchies after the war, recalls the diplomat Mohammed Riad. 'He felt that as there was an outside threat he should not quarrel with other Arab countries.'[983] The President's attitude genuinely changed, according to his daughter Hoda, then working in his office.[984] The key to the relative success of this initiative was the fact that Nasser no longer claimed – or was able to claim – overall Arab leadership.

In particular, Nasser developed a close alliance with King Hussein of Jordan. At the emergency Arab summit in Khartoum, both leaders sought to pursue a relatively moderate policy toward Israel in order to regain their occupied territories. Nasser permitted Hussein to negotiate with the West and supported him consistently.[985] This forbearance stemmed both from a genuine sense of responsibility following Hussein's losses in the June War, and from an objective convergence of interests.[986] Saudi-Egyptian relations also came to be marked by civility, if not warmth. They turned over 'a new page', says Fayek. Egypt's precipitate withdrawal from Yemen was a key factor – although in February 1968 Nasser still felt that, Arab solidarity aside, 'our relations with the Saudis have been overshadowed by the Yemen war, and remain lukewarm'.[987] The limits to this *détente* would become clear at the Rabat summit of December 1969.

In Europe, de Gaulle's France was now seen as distinctly friendly. Over time, there were even substantial improvements in the Anglo-Egyptian relationship. At first, the allegation that British planes had assisted the Israelis in the 1967 War made the UK highly unpopular in Cairo. 'Nothing remains of the old British lion but its tail,' Heikal wrote scathingly on 16 June, 'which the American cowboy sometimes uses to chase away flies. At other times the American cowboy lashes with this tail as if it were a whip in his hand.'[988] However, the British made an intense effort to restore diplomatic relations, and Egypt responded.[989] By December 1967, Heikal was indulgently approving Britain's 'remarkable progress'.[990] In any case, whether friendly or hostile, these countries were all increasingly seen to be irrelevant. The focus had narrowed on the principal enemies: Israel, the 'Zionist' occupier of Arab territory, and the USA, her 'imperialist' protector.

***

After the 1967 defeat, the Egyptian regime at last decided that Israel was the real enemy, without the previous elements of ambiguity regarding the threats from the Western countries and Arab rivals. Michael Barnett explains:

> With unification fading from the Arab agenda the social purpose of the Arab state became more closely defined by the Arab-Israeli conflict, and the Arab national interest became more closely identified with the Zionist threat than ever before.[991]

Under these conditions, Israeli hostility – never precisely a neglected subject – loomed ever larger in Egyptian rhetoric. The occupation of Sinai and the West Bank produced greater emphasis on Israel's 'expansionist' disposition.[992] The war had, said Nasser, less than a month after it ended, 'proved beyond any shadow of a doubt that Israel has an aggressive nature and that it is imperialism's major base in the Middle East.'[993]

Astonishingly, it seemed at first that the war had not caused Egypt to revise her estimation of Israeli capabilities. Some elite comments bear a remarkable resemblance to post-Suez perceptions, when Israel was depicted as behaving arrogantly based on a victory that had been won by luck or by others. Senior army officers saw Israel as 'an arrogant enemy, conceited by a victory won as a result of our own mistakes, and not because of any special military accomplishment'.[994] The Egyptians, they thought, had defeated themselves 'and yielded to the enemy a victory that he did not rightly deserve'.[995] Israel 'became very cocky because of her easy victory in the 1967 war,' the diplomat Ashraf Ghorbal observed, more colloquially.[996]

In the end, however, this desperate attempt to preserve the regime's comfortable view of the world failed. The contrary evidence was too great for Cairo to remain oblivious. Israel did not come to be seen as intrinsically more powerful than Egypt, but her strength and military virtues were more realistically portrayed – not to praise her, but to make the case that Egypt could learn from her in certain respects.[997] 'I follow everything that is currently happening in Israel in detail,' Nasser stated at the Khartoum summit.[998] The army began to study the IDF as a model, copying Israeli methods.[999] In a sense, this was just a more subtle way of rejecting the image of Israeli military superiority. The implication was always that once Egypt had also mastered these few, identifiable, technical achievements, she would finally be in a position to confront her enemy.

***

US-Egyptian relations in the aftermath of the Six Day War were dominated by 'The Big Lie' – Cairo Radio's immediate claim that American and British planes were participating in the Israeli attack.[1000] Nasser was forced to break off diplomatic relations following this allegation, although it is unclear whether he actually believed it.[1001] Baghdadi, who was in Marshal Amer's office on the morning of 5 June, suggests that the President may have been misinformed by Amer, who was in turn given inaccurate data by Sidqi Mahmoud, the air force chief.[1002] More missions were flown, in a shorter time, than Egypt had thought the Israelis could manage. Nasser's initial response was incredulous. 'I will only believe the United States took part if I am shown the wreckage of an American plane,' he said angrily, leaving the room. 'Unless you can do that I will not accept it'. By mid-June, however, Egyptian embassies worldwide were busily issuing 'proofs' of Western intervention.[1003]

Most Egyptian sources suggest Nasser's change of mind was genuine, and it is true that his image of the USA was such that he might well believe the worst.[1004] However, Sadat implies that Nasser only re-thought Amer's charge when he realised the magnitude of the disaster, accusing the US as a political cover-up for domestic consumption.[1005] This was the interpretation of both Western and Eastern observers. The allegation 'was a desperate attempt to save face in the Arab world,' one Soviet official concluded.[1006] 'We know that they and some of their friends know where some of our carriers are,' noted Dean Rusk. 'We can only conclude that this was a malicious charge, known to be false'.[1007] The case for deliberate conspiracy is partially supported by Nasser's prior declaration to Hussein, monitored by Israel:

> By God, I say that I will make an announcement and you will make an announcement and we will see to it that the Syrians make an

announcement that American and British airplanes are taking part against us from aircraft carriers...[1008]

On balance, it seems Nasser believed in the active participation of Western planes only briefly, if at all. However, he saw this as relatively unimportant when set against his fundamental belief in 'imperialist collusion' with Israel.[1009] 'The scenario prepared by the United States and Israel has been carried out meticulously,' he told Sadat on 9 June.[1010] He publicly outlined his case in his resignation speech that evening and in another self-exculpatory broadcast on 23 July. It was a 'murky' business, he complained. The *USS Liberty* (attacked by Israeli planes on 8 June) had turned out to be an American spy ship; the USA had initially accepted Israel's implausible claim that Egypt had attacked first; Johnson had been quoted as saying: 'We have a war on our hands.'[1011] 'The operative words for Nasser were "WE" and "OUR",' Heikal notes. 'All his previous suspicions of Johnson came to the surface...'[1012] Thus Nasser was 'personally convinced' the Americans had deceived him.[1013] 'He did not know exactly how they were involved,' explains Heikal, 'but everything pointed towards it, and he reasoned that as we had not learnt the full facts of the British and French collusion until four or five years after Suez, so American collusion would also be shrouded in mystery.'[1014]

In the summer of 1967, Nasser saw the United States as rejoicing in his downfall and seeking to 'topple the regime'.[1015] This called for desperate measures. 'We are willing to conclude either a secret or an open treaty', he told the visiting Soviet Chairman, Nikolai Podgorny. 'What is important is that we now recognise that our main enemy is the United States and that the only possible way of continuing our struggle is for us to ally ourselves with the Soviet Union.'[1016] Nasser took the same line with his Arab allies and Egyptian aides. 'I do not trust the Americans and their intentions,' he informed Hussein.[1017] 'The American position is clear,' he confided in Farid. 'They want to topple the regime and to destroy Abdel Nasser personally.'[1018] Donald Bergus, the head of the US Interests Section in the Spanish Embassy, saw Foreign Minister Mahmoud Riad only rarely and the President not at all before January 1968.[1019]

Nasser continued to portray the United States as closely linked to Israel. He equated them, telling General Fawzi: 'the struggle with Israel is not over yet. And the struggle with the Americans also is not over.'[1020] However, the seeds of two subtle differences were already present. First, the belief in collusion between the US and Israel led Cairo to conclude that they were even more intimately associated than had previously been thought, now engaging in full 'strategic co-operation' over Middle Eastern issues.[1021] There was a new belief in 'an understanding which had been worked out between the American and Israeli governments,' suggests Heikal.[1022] 'They believe the US is entirely aligned with Israel,' Rostow informed his President.[1023] Second, the Egyptian image of the balance of power between the United States and Israel began to shift. It was difficult to distinguish who controlled whom, remembers Sami Sharaf. 'It's the same thing.'[1024] The Six Day War made it apparent that 'Israel was not a little lamb,' thought Ashraf Ghorbal. 'It was a big military power. Israel did not heed American advice'.[1025]

***

The catalyst for these changes was the ongoing Israeli-Egyptian confrontation across the Suez Canal. This strange, stationary, inherently limited conflict was generally painted as an incomplete intervening stratagem between two wars rather than an end in itself. It is consequently difficult to identify precisely what Nasser intended at each of the separate phases – or even what those phases were. The issue is complicated by the predilection of the Egyptian leadership (particularly the President and General Fawzi) for dividing things 'All into Three Parts'. For example, Nasser once spoke of the conflict as consisting of the stages of 'Resistance', 'Retaliation' and 'Liberation'. However, he used different triple combinations on different occasions and one is forced to the suspicion that the public announcement of a 'new' stage sometimes related as much to the leadership's perception of domestic discontent as to any objective evaluation of the external situation. 'Resistance' was the term most often applied to the initial phase of the post-1967 confrontation with Israel, which lasted until August 1968. It was characterised by the reconstruction of the Egyptian armed forces and the fortification of defences along the Suez Canal.[1026] Concurrently, UN negotiations continued. In the end, however, Egyptian military goals took primacy over political initiatives.

Egyptian diplomats did lay a great deal of emphasis, in the United Nations and elsewhere, on their search for a political solution to the Arab-Israeli standoff. The terminology was precise. A 'political solution' was distinguished both from a 'peaceful solution', which would rule out the use of 'military means'; and from 'political means' (mentioned more frequently in a domestic context), which would not ultimately rule out a 'military solution'. This obsession with language and nuance pervades the contemporary records:

Mr. Parker noted that the UAR also rejected the concept of signature of the same document. This presumably was because Egypt rejected *sulh* (reconciliation), in accordance with the Khartoum formula, although it was now talking of peace (*silm*), at our urging... The Egyptians should realize that without *sulh* there would be no *silm*. If the Egyptians wanted to get the Israelis out of their territory, they had better start thinking about *sulh*.[1027]

The Soviets also were pressing Nasser to come to a solution – 'any solution', says Amin Howeidy, who visited Moscow as Defence Minister in 1967. Brezhnev was afraid Egypt would attack before being ready, and the USSR would be associated with the defeat.[1028] But the President prevaricated. 'I agree,' Nasser told the insistent Soviet Deputy Foreign Minister in July 1967, 'that currently a solution by war is unacceptable... We can accept any political solution, personally I agree to anything, but not to the passage of Israeli ships through the Canal.'[1029]

This stated desire for a solution is only partially borne out by the course of the UN negotiations. Although Mahmoud Fawzi's opening speech in New York on 19 June was moderate compared to those of the other Arab representatives, he proceeded to reject the text of a Latin American resolution (which the US was at that point prepared to endorse) unambiguously calling for a full withdrawal in return for recognition of Israel's right to exist.[1030] Foreign Minister Mahmoud Riad later claimed that Fawzi acted against orders, but this is contradicted by Salah Bassiouny, who remembers that Fawzi sent a telegram arguing it was the best proposal Egypt could expect in current circumstances. He blames Riad – who returned from a meeting with Nasser saying that the text should be refused and that he agreed with the refusal – for influencing the President against it.[1031]

***

In fact, however, the rejection was entirely in tune with the new political orthodoxy in the Arab world. The Arab summit at Khartoum in August famously resulted in the 'three noes' – no negotiation; no recognition; no peace with Israel. At the time, the declaration was generally cited as evidence that Nasser was resolved on another war. The Arab rulers were 'dug in behind a barrier of self-imposed prohibitions', wrote Yitzhak Rabin, then Israeli Ambassador to Washington. They called for Israeli withdrawal so they 'could pick up their fight from the same positions they had held at the beginning of the last round'.[1032]

However, many historians now see the agreement as a victory for the 'moderates' Nasser and Hussein, since it legitimised the use of diplomacy and prioritised the return of the occupied territories over Palestine. When the PLO leader objected, noted Harold Saunders of the US State Department, who had seen the transcripts:

> they literally shouted him down. They insisted that the only subject they were discussing was how to get the Israelis out. They talked about rebuilding military strength, but mainly so they don't have to negotiate flat on their backs and in order to use force eventually if political means fail.[1033]

Egyptian diplomats downplayed the summit's importance. 'So far as the interpretation of the Khartoum Resolution was concerned Fawzi said he would prefer to get away from this controversy,' Harold Beeley reported from Cairo in October 1968.[1034] Simultaneously, Mahmoud Riad told the British Foreign Minister that 'the words used in the Khartoum Declaration were not important in the context of a peaceful settlement'.[1035] Robert Stephens argues:

> Arab spokesmen later interpreted the Khartoum declarations to mean no formal peace *treaty*, but not a rejection of a state of peace; no *direct* negotiations, but not a refusal to talk through third parties; and no *de jure* recognition of Israel, but acceptance of her existence as a state.[1036]

This was not the public perception. When Nasser returned from Khartoum, his Information Minister asked how he was supposed to sell the slogan 'No Peace'. The President corrected him. The message was: 'No Peace Treaty'. A treaty would constitute recognition of the Arab defeat. 'I cannot negotiate now,' he explained. 'But this doesn't mean that I am not going to negotiate forever.'[1037]

Nasser was in a tight spot at the Arab summit. He needed to adopt an attitude that was sufficiently intransigent to persuade the oil states to subsidise his fight against Israel and the Palestinians not to denounce him, as well as to safeguard his precarious domestic position.[1038] He was also genuinely sceptical about the prospects of a peaceful solution.[1039] Nasser might have been trying to placate the Arab radicals when he spoke at the summit of plans 'to carry out the only action that Israel understands well, and that is the liberation of land by force.'[1040] When he met King Hussein alone at the end of September there was less need for such language, however. The two rulers agreed on a relatively moderate platform to be presented to the Americans. They would recognise Israel's right to security; they would end belligerency; they would even allow passage through the Suez Canal, in return for full Israeli withdrawal and return or compensation for the Palestinian refugees.[1041] 'We want a solution to this crisis,' averred Nasser. But he was not optimistic. 'I do not think that you can do anything. But I agree that you can travel to America and negotiate with them, despite the fact that I am sure that you will not find a solution.'[1042]

While Hussein headed for Washington, negotiations were also continuing at the UN in New York. At last, on 22 November 1967, agreement was reached on a British text for Resolution 242, calling for a 'just and lasting peace' based on the twin principles of Arab acceptance of peaceful coexistence with Israel and Israeli withdrawal 'from territories occupied in the recent conflict'.[1043] Egypt accepted this resolution only on the basis of her own declaration that the deliberately ambiguous language mandated Israeli withdrawal from *all* occupied territories. In the ongoing UN discussions, moreover, Egyptian Foreign Minister Riad tended to paint such a full withdrawal as a precondition rather than a *quid pro quo*, resisting direct negotiations at all costs.[1044] The resolution also required that a UN Special Representative should proceed to the Middle East to promote a settlement, and Gunnar Jarring, formerly Swedish ambassador to Moscow, was soon dispatched to make an attempt.

Syria refused to receive the Jarring Mission at all; and Israel, while officially co-operating, had rather low expectations of success.[1045] Nonetheless, Jordan was hopeful, and even the Egyptian attitude sometimes seemed more flexible than the official rhetoric would imply. On balance, however, Cairo's acceptance of Resolution 242 seems to have been a tactical move, based on the fear that a rejection would give Israel a pretext for annexing all or part of Sinai. Just three days later, Nasser told his military commanders:

> Everything you hear us say about the UN resolution is not meant for you... Please remember what I have said before – what has been taken by force can only be recovered by force. This is not rhetoric: I mean it... So you don't need to pay any attention to anything I may say in public about a peaceful solution.[1046]

***

Preparations for a renewed battle with Israel therefore continued apace. Egyptian sources argue that Nasser from the outset saw war as his only option, believing he could not negotiate with Israel from a position of weakness.[1047] It would be 'impossible to reach a reasonable political solution,' he announced, without the inevitable military battle.[1048] After all, as Heikal noted, 'we no longer live in an age of miracles'.[1049] Nasser's reported estimates of how long it would take to prepare for this battle range from one to eight years.[1050] At first he 'had been thinking in terms of months,' he told his commanders in November 1967; 'now he had come to the conclusion that, with a miracle, they could mount an offensive in three years, but... all the facts pointed to five years as a more realistic estimate'.[1051] Once he had got over the initial shock, it is certain that Nasser did not expect Egypt to be ready immediately, nor did he expect the war to be easy. 'I've got the Israelis on the Canal,' he told his Yemeni protégés, justifying the Egyptian military withdrawal. 'If they wanted to, they could come all the way to Cairo. They could come all the way up to my house and pick me up if they wanted to.'[1052]

'I believe that a continuation of the war is inevitable,' Heikal wrote, 'but that this does not necessarily mean fighting should be resumed tomorrow or the day after. Most probably we shall face a long and bitter war.'[1053] Even the Foreign Minister later said he had 'felt that diplomacy held no hope', believing the 'only solution was to rebuild the army and proceed to take back by force what had been lost'.[1054] The war would be 'violent, savage and protracted,' General Fawzi predicted, and would depend on combined Arab operations.[1055] The Egyptian military establishment was desperate to show its mettle, believing that confrontation was the only option.[1056] The armed forces were in extreme disarray, however, having lost many soldiers and more equipment.[1057] Nasser spent hours at his desk with the two newly-promoted martinets, Generals Fawzi and Riad, working day and night to organise, train and expand the army.[1058]

Assistance from the USSR was vital to this endeavour. The Russians, however, felt deeply shamed by Egypt's poor performance – despite the latest Soviet equipment – in the June War. The Egyptian Ambassador to Moscow, Mourad Ghalib, was insulted in the streets. When the Politburo eventually agreed to provide renewed military support, it insisted on starting again 'from the beginning', rather than sending advanced weapons.[1059] It also expected to be paid in Egyptian exports. 'We have sold our cotton so far in the future that I don't know how we will meet all our obligations,' Foreign Minister Riad complained.[1060]

Soviet arms came with a few thousand Soviet personnel. 'Very soon,' Brezhnev told Eastern bloc leaders in July 1967, 'Moshchenko, a military district commander, will be heading for the UAR with a large group of Soviet advisors... Our people are helping in the reorganization of the army, in the preparation of the officer cadres, to teach the correct deployment of troops, conducting training in military techniques and modern methods of operations.'[1061] Nasser asked his Russian-speaking officers to play their part in lobbying these advisors for better arms.[1062]

Brezhnev claimed that Nasser had asked for even more assistance to repel an imminent Israeli attack, seeking Soviet planes and pilots and begging the USSR to take control of the Egyptian air force; but that the Soviet Union had seen no call for such a dramatic move.[1063] Heikal dismisses this request as merely an emergency measure. It was the Soviets, he says, who insistently sought base privileges at Alexandria.[1064] Minister of Defence Amin Howeidy telephoned Nasser at 2am to complain about this clause in the proposed agreement, and the President duly rejected it.[1065] But the affair was not over. Speaking to Birdsall in December, Nasser apparently 'hinted at strong Russian pressure' regarding the use of Alexandria, 'possibly involving permanent fueling facilities and barracks for Soviet naval personnel'.[1066] The USSR, now identifying a Mediterranean base as a major policy objective, continued to ask piecemeal for privileges such as air force facilities at Suez and a base at Mersa Matrouh from which to monitor the US Sixth Fleet.[1067] In return, however, most Egyptian war losses were replaced by October 1967.

***

Over the summer, a series of small military incidents had flared up along the Canal. These enabled Cairo 'to maintain the fiction that the fight is still on', thought the British. The Americans, however, 'were not ruling out the risk of a UAR strike against the Israelis across the canal, however wild and improbable this might seem,' as the British Ambassador reported from Washington. 'The indications that this might be on the cards had been sufficiently serious for the Americans to warn the Israelis yesterday on the intelligence net of the possibility.'[1068] In the event, UN observers arrived and a new ceasefire was agreed, leading to a lull at the end of July.[1069] In August, however, Nasser promised arms, training and supplies to leaders of the Palestinian *Fateh* movement. 'You', he told them, 'must be our irresponsible arm.'[1070] The exchanges of fire started up again, continuing into

September. Canal Zone towns were devastated, and the civilian popula-tions evacuated. Korn concludes that 'Nasser was clearing the decks for war.'[1071]

The key moment that is often identified as signalling the resumption of hostilities was the Egyptian sinking of the Israeli destroyer *Eilat* on 21 October 1967. However, it is not clear that this constituted part of a deliberate plan. The assault was certainly approved in Cairo, and Nasser was very probably that aware of it, despite his denial to Anderson in November: 'It was all finished and done with before I even heard about it.'[1072] The President's relations with High Command were not such that he would have been left ignorant. He 'obviously' gave the order, says Sami Sharaf; after all, it was a big operation that risked sparking off another war.[1073] When Defence Minister Howeidy was informed that the Israeli destroyer was approaching and the Navy was preparing an attack, he immediately told Nasser, who gave the order. 'Go shoot.'[1074]

There were various speculations over Egyptian motives. They may have hoped 'to fend off a potentially dangerous reconnaissance mis-sion on a sensitive area,' thought the Cairo-based British diplomat Robert Tesh; naval officers might want 'to make up for their poor showing to date by a successful action'. The Israeli Foreign Ministry suggested that the attack was an attempt to induce the West to press Israel to withdraw by showing the world that otherwise 'there would be serious trouble in the area'.[1075] Israel launched a crushing retaliation against the Suez oil refineries on 24 October. The Egyptians claim to have anticipated such a response. Howeidy ordered firemen to be put on standby.[1076] 'I started clearing my Suez to be ready to face these problems,' remembers the Governor, Hamed Mahmoud. When the Israelis attacked, 'Suez was not to be burned as if we had not taken these measures in order to secure Suez.'[1077]

However, the Egyptians did not retaliate in force, which implies that the *Eilat* incident was not a major planned escalation. There had been a long-standing order to sink the destroyer if she ventured into Egyptian territorial waters.[1078] Howeidy portrays the move as part of a deliberately limited strategy, 'like a game of ping-pong', but says that Egypt's defences were not yet strong enough for the next step.[1079] Tito told colleagues that the other Arab countries had wished to seek a 'military solution' after the bombardment of Suez, but that 'Nasser is decidedly against it.'[1080] It was not until November 1967 that Nasser, informed by the Soviet Marshal Zakharov that Egyptian defences could now withstand an Israeli attack, rescinded his order forbidding the ini-tiation of fire across the Canal. 'The actual strength of our armed forces now exceeds their actual strength before the start of the fighting,' he told the National Assembly. General Riad began to prepare training exercises in crossing the Canal and establishing a bridgehead on the east bank.[1081] Nasser wanted the front to remain active, and small exchanges of fire continued through December and into the following year. But there was nothing else as significant as the attack on the Israeli destroyer.

***

The principal Egyptian aim during this period was to prevent the front from 'freezing' and Israel from consolidating her possession of Sinai. As time passed with no speedy Suez-type withdrawal, images of the enemy as evil and expansionist were intensified. Israel was seen as likely to exploit any sign of Arab weakness, such as an agreement to direct negotiations. (This did not preclude indirect contacts through the UN mediator Gunnar Jarring, the United States and certain self-appointed – generally unwelcome – private messengers.)[1082] On the other hand, 'as long as the Israelis cannot sign a peace treaty with us,' Nasser told the Council of Ministers, 'Israel will not consider that it has won the war. The Zionist strategy is to force a settlement.'[1083] Nasser may have been afraid Israel might seize the west bank of the Suez Canal and operate it herself.[1084] He was certainly convinced that she would not willingly return the Sinai, telling his army that the fundamental objective of their 'deceptive', 'cunning', 'vicious' and 'depraved' enemy was 'expansion at the expense of Arab territory'.[1085]

'Israel is intoxicated by its cheap victory,' Heikal wrote in early 1968. 'Like one drunk on adulterated wine, it is being stupid and quarrelsome and will not heed the logic of peace based on justice.'[1086] Nasser himself complained of Israel's 'arrogance and indifference', which he attributed to the knowledge that Egypt was not yet militarily prepared.[1087] Israel, he pointed out, was not 'the dreadful unconquerable enemy' and was in no way 'extraordinary'. She had simply mastered certain military virtues. The Egyptian army could now correct its known defects 'to become equal to our enemy, who is continually training, who has been described by all writers as shrewd and wicked'.[1088] The June War had induced a semi-mystic belief in the innate military superiority of the IDF among the army's rank and file. However, this was undermined by the ongoing confrontation across the Canal, which encouraged a more realistic assessment of Israeli advantages and errors.[1089]

An expansionist and arrogant Israel would not, it was assumed, be dislodged from the occupied territories by political means alone. The conviction that a renewed military confrontation would ultimately be necessary was reinforced by the Egyptian elite's re-evaluation of the US-Israeli relationship, which had begun – with some false starts – soon after the June defeat. Israel was 'not merely a blind imperialist instrument,' Heikal wrote in *Al-Ahram*, but also 'an independent entity with its own ambitions, based on its racialist principles'.[1090] He suggested that deteriorating US-Israeli relations might therefore allow Egypt room for manoeuvre. By the end of the year, this cheering possibility had vanished, and the links were seen to be as close as ever. But the balance of power had changed, at least temporarily, in what Heikal saw as a very dangerous direction. 'Before the 5th June, Israel was virtually a tool in US policy. After the Six Day War, Israel became almost a partner in US policy.'[1091]

***

Perceived American hostility cemented Egypt's re-revaluation of US-Israeli relations. Both diplomatic and secret channels between Cairo and Washington did remain open, facilitating discussions that were wide-ranging and sometimes seemed potentially productive. 'We cut our relations with the Americans,' Howeidy claims to have told Nasser when, as head of General Intelligence, he set up a conduit to the CIA in 1967–8. 'We have to make many channels with them.'[1092] This was a high priority for the President, who – despite his urgent need for military assistance from the USSR – did not want to fall entirely into Russian hands.[1093] 'We are eager for a political settlement, for a political peace,' he told unofficial US envoy Robert Anderson in November 1967.[1094] He emphasised, according to Anderson, 'that he would welcome any attitude on our part that would give him an excuse to turn away from the Soviets'.[1095]

The ubiquitous James Birdsall returned to see Nasser the following month, and was given a short, polite letter to pass on to President Johnson, together with the proffer of a 'state of non-belligerency' with Israel, expressed in a vague verbal message – although US officials noted it was difficult to tell how much was Nasser and how much Birdsall, who seemed dreadfully eager to become a permanent back-channel.[1096] Nasser allegedly told Birdsall that he also wished to resume diplomatic relations with the US, suggesting that he might even exchange ambassadors with Israel if the Palestinian refugee problem were solved. He blamed his previous hostility on fear of a coup by left-wing domestic elements headed by Ali Sabri and on the need to placate the Soviets.[1097] Johnson, however, was sceptical, and when Nasser received the US chargé Donald Bergus for the first time in January 1968, he denied making any such request via 'Birdswell'. He emphasised that the resumption of diplomatic relations would take time, 'despite the fact that there were good intentions on both sides'. Amicable and relaxed, with his characteristic 'little giggle', he took the opportunity to complain once more of American support for Israel. 'If I told you that it was now possible to move into a new period of friendship based on trust, I would not be myself,' he confessed. 'It is impossible for me to say that as of today I now have full confidence and trust in US Government. I think we can get there but it needs time.'[1098]

In fact, Nasser never gave the effort concerted time and attention, sending a series of mixed messages. Farid portrays him as deliberately refusing diplomatic relations with an importunate United States. 'The Americans want to return to the region at any price,' the President told his Council of Ministers, 'and they understand that they cannot return except through us.'[1099] *Look* magazine published an interview with Nasser in which he admitted that the US had never participated in the June War. This public statement had assumed symbolic importance as a precondition for the resumption of relations.[1100] However, as Saunders noted, it was 'fudged' in the Egyptian press:

> First, they altered the crucial admission to read – instead of 'you could say that, yes' – 'you could say that, but someone else may say something else.' Then their spokesman said that resumption of US-UAR relations is 'not at present an issue that is being considered'.[1101]

The United States might have overlooked even that, but by April 1968 Nasser emphasised that he was 'unwilling' to restore formal diplomatic relations. He told King Hussein that he had just refused such an opportunity 'and would continue to do so'.[1102] Throughout the year, the Cairo regime continued to ask, in an increasingly less positive manner, for the USA to make some sort of 'gesture' – preferably by limiting arms sales to Israel. Nasser informed Anderson in May that, although a resumption was desirable:

> it ran contrary at this moment to public opinion until there was at least some signal from our side that we wanted to implement the

Security Council resolution and would not continue to talk in such terms as 'in the context of' or other terms which he described as vague and as supporting the Israeli view.[1103]

Nasser seems to have been genuinely convinced that the United States was biased in favour of Israel. She was, he claimed at Khartoum, 'planning to facilitate Israel's domination of the Arab area'.[1104] Nasser 'doesn't trust the Americans, considers them as crooks, thieves, says he knows them long enough, etc.' reported the Soviet Ambassador in November 1967.[1105] The following month, there was an outcry in the Cairo Press when the US (vilified by Heikal as 'the world's problem') exported military aircraft to Israel.[1106] Nasser complained that the stance of the US delegate Arthur Goldberg in the UN negotiations was '100% identical to Israel's position', concluding that 'America's aim at the present stage is to freeze the situation and to leave it unresolved'.[1107] He told Hussein in April 1968 that 'the Americans are playing a very despicable game, and want all of us Arabs to sell out'. The next day, he confirmed to the Council of Ministers that, having failed to overthrow the Egyptian regime by military or economic means:

the Americans have turned to attempts to overthrow us internally through domestic instability. I estimate that next year they will spend between £E15 and £E20 million on certain domestic elements in order to achieve this goal.[1108]

***

Nasser's options after the June defeat had been limited. He was constrained by public opinion, by the need to retain elite support, by Arab regional proprieties and international power realities. His primary foreign policy goal was formulated in his resignation broadcast and remained constant thereafter; namely, 'to remove the traces of the aggression'.[1109] Unfortunately, it was unclear how this might be achieved. At first, Nasser was preoccupied by his extreme vulnerability to Israeli attack and Egypt's lack of any viable military option. (Chairman Mao suggested guerrilla fighting in Sinai, which Nasser found unhelpful. 'It is a desert,' he explained, 'and we cannot conduct a people's liberation war in Sinai because there are no people there.' But Mao did not believe him, insisting on training the Palestinian fighters along classic revolutionary lines.)[1110] However, if the Egyptian

President could not make war, neither could he make peace. Anything that could be interpreted as acceptance of defeat – giving up territory, sitting down to negotiate at the same table as the Israelis, coming to a separate agreement, or signing a treaty – would have upset his precarious domestic and regional balance.

As a result, Nasser formulated a sophisticated strategy that attempted to combine (and sometimes confound) military and political action. The latter was explained to his domestic constituency in terms of the need to placate international opinion; the former was explained to foreign diplomats in terms of Arab pressures. To some extent, the two strategies were complementary. 'Actually we believe that reaching a sufficient degree of strength may obviate the need to use it in practice,' Nasser told the National Assembly.[1111] 'Political action cannot be separated from military action,' explained Heikal. 'Policy must be backed by force, whereas force alone is ineffective if not preceded by political action.'[1112] The essence of political action was to persuade the United States to press Israel to withdraw. This necessitated a delicate diplomatic game. Maintaining contacts both with various US representatives and with Jarring, the Egyptians generally emphasised that Israeli withdrawal was a necessary precondition for any progress. Occasionally, however, they dropped hints that a declaration of intent to withdraw could be the starting point for a comprehensive settlement.[1113]

Nasser sometimes seemed to prioritise the political option. Since Egypt was 'unable to launch an attack to liberate the land,' he explained to the Iraqi President, 'we have no alternative at the present time except a political initiative'.[1114] He took a similar line with ASU leaders in November. 'I preferred the peaceful solution,' he confessed, 'despite the fact our armed forces refuse it, safeguarding their honour and Egypt's honour. I said to them that war is not for the sake of war only, but it is a means for the achievement of political and strategic aims.'[1115] The basic problem was that Nasser was not consistently prepared to make substantial concessions for a political solution. If his motives remain a matter of controversy today, with so much new material available, it is hardly surprising that contemporary world leaders were not convinced that he was serious. Despite the tactical rhetoric, 'it was understood', Malcolm Kerr argues, that Nasser 'was seriously committed to the principle of coexistence with Israel, in exchange for the return of lost territory.'[1116] Yoram Meital similarly notes a 'gradually widening gulf between the declarative level and the realm of practical action'.[1117] In fact, however, it was *not* always understood; while the declarative rhetoric drew increasing international attention.

Perhaps a political settlement acceptable to Egypt was never achievable. Nonetheless, there were moments when Nasser could have given it a better chance without incurring excessive domestic costs. He might have agreed to the Latin American text for the UN Resolution, or consistently offered the occasional concessions that were suggested and then withdrawn. The reason he failed to do so is that, increasingly, it did not seem to him to be worth it. This development is related to his changing images of the United States, Israel and the relations between them, which brought him to the belief that the USA would not force Israel to withdraw from the occupied territories, and underlined his existing conviction that the Jewish state would never withdraw voluntarily from land on which 'he had set his boots'.[1118] These images caused Nasser to conclude that he had even less room for manoeuvre following the June defeat than he really possessed.

Thus Nasser's dual approach became unsustainable when he no longer believed that political means would serve any more than tactical purposes. 'We are going to do everything to solve it peacefully,' he told his Information Minister, 'but I *never* expect that this will be possible'.[1119] A US representative, visiting for an exchange of views in July 1968, suggested that Nasser's prior remarks indicated an underlying belief that no political solution was in sight. 'Then there is only one other solution,' the Egyptian President hinted darkly.[1120] On the other hand, the fact that Nasser was sceptical about the prospects of diplomatic success did not necessarily mean that a military solution would be feasible either. It was merely the only thing left to try. There is a kernel of truth in the contemporary Egyptian joke, which tells how the Commander-in-Chief:

> was horrified to see President Nasser ordering a tattoo artist to print on his right arm the names of all the territories seized by Israel like Sinai, Gaza, Sharm al-Shaykh, Jerusalem, the Golan Heights.
> 'Why are you doing this?'
> 'Lest I should forget them.'
> 'But why tattooed? What will you do if we get them back?'
> 'If we get them back I'll cut off my right arm.'[1121]

9
No Alternative to Battle: The War of Attrition

It has now become clear to us all… that there is no alternative to battle. Despite his losses, the enemy continues his pressure and arrogance. The enemy's friends, with the USA foremost among them, continue to give him aid, thus helping him continue his aggression.[1122] – Gamal Abdel Nasser

The stage of 'Resistance' was complete, President Nasser announced in September 1968. The armed forces had been rebuilt, and 150,000 Egyptian troops were facing the Israelis across the Suez Canal. The phase of 'Deterrence' could now begin.[1123] This was meant to be more energetic than it sounded. Egypt would begin to engage with the enemy, to restrict her movement, to inflict casualties and to destroy equipment (collectively known as 'preventive defensive operations').[1124] The new stage began on 8 September, when Egyptian forces opened fire, breaching the UN ceasefire and provoking a major artillery duel along the canal that resulted in relatively high Israeli losses.[1125] Smaller incidents followed throughout the month, and the Cairo press began to discuss a new strategic concept: the 'War of Attrition'. General Fawzi held a series of exercises designed to prepare the army for war.[1126] The next step would be 'Liberation'.

In some ways, the whole affair was a little haphazard. The situation on the canal apparently prevented Nasser from returning to Moscow as he had intended. He was in increasingly poor health, and Soviet doctors had advised him to spend some time in a spa.[1127] Foreign diplomats in Cairo were unsure whether the escalation had been planned in advance. Sir Harold Beeley, the senior British diplomatic representative, originally concluded it was not. The first exchange of fire might have been 'sparked off by one small incident', he suggested, since the

144

Egyptian defences were 'in a maximum state of alert and nervousness', expecting Israeli retaliation for a commando attack that had taken place on 26 August. The mood of Egyptian officials seemed 'nervous and defensive rather than offensive'; they must surely be 'very conscious of the vulnerability of the Suez refineries'.[1128] By mid-September, Beeley was positively stating that the Egyptians were 'not looking for trouble', although they were 'apprehensive about attack from Israel'. They maintained 'top alert on the Canal with orders to the army to give as good as they get'.[1129] When he called on Mahmoud Fawzi to discuss possible conditions for peace talks in late October, the former ambassador was told yet again that Egypt 'sincerely wanted a termination of the state of war and a situation in which both the Arab states and Israel could feel secure'.[1130]

Two days later, however, on 26 October 1968, the Egyptians instigated another massive artillery barrage and a commando operation in the Mitla Pass.[1131] Thereafter, even Beeley grew sceptical. Cairo made less effort to maintain the fiction that it was not playing an initiatory role. Heikal said that:

> he accepted the denial of the UAR military authorities that they had started the shooting but he believed they had been responsible for widening the area of the engagement because they had been looking for an opportunity of attacking the rocket sites established by the Israelis opposite Ismailiyya and Suez.

On the whole, Beeley believed Heikal when he added that the Egyptian motives were military rather than political. He thought that they aimed to raise morale and harass Israel, but not to reject UN mediation or the prospect of a peace settlement. Instead, he accounted for the raids on the grounds that Nasser's 'basic idea has always been that a settlement can only be reached after a military balance of power has been established.'[1132] If this was indeed the aim, the Egyptians were to be disappointed. On 31 October, a crushing Israeli response brought this premature phase of confrontation to an abrupt end.

***

There is evidence that a more radical departure from existing policy than Sir Harold Beeley realised was planned in September 1968. The incidents must be seen in the context of a slow escalation – involving artillery duels, attempted overflights and guerrilla activity – that had been mounting since the summer.[1133] Nasser apparently gained Soviet consent to an intensification of the conflict during his July 1968 Moscow visit.[1134] Arab guerrillas waylaid a group of Israeli jeeps on 26 August, capturing one soldier and igniting a diplomatic controversy. Tel Aviv 'had reliable information that, a few days before the ambush, the Egyptians had reinforced their position along the canal with additional guns and had raised their general state of alert'.[1135] There was speculation that a major move might be imminent. Even as the Egyptian envoy, Ashraf Ghorbal, told the US State Department that Israel was 'throwing up a smoke screen and manufacturing these incidents' as part of a 'ridiculous little cops and robbers business' to conceal their own lack of co-operation, he appeared to contradict himself. 'People in the Arab world,' he warned, were 'becoming generally frustrated and an increase in incidents like this is exactly what we must expect from now on.'[1136]

The case for an intended change of strategy is reinforced by the increasingly activist language adopted by the Egyptian regime that autumn. Nasser informed the National Congress on 14 September of 'the intensification of the war of nerves'. One week later, the Congress asserted in its own closing statement 'not only the inevitability of the battle with the enemy but also the inevitability of victory in the battle'.[1137] Heikal wrote in his weekly editorial that war was now 'almost the only remaining possibility because of the enemy's intolerable intransigence and arrogance in which he is encouraged – or rather instigated – by the imperialist powers'.[1138] In New York, Foreign Minister Riad was also oddly (given Egypt's relative military capacity) belligerent. 'You haven't seen anything yet,' he warned the US. Showing little interest in diplomatic solutions, Riad predicted that such incidents would continue for as long as the Israeli occupation endured:

> Egypt would not acquiesce in the indefinite occupation of its territories, and no-one had the right to raise firing incidents with the UAR unless the question of aggression and occupation was taken care of first.[1139]

Cairo's attempt to raise the stakes in late 1968 appears to have had a dual motivation. First, there were important local reasons to escalate. The reinvigorated army was straining at the leash, and the student riots indicated a corresponding need to raise civilian morale. There was pressure also from the wider Arab arena. The Saudis wanted to see their subsidy well spent, while Jordan complained that Egypt was once again sending all the commandos to Amman while her own front remained quiet.[1140] The second reason for the change in strategy, however, was that the diplomatic option seemed ever less promising. Cairo had lost faith in it, and it showed. Western observers began to attach the adjective 'gloomy' to Foreign Minister Riad with the consistency of Homeric epithet.[1141]

As election fever mounted in the USA, the two presidential candidates vied with one another to promise Israel all the arms she wanted. Richard Nixon specifically undertook to ensure permanent Israeli military superiority.[1142] In her relationship with the United States, Israel had become 'a junior partner who no longer takes orders even when subjected to pressure from the major partner,' wrote Heikal, arguing that her 'arrogance and immoderation' had 'reached the point of madness'.[1143] The Arabs knew by experience, Riad told his British counterpart, that Israel's policy was expansionist.[1144] The Israelis didn't want a settlement, he claimed to former Ambassador Lucius Battle, when the latter visited Cairo. They published maps showing Sinai as part of Israel; they refused to accept Resolution 242; they made ominous public statements. When Battle pointed out that Tel Aviv had repeatedly disclaimed any desire to retain Arab territory, Riad simply replied: 'we don't believe them'.[1145]

Why, in that case, did Cairo's new confrontational strategy fizzle out after only a month and a half? The explanation seems to be that the Israeli reprisal was much more severe than anticipated, breaking out of the previous paradigm limiting hostilities to the canal area. On the night of 31 October, the IDF performed a deep-penetration commando raid on the transformer and bridges at Nag Hammadi. This provoked civil disturbances and demonstrated to the regime that Egypt's economic infrastructure was vulnerable. More time was needed to prepare the army and the local population to counter such actions. Coupled with the ongoing attacks on Suez, the raid also created a domestic problem of energy shortages that required urgent solution. As a result, Egyptian troops were once more ordered to keep the ceasefire, while a 'popular militia' was set up to protect key national installations.[1146] Sadat wrote that Egypt 'had to stop until March 1969, when we had completed a network of internal defenses around all vital civilian targets'.[1147]

***

The 'War of Attrition' proper was therefore merely the resumption of a strategy that had been temporarily abandoned in practice, but not in conception.[1148] Although Nasser told Robert Anderson in November 1968 that he was 'more anxious than ever to have some kind of peace', he also dropped hints of heavy pressure from the Soviets and left-wing domestic elements.[1149] Even as he spoke, he was setting up a National Defence Council to prepare for war and promising the SEC that 'sustained campaigns of attrition', consisting of two or three-day patrols within the occupied territories, would begin within a month.[1150] In December, Nasser publicly explained the delay. 'We need time to rebuild our armed forces. At the same time we are working for an honourable political settlement. This is not surrender.'[1151] However, important developments that month cemented the Egyptian determination to resume the fight as soon as possible.

First, the Israelis began to construct the 'Bar Lev' line of defences along the canal front. Although this was principally a defensive measure following the events of that autumn, it was seen as an attempt to fix the border and the *status quo*.[1152] Still regrouping after the Nag Hammadi raid, the Egyptians simply watched.[1153] When the High Command realised the scale of the project in January 1969, there was a debate over the most appropriate response. Some argued for immediate confrontation, although the cautious General Fawzi was not convinced his troops were ready.[1154] Nasser himself saw the Bar Lev Line as confirmation of his belief that there was 'no hope of a political solution unless the enemy realises that we can force him to withdraw by fighting'. His announcement to this effect in front of the Egyptian National Assembly on 20 January immediately preceded a presentation by General Fawzi in closed session, which presumably laid out the regime's revived military plans.[1155]

Nasser's conviction that no political solution was possible had been reinforced by the Israeli commando raid on Beirut airport of 28 December, which destroyed 13 Arab planes on the ground. The raid was a response to the Palestinian guerrilla attack on an El Al airliner at Athens airport two days earlier.[1156] Nevertheless, Foreign Minister Riad saw it as a 'huge' turning point. It constituted 'new evidence that a peaceful settlement was neither expected nor even possible', he explained to the Council of Ministers.[1157] Nasser also laid considerable emphasis on the raid. He thought it showed the Israelis were 'desperate' and 'reckless'. Currently 'in a state of tension and anger', they were 'dying to take any sort of action'. It finally proved 'that it is Israel which exerts pressure on America and not the other way round.'[1158]

Peace was impossible. 'Unless the Arab nation moves to change the status quo balance,' wrote Heikal that month, 'Israel will attempt to change it first.'[1159] By February, frontline troops had been authorised by General Fawzi to use small-arms fire. The General Staff was ordered to prepare for battle, a State of Emergency was declared, and the Popular Defence Army was placed on maximum alert.[1160] A major operation was clearly being prepared.

At last, on 8 March 1969, Egyptian forces opened a massive artillery barrage across the Canal. Four days later, a government spokesman announced that Egypt would no longer be bound by the ceasefire.[1161] There was an immediate setback when the Chief of Staff, General Riad, was killed, and the front was relatively quiet for the rest of the month. The luckless UN mediator Gunnar Jarring took the opportunity to make yet another failed trip to the region, leaving each side a 14-point questionnaire.[1162] The escalatory rhetoric, however, continued. On 27 March, Nasser announced to the National Congress that Egypt was entering a new and dangerous stage of confrontation.[1163] It was a critical turning point, he told them three days later:

> There was a time when we used to ask our soldiers at the front to account for their actions if they fired at the enemy on sight for we were not prepared for complications. Now the picture has changed. We ask every soldier at the front to account for his action if he sees the enemy and does not fire at him.[1164]

At the same time, General Fawzi and the new Chief of Staff, General Ahmed Ismail, stepped up pressure on the Bar Lev Line, ordering artillery barrages and commando raids. Heikal led the call for a 'limited' battle – in which the Egyptian army would modestly 'destroy two or three Israeli Army divisions, annihilate between 10,000 and 20,000 Israeli soldiers, and force the Israeli Army to retreat from the positions it occupies to other positions' – in order to jolt the United States out of its complacency.[1165] On 29 April, the Israelis launched a second raid on Nag Hammadi, but this did not have same deterrent effect as the first, a circumstance attributed by Nasser to the fact that Egypt's Popular Army was now ready and waiting.[1166]

There were some indications Egypt might draw back in May 1969. US sources hinted at an internal regime struggle 'between those who wish to pursue an aggressive policy along the Suez Canal and those who want to calm things down'.[1167] There is even evidence that the Soviets – who had previously (albeit hesitantly) accepted the War of

Attrition as 'militarily and politically necessary' – now begged Nasser to 'use every effort' to halt it.[1168] If there ever was a 'peace party', however, it seems to have lost the argument. On 5 June, General Fawzi announced the beginning of yet another new stage, that of 'Active and Positive Defence'.[1169] The Grand Old Man of Egyptian diplomacy, Dr Mahmoud Fawzi, told a British representative in July that he believed the prospects of a peaceful settlement were considerably less good than a few months previously.[1170] At last, from 20 July, the mounting incidents provoked a massive retaliation by the Israeli air force, which would ultimately devastate the Egyptian air defence system.[1171]

***

Nasser had three aims in the confrontation across the canal that began in March 1969.[1172] The first was domestic. It was 'a practical and moral preparation for battle', which would 'inoculate' the troops by instilling an aggressive spirit and giving them practical training in crossing the canal and overpowering the enemy.[1173] It would also mobilise the public – who were, according to the former Information Minister, 'so frustrated that they cannot wait till you are ready and then after three years you go'. They needed to see 'that there is a war already: there are casualties from the Israelis'.[1174] That problem had been brought home to the regime by the severe student riots that forced a suspension of studies in Egyptian universities the previous November.[1175] The Popular Army that the Egyptian government had been obliged to raise after the first Nag Hammadi raid presented a potential danger in this respect, while the 4000 *fidā'iyūn* from the Palestine Liberation Army (PLA) in the Canal Zone were repeatedly cited by Cairo as a constraint. 'After another six months,' Nasser told Beeley in December, 'they would be uncontrollable'.[1176] There was also the problem of the Egyptian army itself, which was visibly impatient and – as Mahmoud Fawzi put it during a UK visit – 'importunate'.[1177]

The second aim was to convince Israel that staying in Sinai would not bring her long-term security, by demonstrating that the costs were too high to stomach, both economically, due to the impact of long-term mobilisation, and psychologically, in terms of loss of life.[1178] Thus the ground might be laid for a political settlement on Arab terms. It has been suggested that the War of Attrition was originally intended to facilitate the immediate military liberation of Arab territory. Bar-Siman-Tov argues that the Egyptians thought they would be able to institute raids into Sinai (first by commandos and then by larger units) after several weeks of bombardment, following which the army would perform a canal crossing at two locations in the swampy northern sector, supported by the air force.[1179] It is true that, in June 1969, Heikal predicted 'a dangerous summer' spent mobilising the Arabs, to be followed by 'a hot winter of explosions, flames and fire'.[1180] Furthermore, Egyptian sources confirm that a plan to establish two bridgeheads across the canal *was* then under consideration, and troops were trained accordingly. 'We had many plans,' remembers General Talaat Mosallem. He adds, however, that they were 'for study more than for execution'. The Egyptians knew that they must first secure their weak air defences. Given the military balance at the time, and the inherent nature of attrition as a long-term strategy based on the avoidance of escalation, it seems unlikely that immediate offensive plans could have been taken seriously for long.[1181] They certainly became unfeasible in very short order after 20 July.

The third and final aim was to destabilise the region and involve the superpowers, convincing the world that Egypt would fight to regain Sinai if – as seemed increasingly likely – political channels failed.[1182] Egypt needed to maintain tension along the Canal to disprove the US-Israeli case that there was no crisis in the region, Salah Gohar, the Egyptian Under-Secretary for Foreign Affairs, told the Canadian Ambassador.[1183] The regime still saw the Israelis as aggressive, conceited and irrevocably hostile. They 'really do want to expand', Nasser assured the SEC, reiterating that 'the military in Israel have become remarkably affected by arrogance'.[1184] He emphasised the same point to Beeley the following month, insisting that Tel Aviv 'wanted to get rid of him'.[1185] The enemy was 'treacherous', agreed General Fawzi. However, he added, practical experience proved that she was 'not invincible'.[1186]

There had been clear indications, in the spring of 1969, of a change in Egyptian perceptions of the Cairo-Tel Aviv military balance. Visiting London, Mahmoud Fawzi went so far as to dismiss Israel as 'a pampered baby'.[1187] This did not constitute a return to the old underestimation of the enemy that had preceded the 1967 War. Nasser was still insisting to the SEC that military confrontation was 'not easy', since 'we should not forget that the Israelis are well trained in offensive combat'.[1188] On the other hand, the Egyptians had improved their own capabilities since the defeat, in both quantitative and qualitative terms. Moreover, the strategic conception of a war of attrition posited a confrontation with Israel on the canal front *only*, where Egyptian forces were highly concentrated.[1189] Tolerance of casualties, in which regard

Egypt – as a much larger country – had a relative advantage, also emerged as a major issue. Nasser was wrong when he claimed on 1 May that Egyptian artillery had destroyed 60 per cent of the Bar Lev Line.[1190] In fact, the barrages had done comparatively little damage. The Israelis were concerned, however, because he seemed genuinely to believe his announcement.[1191]

***

The Egyptian perception of the United States at this time was characterised by a marked disappointment, attributable to two factors. First, the US agreed to increase the supply of arms to Israel on 2 November, causing Riad to leave New York in disgust, and Nasser to exclaim that there could be 'no coexistence' between Egypt and the USA, because 'the Americans are first and foremost sympathetic to Israel'.[1192] In particular, Cairo objected to the proposed American sale of advanced 'Phantom' fighter planes, which became a recurrent source of friction. Limiting the export of arms to Israel was repeatedly suggested as the friendly 'gesture' through which Egypt might be persuaded to exchange ambassadors with the United States.[1193] (The new National Security Advisor, Henry Kissinger, was notably unimpressed by this idea.)[1194] Nasser's image of the balance of power in the US-Israeli relationship shifted further toward Tel Aviv. He complained to Beeley that 'the Americans were still playing the Israeli game'. They had 'finally reached total partiality for Israel and complete agreement with Israel's views,' he told the Council of Ministers.[1195]

The second cause of Egyptian disenchantment was the discovery that the Nixon Administration's Middle East policy would not be substantially different to that of Johnson.[1196] Nasser had sent a message of congratulation to the President-elect in November 1968. He dropped heavy hints that he expected a reply, and was 'obviously pleased' when these were heeded and he received a polite note of acknowledgement.[1197] The following month, the Egyptian leader found further food for optimism in his talk with Governor William Scranton, who was touring the Middle East at Nixon's behest.[1198] By February 1969, Heikal began very cautiously to suggest that there might be an improvement in the American attitude; and over the next few weeks Nasser granted several interviews to US publications such as *The New York Times* and *Newsweek*.[1199] In March, however, Mahmoud Riad was (still) gloomy, noting that 'so far there was no sign that the Nixon regime would be any better than Johnson'.[1200] His colleague Mahmoud Fawzi agreed that 'there had not even been the minimum of improvement in the American position'.[1201] Nasser resumed loud complaints about arms sales. 'I do not,' he notified the National Congress, 'see any indications of a change in the US attitude, which supports Israel all the way.'[1202]

In 1969, Nasser also revived his claim that the United States was seeking to overthrow him. He warned ministers of American plots and lavish bribes to stir up domestic opposition, and was even wary of giving detailed information to World Bank, believing that many of the delegates worked for the CIA. The Americans 'will continue to work against us and will not leave us alone,' he told his government, 'unless we adopt a completely rightist philosophy'. He claimed to 'have received new information about increased activity inside Egypt by American intelligence and about a serious attempt that has been made to approach certain officers in the armed forces'.[1203] He was almost certainly mistaken. The United States would not have been devastated to see Nasser overthrown, but officials were wary of being associated with internal Egyptian conspiracies.[1204] Nonetheless, the case that Nasser may have *believed* these allegations is credible, given the relatively private forum in which they were uttered. They were not reflected to the same extent in his public speeches.

Believing, therefore, that the US was both hostile and unable to break away from Israel, the Egyptian regime became ever less optimistic about the prospect of a peaceful settlement. Consequently, the diplomatic game was played with reduced enthusiasm. Dean Rusk had offered a generous 'Seven Point' agreement, apparently conceived without consultation, on 2 November 1968, including full Israeli withdrawal from Sinai. More than a month later, Egypt finally presented a legalistic and noncommittal answer, which was interpreted as a rejection. Parker speculates that the negative response may have been based on a misapprehension that Rusk was suggesting a separate peace, or the Egyptians may simply have been waiting to discover the attitude of the new Nixon Administration.[1205] However, Cairo's wariness was also rooted in a broader scepticism regarding US intentions.

The Egyptian leader adopted a similarly uncompromising attitude to third-party mediation attempts – by eager go-betweens such as Romanian President Ceausescu – in late 1968.[1206] Heikal portrays Nasser as politely repelling such would-be peacemakers by telling them to ask Israel to provide a map of her desired final frontiers. None of them ever came back.[1207] Visiting the UK in March 1969, Mahmoud Fawzi explained that Egypt would prefer to wait longer for a good settlement, rather than getting a bad one in a hurry.[1208] The following month,

Fawzi was in Washington for Eisenhower's funeral. He took the opportunity to meet Nixon, but he had no power to offer any concessions *vis-à-vis* Israel, and was ordered by Nasser, possibly at Soviet behest, to say that 'the time was not yet ripe' for the resumption of diplomatic relations.[1209] Kissinger avers that 'the United States would have pursued the peace process more energetically early in the Nixon Administration had Nasser been more flexible' – although he also admits that the stalemate in the Middle East suited his own Cold War strategic conception.[1210]

***

Conversely, that stalemate began to prove increasingly awkward for Egypt after 20 July 1969. At that time, Marshal Gamasy recalls, the military leadership 'realised that its assessment of the expected Israeli response to the War of Attrition was over-optimistic. It had not expected Israel to put its entire air potential into the war, a move which quickly gave the Israelis a tremendous advantage.'[1211] Although the destruction wreaked on Egypt's missile batteries came as a shock, it was met with a belligerence that was equally unexpected from the point of view of Egypt's enemies. 'Our military force and military action are now beginning a new stage,' Nasser announced to the National Congress on 23 July. Despite the fact that Israel was 'scheming' for a 'cheap victory', he said, 'we are now in the position of one determined to fight the battle of liberation.'[1212] The following day, with his air defences collapsing around him, he replaced his air force commanders, which at the time was interpreted by some as a signal that battle was ahead – although in retrospect it seems more like a response to perceived incompetence.[1213]

Nevertheless, Egyptian attacks continued throughout the following month, shifting from artillery to mortars and small arms. Israel responded with humiliating deep-penetration commando raids on 27 August and 9 September. The second – launched just 96 hours after the first US Phantoms were delivered to Israel – was a major blow, resulting in the destruction of two major radar installations and the deaths of hundreds of Egyptians. Egypt tried to strike back two days later, but lost 18 planes in a major air battle. From this point onward, Egyptian positions on the canal were subjected to regular bombing by the Israeli air force. A furious Nasser dismissed yet more senior officers, including the new Chief of Staff, General Ismail, who was replaced by the more activist Director of Military Intelligence, Mohammed Sadeq.[1214] On the same day, 18 September 1969, Nasser cancelled his

planned visit to the Soviet Union on the grounds that he had influ-
enza. In reality, he had just suffered his first heart attack.[1215]

Nasser was laid low for eight weeks. Quite apart from their leader's
state of health, however, the Egyptians knew that they were in no position to confront Israel as yet. At a meeting of the Arab 'confrontation
states' in September, General Fawzi presented a report concluding that,
even with full co-ordination among the Arab armies, they would not
be battle-ready for 18 months. The recent Libyan Revolution, instigated by that over-enthusiastic young Nasserist, Colonel (formerly
Captain) Mu'ammar Gaddafi, was also something of a burden. Nasser
felt he must scale down the confrontation in order to give the new
regime time to consolidate.[1216] As the first Egyptian pilots began to
return from training in the USSR, the President informed them that
their air force was still unable to match Israel's.[1217] If there ever had
been a serious plan to establish a bridgehead across the canal, it was
definitively shelved.[1218] On the contrary, Heikal announced in November that a major Israeli strike was imminent – and he was not mistaken.[1219] By December, the Egyptian SAM-2 air defence system had
been wiped out, along with a substantial proportion of her air force.
It was clear, fiery propaganda notwithstanding, that the strategy of
attrition had failed. The war was being lost.[1220] At the end of 1969,
therefore, the Egyptian regime was faced with only three options.

***

First, Cairo might have accepted an American peace plan. Throughout
the summer and autumn of 1969, however, the Egyptian attitude to
the United States had remained extremely chary. At the end of July,
Egypt rejected the Sisco Plan – which was, Nasser told his Cabinet, 'not
much different from the American plans that preceded it, all of which
seek our surrender to the Americans and to Israel'. After all, he explained, the US was '99% in Israel's embrace' – although it was worth
keeping in contact, 'if only for the remaining 1%'.[1221] 'Don't suppose
for a minute that when I'm gone the Americans will leave us alone,'
the President warned Sadat and Heikal, walking in his garden at
Alexandria. 'Somewhere at this moment they are grooming a Suharto
in the ranks of the army.'[1222] By the end of August, Mahmoud Riad was
complaining to the British of the USA's 'threatening tone', while
Heikal blamed the American attitude for killing any chance that Cairo
might consider resuming diplomatic relations. 'Our enemy's friend,' he
stated, 'is our enemy.'[1223] As if to prove him right, in September, the
United States finally began to deliver advanced Phantom jets to Israel.

At the end of October, another US peace initiative, the Rogers Plan, was delivered to Ambassador Anatoly Dobrynin, the Soviet representative at the Four Power talks on the Arab-Israeli impasse – which had by now become Two Power talks between the US and the USSR, negotiating for their respective clients. The previous month, the Soviets had accepted, in Egypt's name, the concepts of a binding agreement, recognition of Israel's right to exist and 'Rhodes-style' talks (which implied the possibility of direct negotiation). In response, US Secretary of State William Rogers now offered this 10-point plan, which included full Israeli withdrawal from the Sinai.[1224] On 6 November, however, Nasser made a speech that branded the United States as Egypt's enemy and appeared to constitute a comprehensive rejection of the Rogers Plan, asserting that there was now 'no alternative to battle'.[1225] The rebuff was confirmed by a National Assembly resolution later that month and a formal Soviet refusal in late December. Nasser, Dobrynin stated firmly:

> would not negotiate with Israel about anything, about demilitarisation, free maritime passage or security arrangements. And he would not agree to the language on peace that the United States had made a condition for its endorsement of total Israeli withdrawal from Sinai.[1226]

There has been much debate over Nasser's reasons for rejecting the Rogers Plan.[1227] It is, of course, possible that the content was simply unacceptable. But the Egyptians themselves suggested their motivations were tactical. They could not accept any plan under conditions of strategic inferiority, when Israel was in such a dominant military position. Nasser's scepticism about the chances of an acceptable agreement when Egypt could not face her enemy on equal terms was founded on his disbelief that the United States would be prepared to enforce such an agreement fairly. Before delivering his inimical 6 November speech, the President had been notified by Ghorbal of reports current in Washington that the Nixon Administration was already backing away from the plan.[1228] The US sale to Israel of the very Phantoms that were bombing Egyptian territory continued to be painted as highly significant, as was the controversy in October over American citizens serving in the Israeli armed forces.[1229] 'It is clear from all sources,' Nasser told the Council of Ministers on 12 November, 'that the United States still insists on putting our area under its influence and control'.[1230]

***

A second option might have been to persuade the other Arab countries to provide support. This was discussed during the Arab summit at Rabat in December 1969. Comprehensive action-plans through which Jordan and Syria could activate a second front were considered; while the oil-producing states were asked to donate additional funds for the purchase of the advanced electronic weapons systems that the USSR had thus far refused to provide. Hopeful suggestions ranged from $70 million to $250 million in hard currency. Nasser had been trying to organise another Arab summit for some months, but in the event it was a major disappointment. The leaders could not agree, failing even to issue a final communiqué.[1231]

The reasons for the collapse are disputed. It has been suggested that Nasser himself did not seek co-operation at the summit, browbeating the other rulers and seizing the chance 'to excoriate the Saudis implicitly but clearly for their association with the United States'.[1232] Some interpret this seeming belligerence as a deliberate strategy to *avoid* war. When the other Arab states dragged their feet on the issue of immediate confrontation, Egypt could flounce out threatening to act alone, the ultimate implication being 'that without the means for war, the thing to do was to make peace.'[1233] However, this argument is weakened by the fact that Egypt did not then proceed to make concessions in order to achieve such a peace. Moreover, Farid testifies that Nasser made a genuine effort to improve relations with Faisal, giving very specific instructions for his welcome when he came to Cairo.[1234] The President's subsequent anger rang true. 'I believe that King Faisal's visit to our country last month was for the purpose of throwing dust in our eyes,' he told the SEC in January 1970, 'because they are still plotting against us.'[1235] Nasser may never have had much hope of the summit's success, but he did not deliberately sabotage it.[1236]

The failure at Rabat is better viewed as the culmination of a long series of squabbles between the 'confrontation states' and the providers of Arab aid. As early as November 1968, Nasser had emphasised to Anderson that his financial support from Kuwait, Saudi Arabia and Libya came with strings attached. These countries would welcome any 'pretext to discontinue their aid'.[1237] The following year he resisted a British initiative to set up secret talks with Israel on similar grounds – the oil producers would object and 'you could not gamble with all that money'.[1238] In September 1969, Saudi Arabia had requested that Egypt and Jordan present ongoing reports detailing the use of Arab funds, and subsequently demanded that the money should be transferred directly to the banks involved in the arms deals.[1239] King Faisal's deep suspicion of the Soviet presence in Egypt contributed to the decline in aid.[1240] It was therefore ironic that, once the Rabat summit had definitively ruled out any possibility that the other Arabs might rescue Egypt, Nasser, according to his Foreign Minister, 'found himself with no choice but total dependence on the Soviet Union, economically and militarily'.[1241]

***

By now, the situation was desperate, requiring desperate measures. In December 1969, the Egyptians had begun to move new SAM-2 missile batteries into the Canal Zone, but most of these were destroyed in a massive attack by the Israeli air force at the end of the month. Israel went on to humiliate Egypt farther by stealing an entire radar installation from Ras Gharib. Nasser was furious, and had the officers responsible severely punished.[1242] He also called a series of meetings of the Supreme Council of the Armed Forces, beginning on the evening of 6 January 1970. 'Why are the Israelis superior to us in planning and execution?' Nasser demanded of his generals. In response, Fawzi presented a report on the condition of the Egyptian military, pointing out that it suffered from a shortage of pilots, long-range bombers and medium-range missiles. He added consolingly that morale was high, and the army was ready to continue the escalation. But it was agreed that there was no imminent prospect of Egypt being able to cross the canal. As the Chief of Staff noted, however, they must take some action to defend the honour of the armed forces. Nasser, acquiescing, resorted to his final option. He asked the Soviet Union to take control of the Egyptian air defences.[1243]

Such a move would involve a momentous policy shift for both countries. Nasser was demanding not only advanced SAM-3 air defence missile bases and MiG-21J bombers, but also missile crews and pilots. It meant the first-ever dispatch of Soviet combat personnel to a noncommunist country. It also constituted a substantive abandonment of Egyptian territorial sovereignty as Nasser conceived it. The necessity of the request was underlined on 7 January, however, by a major escalation on the part of Tel Aviv. Israeli planes began a series of 'deeppenetration' bombing raids, devastating military bases in the Egyptian heartland. To add insult to injury, on 22 January Israeli forces occupied

Egypt's Shadwan Island for 24 hours. Members of the Cairo regime were not necessarily surprised by these developments, but they were increasingly perturbed.[1244]

In Egypt, the deep-penetration bombing was perceived as part of a strategy of psychological warfare, the ultimate aim of which was to overthrow Nasser, forcing a settlement that would perpetuate the ceasefire lines. It was believed that the bombing would not stop until that goal had been achieved.[1245] The official line from Tel Aviv was that Israel was *not* specifically aiming to bring down Nasser – but that was certainly the implication of various statements made in private and sometimes even in public by the Israeli leadership, particularly in the initial phase.[1246] Egyptians further speculated that the entire strategy had been planned in advance by the United States, which sought to strengthen its own position in the Arab world at Egypt's expense. In his speeches of early 1970, Nasser blamed the USA – who wanted Israel 'to crush the peoples of the Arab nation' and provided her with Phantoms to that end – for the whole Middle Eastern situation, including the deep-penetration bombing.[1247]

***

On 20 January, Nasser urgently summoned the Soviet Ambassador, and just two days later he secretly flew to the USSR. Heikal, Fawzi and Moscow Ambassador Mourad Ghalib, all of whom were present, provide reasonably consistent accounts of the conversations that then took place. Nasser asked the Soviet leaders to furnish Egypt with the more advanced SAM-3 air defence missiles. Since the Egyptians were not trained to operate these, he also asked for Soviet missile crews, a request for which the USSR was apparently unprepared. The Russians argued that they could not send crews, because the missile bases were part of an integrated network requiring protection from the air. Unfazed, Nasser asked them also to send aircraft (the advanced MiG-21J, reputed to be a match for the latest Phantom), to be flown by Soviet pilots.[1248]

The initial response was negative. However, Nasser threatened to step down as President, recommending he be replaced by someone able to make peace with the United States, since that would then be Egypt's only remaining option. Eventually, the Politburo gave in and agreed to send it all: missiles, crews, planes and pilots – although, according to Soviet sources, Brezhnev insisted that they should arrive on a covert basis, rather than openly, as Nasser wished.[1249] Soviet combat personnel began to be dispatched to Egypt in March, and several thousand troops had arrived by the early summer, housed with their equipment in special bases. In effect, the USSR had taken operational control of most Egyptian airfields and much of the armed forces.[1250] Nasser, however, had also achieved his goal of deterring Israeli raids – both militarily and politically.

Should Nasser's request for Soviet troops therefore be viewed as an integral part of his strategy? Or was it a defeat for his longstanding policy of Egyptian independence? Nasser had indeed vainly attempted to persuade the Soviet Union to deepen its combat role in Egypt in the summer of 1967. 'Let the USSR take upon itself command of anti-aircraft defense and bring to the UAR military aircraft together with crews,' Brezhnev depicted him as begging.[1251] Kosygin was surprised, Ghalib remembers, by Cairo's 'childish' request for fully equipped planes to assist at once, in the heat of battle.[1252] However, this was a desperate petition made 'under the impression of the defeat', when Nasser feared a renewed Israeli attack across the canal at any moment.[1253] Once the situation had stabilised, he would not have welcomed as an unmixed good the loss of policy control – particularly as regards the options *either* of launching a full-scale attack, *or* of seeking an accommodation with the United States – that a major Soviet military presence denoted. Already, there were differences of opinion with Soviet advisors and KGB officers on the ground.[1254] By April 1970, Nasser's increased dependence on the USSR would necessitate a left-leaning government reshuffle.[1255]

The Egyptian decision to seek SAM-3 missiles was taken in extremity, but it was not solely motivated by the Israeli deep-penetration bombing – although that development made the need vastly more urgent.[1256] As the situation worsened in late 1969, additional Soviet assistance had seemed ever more necessary. In December, General Fawzi led a high-level mission to Moscow to seek additional aid, but – although he was received with sympathy – the response at that point remained firmly negative.[1257] In this respect, it was the USSR, not Egypt, which changed its mind because of the events of January 1970. One question, however, remains. Did Nasser seek Soviet help as part of a coherent long-term strategy to institute offensive operations and liberate the Sinai? The answer can only be determined by examining the events of 1970 in some detail.

***

That spring, as Egypt once again began to provoke incidents along the Suez Canal, the United States and Israel slowly realised that Soviet military personnel were being deployed in the Egyptian interior. On 19 March, the Tel Aviv media broke the news publicly. Israeli Defence Minister Moshe Dayan predicted an 'electronic summer' in the Middle East, as the superpowers' most advanced missile guidance and detection systems battled it out for the very first time. Four days later, one of the new SAM-3 batteries went operational. Its opening move was accidentally to bring down an Egyptian plane – but it still raised a cheer from the spectators.[1258] Meanwhile the Israelis, hoping to avoid a direct confrontation with the Soviets, who were thus far staying away from the Canal Zone, scaled back the deep penetration bombing, ending it entirely after 13 April 1970.

They very soon realised, however, that their hope had been in vain. A massively effective air assault was launched against the Bar Lev Line in mid-April, and the pilots were overheard communicating in Russian.[1259] Throughout May, the Egyptians and Soviets continued to build their missile wall, sometimes installing dummy missile batteries to divert the constant Israeli air strikes. At the same time, they maintained the offensive, keeping up a relentless artillery bombardment of the Bar Lev Line. At the end of the month, the first successful Egyptian commando raid against the east bank of the canal wiped out an Israeli platoon.[1260] By 30 June, the network of missile bases had been constructed and the first SAM-3s brought in. That night, two Phantoms were shot down, heralding the beginning of the high-casualty 'electronic war'.[1261]

On the surface, it seems strange that it was during this period of tension and confrontation that progress was finally made towards agreement on an American-brokered ceasefire. The USA had been held responsible for the deep-penetration bombing, which would, the National Assembly predicted in March, 'drive the entire area towards a new war of unpredictable consequences'.[1262] Even US messages of condolence on civilian deaths were seen as veiled threats.[1263] Heikal wrote that US-Israeli relations 'have now reached a point where US policy is no longer able to exercise any amount of independence from the Israeli will'.[1264] Israel wanted, he concluded, to be America's 'hand acting in the Middle East' and was 'trying by all means to be ahead of the USA in what it wants and to achieve for it whatever it can'. Recent Israeli actions, he implied, were primarily devised to please the United States.[1265]

The portents for US Assistant Secretary of State Joseph Sisco's visit to Cairo in April were consequently unpromising. Nasser's remarks on the possibility of peace with Israel were vague and downbeat. It would depend, he continued to insist, on an Arab-wide solution incorporating the Palestinian refugees and Jerusalem. The 'bitter' Egyptian President emotionally condemned the USA's ongoing export of Phantoms and commitment to maintain Israeli military superiority, declaring his lack of confidence in the US government.[1266] On the other hand, there were indications that the Egyptians were once again beginning to distinguish between different groups in the US, rather than portraying it as a hostile monolith. Nasser himself separated those in the Nixon Administration who sought a solution to the Arab-Israeli problem, such as William Rogers and the State Department, from Kissinger and his ilk, who thought that US interests were unaffected by the conflict.[1267] In his relatively conciliatory May Day speech, the President said that, although the USA was behind Israel, 'Israel is deceiving the public in the USA as well'.[1268] Egypt naturally leaned more towards the West than the East, he told a group of Egyptian diplomats later that month, discussing ways of improving relations with America.[1269]

The turning point came with Nasser's speech of 1 May 1970, which was partially framed as a message to Nixon. Egypt was at last in a position of strength, Nasser stated, since 'our armed forces have regained the initiative with bold military operations in the air and on land'.[1270] Under these circumstances, he might be open to dialogue – provided that the United States ceased supplying Phantoms to Israel. The tone was still belligerent, but the message was reinforced the following day, when the US chargé, Donald Bergus, was summoned to see Foreign Minister Riad. Greeted by a surprising number of photographers who were somehow aware of his appointment, he was handed a letter echoing the words of Nasser's speech to pass on to his President. Over the next few weeks, Bergus received further hints that the Egyptians would welcome a limited truce; and in June Nasser announced in a US television interview that he would accept a six-month ceasefire, provided that the time was used to arrange a full Israeli withdrawal.

***

In response, on 19 June, William Rogers announced a new, extra-simple plan, which he called his 'stop shooting, start talking' proposal. It required merely that both parties express their acceptance of Resolution 242, their willingness to negotiate, and their agreement to a ceasefire of at least three months. There was an additional clause mandating acceptance of a military standstill within the combat zone, which was not mentioned in the letter outlining the plan presented by Bergus to the Egyptian negotiator Salah Gohar but was included in the draft agreement that accompanied it.[1271] Finally, the USA committed herself to deliver no more planes to Israel than had already been agreed. Nasser was informed of Rogers' proposal while on a visit to Libya, and his initial private response was non-committal. But his belligerent speech in Benghazi on 25 June, in which he animadverted as usual against the 'American imperialism' behind 'Israeli aggression', seemed like an informal rejection.[1272]

'I have no opinion,' Nasser told the SEC blandly, asking for their reaction to Rogers' proposal during his brief return to Cairo before heading for Moscow on 29 June. The members all averred that – like Foreign Minister Riad, who had been consulted in Libya – they opposed acceptance.[1273] The initial reaction of Cairo Radio was also negative. 'This is not the first time that Washington has hinted at a change in policy and pressure and concessions, and it has later become clear that there are no changes and concessions,' it noted, suggesting that the US purpose was merely to mask the latest Phantoms deal.[1274] Heikal's editorials in early July were equally dismissive.[1275] On 23 July, however, following his return from Moscow, Nasser suddenly announced that he planned to accept Rogers' proposal. He presented it as a matter of form: the initiative contained 'nothing new', and Egypt's rejection would have been exploited by the US. Otherwise, his speech took a hard line, reasserting that Israel's nature was expansionist, and 'we must be prepared to reply with force to the enemy who only understands the language of force'. Nasser also emphasised once more that 'the USA is co-operating fully with Israel'.[1276]

The President's claim that agreement to the ceasefire involved no new concession was not strictly true. It constituted a separation from the positions of the other Arabs, and an acceptance of progress without Israeli withdrawal as a precondition, not to mention a commitment to negotiations before the same had been accepted by Israel.[1277] Thus his decision had significant domestic and regional costs. Although Nasser was still popular in Egypt, the army was restive, particularly the lower ranks.[1278] The announcement jeopardised the Arab subsidies. Finally, it further radicalised Yasser Arafat's *fidā'iyūn*. The ten most important Palestinian organisations rejected the move, and their public complaints forced Nasser to close the *Voice of Palestine* radio station. Palestinian fighters surrounded the site, but were arrested. The next day, it is alleged, Arafat apologised on his knees, trying to kiss Nasser's hand. The President was having none of it. 'You idiot!' he exclaimed. 'Do you think I am King Hussein? Do you think I am the King of Jordan?' Arafat appears to have taken the hint. By the end of July, he was leading demonstrations against the initiative in Amman.[1279] Despite all protests, however, the ceasefire came into effect on 8 August, following Israeli acquiescence under considerable US pressure.

Given these costs, what motivated Nasser's *volte-face*? It is noteworthy that the Egyptian leader spent 20 days in the Soviet Union before announcing his acceptance. This was longer than had been planned – although it is possible that the delay was merely to allow Nasser to receive medical treatment.[1280] Based on Cairo's apparent change in policy after the visit, some historians suggest that Nasser accepted the ceasefire because of pressure from the USSR.[1281] It is true that the general trend of Soviet policy at this time was to restrain Egypt from aggressive action.[1282] However, this did not usually extend so far as encouraging Nasser to come to an agreement with the United States. Indeed, Egyptian eyewitnesses suggest that this aspect startled and disturbed the Soviets.

'Do you mean to tell me that you are going to accept a proposal with an American flag on it?' Brezhnev asks in Heikal's account, glaring over his spectacles at Nasser, who had just made his intentions known. 'Exactly,' replied the Egyptian President, 'I am going to accept it just because it has an American flag. We must have a breathing space so that we can finish our missile sites. We need to give our army a break, and to cut down our civilian casualties. We need a ceasefire, and the only ceasefire the Israelis will accept is one proposed by the Americans. But I wouldn't rate its chances at more than a half per cent.'[1283] The Soviets still took some convincing. 'What about the battle?' Brezhnev asked. Nasser apparently pointed out – perhaps not *quite* so boldly as his hagiographers suggest – that it was his country and his battle, and he would resign if Brezhnev did not accept that. He also took the opportunity to request more military equipment. After lengthy consideration, Moscow reluctantly approved Nasser's decision.[1284] He was not particularly grateful. 'Anwar!' he allegedly exclaimed to Vice President Sadat on his return to Cairo. 'The Soviet Union is a hopeless case.'[1285]

***

The most important question regarding Egyptian acceptance of the Rogers Initiative concerns its ultimate goal. The international aim, of course, was that it should lead to a lasting peace, and some suggest Nasser shared this hope.[1286] The costs of the War of Attrition for the Egyptian economy and armed forces had been prohibitive. 'Listen, Anwar, whether we like it or not, all the cards of this game are in America's hands,' Sadat later quoted Nasser as telling him before the 1 May speech. 'It's high time we talked and allowed the USA to take part in this.'[1287] However, the balance of evidence suggests that Nasser's motivation was tactical. He admitted to 'no hope at all' of a 'far-fetched' political solution, suggesting his main purpose was to wrongfoot his enemies.[1288] 'Our acceptance of the initiative would pressure the Americans and put them in a corner,' the President informed his SEC colleagues.[1289] There was 'a great possibility that the three-month period will end in absolutely nothing,' he added to Riad. 'When Jarring resumes his mission, we shall never agree to talk for another year.'[1290]

Nasser saw the initiative as a respite allowing him to move his missiles towards the Suez Canal despite the standstill agreement, rather than as an opportunity for negotiation. The critical importance of the missile movement – in order to prepare for renewed battle in Sinai – is underlined by almost every Egyptian source.[1291] Even the minority who claim that Nasser *wanted* the ceasefire to bring peace suggest the missiles remained an important motivation, since 'he was not particularly optimistic about this new American move given his previous experience with American plans'.[1292] He estimated its chances of success at 'a mere half of one per cent', suggests Heikal.[1293] Foreign Minister Riad later explained:

> Nasser saw the US proposal as a situation in which we could not lose. On the one hand, we give the Americans the chance to try for a diplomatic solution. If that doesn't work, we will have improved our military position.[1294]

In the broadcast ASU proceedings of 24 July, Nasser began to read out a written question. 'Will the ceasefire enable us to install a network...?' Then he broke off. 'This we shall answer in the closed session.'[1295] In that session, British Embassy officials were informed, he duly promised to install the missile network during the ceasefire. They wondered, since the questions were submitted in advance, whether the apparent slip was deliberately planned to placate domestic opinion.[1296] The Egyptians were rushing missiles into the Canal Zone from late July, while the conflict between MiGs and Phantoms heated up and the

Israelis sought to clarify the text of the standstill agreement.[1297] They did not even pause in their construction of additional missile sites when the ceasefire began on 8 August. Many Egyptians therefore argue that Nasser's acceptance of the Rogers Initiative was merely a temporary tactic. It is portrayed as part of a comprehensive plan to regain the Sinai by force, which would surely have been implemented shortly thereafter, had the President not suffered a final, fatal heart attack.

10
Conclusion: Ambiguous Legacy

I did not find what I expected.[1298] – Gamal Abdel Nasser

What did President Nasser really intend, on the eve of his death in September 1970, to do about the Israeli occupation of Sinai? This question lies at the heart of his legacy. His remaining adherents fervently contend that Nasser's acceptance of the Rogers Initiative was merely a stratagem. He hoped to allow time for the final preparations so that his secret scheme to retake Sinai by force could at last be put into effect.[1299] They do tend to disagree on the details. The plan was called 'Granite One', say some.[1300] According to others, it was 'Operation 200'.[1301] Most claim it was 'nearly exactly the same plan' as that implemented by Nasser's successor, Anwar Sadat, in the (relatively) glorious October War of 1973.[1302] A few, such as the Minister for Presidential Affairs, Sami Sharaf, insist that it was much better. It would have been a truly united Arab operation, co-ordinated with the Syrians, Jordanians and Lebanese.[1303] Egypt would not merely have established a bridgehead across the canal to improve her negotiating position. She would, the Nasserists wistfully avow, have taken the mountain passes and regained the entire Sinai by force of arms.

They broadly agree on the question of timing. Nasser rehearsed the canal crossing a few weeks before he died, remembers Abdel Magid Farid.[1304] Sharaf states that the plans were fully prepared for a two-phase attack to retake Sinai even before the acceptance of the Rogers ceasefire in July, and all that was needed was this opportunity to install the new air defence system. The offensive, he says, would have begun in early October 1970 or April–May 1971, depending on the weather, the tides and the other Arabs' preferences.[1305] 'There was a plan which was ready and it was supposed to be the spring of '71,' specifies

Mohammed Fayek. 'This was definite. It was very important that it should take place... before the end of 71.' By the following year, the United States would have armed Israel with more advanced aircraft, and the opportunity would have passed.[1306] 'We have to begin the hostilities and cross the canal in 1970 or 1971 at the very latest,' Nasser himself had told Colonel Gaddafi in February.[1037]

This nebulous offensive plan is said to have been shelved after Nasser's death on 29 September 1970. The following day, Vice President Anwar Sadat had a meeting with key insiders, including Heikal, Fawzi, Riad, Howeidy and Sharaf, at which they discussed whether Egypt should extend the ceasefire. Given the conditions of internal uncertainty, and General Fawzi's assertion that – although he would attack now if given written orders – the armed forces would be in a better position in two months' time, they agreed to do so.[1308] Even at Nasser's funeral, however, Sadat was sending plaintive messages to the US Ambassador asking for peace.[1309] By November, with Fawzi still cagey about Egypt's military readiness, the new President had entirely rejected the idea of regaining the Sinai by force. It would take months of Soviet shiftiness, Israeli intransigence and American indifference before he abandoned hope of a purely political solution.[1310] Thus Nasser's legacy became a matter of deep controversy in Egypt during the Sadat era.

As a result, no eyewitness assertions can be taken at face value. Most of the Nasserists quoted at the beginning of this chapter lost power and influence under the new President. Some were even imprisoned. They have an obvious motive to depict Sadat as betraying Nasser's legacy, and taking credit in 1973 for implementing an inferior version of a pre-existing plan. Sadat's subordinates, by contrast, argue that Nasser's original plans would never have worked, so it was just as well that the new President made substantial changes.[1311] When he became Chief of Staff in May 1971, claims General Shazly, no offensive strategy had been prepared. The plan code-named 'Operation 200' was purely defensive, while 'Granite' included raids into Sinai, but no proper canal crossing. In any case, the critical Soviet personnel were not permitted to involve themselves in offensive operations; indeed, Moscow's stipulation that Soviet planes should stay away from the Suez Canal would have made that rather difficult.[1312] 'As I remember,' agrees General Talaat Mosallem, 'Plan 200 was a defensive one.' Before Nasser's death, he adds, there were no 'serious' plans at all, only 'plans to think about'. An attack in late 1970 would have been logistically impossible.[1313]

The probability is, therefore, that the plans mentioned by Nasser's supporters were vague contingency scenarios, which would have been deferred yet again as the critical date approached. This process had recurred throughout the conflict. It is possible that Nasser would have accepted a 'reasonable' peace offer, now he believed Egypt was no longer in a position of inferiority. He went out of his way, as late as 9 September, to inform the United States that he was still interested in peace.[1314] Nonetheless, the evidence is very strong that he expected no such offer, given his images of the United States and of Israel, and that he thought a war would be necessary in the end. Nasser's acceptance of Rogers' ceasefire, although it kept various options open, was primarily a tactical move in an ongoing confrontation. He did not expect it to be his final one.

***

Of course, if Nasser had lived, it is hard to see where this tactical move could have led him. The history of the War of Attrition is one of subtlety turned to stasis. Arab nationalism – as Nasser himself had defined it – mandated that certain concessions could *not* be made, in defiance of all rational calculations based on the concrete balance of forces. This may have begun as a rhetorical tool or a negotiating position, but in the end it became the truth. Nasser's hands-tying debate tactics had left him cuffed to an inconvenient ideology – and despite all later claims made on his behalf, it was becoming increasingly clear that he was not going to pull another Houdini. His health was deteriorating. He had developed diabetes some years previously; now he suffered two serious heart attacks. The USSR provided medical assistance – but the Soviet Union was itself another source of pressure, relayed through the burgeoning ranks of 'advisors'. The Egyptian President was isolated, having forced most of his former revolutionary colleagues out of power, culminating in the death of Amer, his oldest, closest friend. Almost the only one left was Anwar Sadat, too much of a nonentity to quarrel with, who – apparently on the spur of the moment – had just been dubbed Vice President. In many ways, Sadat himself was Nasser's unlikeliest legacy.

The final week of Nasser's life demonstrated in a microcosm how much his world had changed. It was 'Black September'. The Palestinian question was now at the vanguard of Arab political consciousness – indeed, Nasser had just obliged the British Prime Minister, Edward Heath, by helping to negotiate hostage releases following the simultaneous hijacking of three international airliners by the radical Popular Front for the Liberation of Palestine (PFLP).[1315] Meanwhile, Yasser Arafat's own PLO insurgents had driven Jordan to the verge of civil war, and King Hussein's security forces were cracking down hard. As the fractious Arab leaders met to discuss the crisis in the rarefied surroundings of Cairo's Nile Hilton hotel, Nasser found himself playing an unaccustomed role. He was the moderate elder statesman, trying to restrain both radicals and reactionaries to avert an open break. The region's replacement firebrand, the Libyan leader, Colonel Gaddafi, was outraged by the whole situation. 'If we are faced with a madman like Hussein who wants to kill his people, we must send someone to seize him'. But this offended the Saudi monarch's sense of propriety. 'I don't think you should call an Arab King a madman who should be taken to an asylum.' It fell to Nasser to defuse the tension with a wry joke. 'I suggest we appoint a doctor to examine us regularly and find out which ones are crazy.'[1316] After the summit, Nasser exhausted himself escorting various Arab leaders to the airport, placatory to the end. On his return, he suffered his last heart attack.

'I did not find what I expected,' observed President Nasser, as he lay on his deathbed.[1317] Although in fact he was merely exhibiting mild surprise at the evening radio headlines, the words have a deeper resonance. Twenty years before, who could have dreamt of such a future for the reserved young officer in the Egyptian army, who smoked incessantly and listened more than he spoke? Even after the revolution, surprise twists of fate and disappointed expectations had been a recurring theme in Nasser's foreign policy. Courted and hated by East and West, Palestinians and Israelis, revolutionaries and kings, he remained ultimately elusive. What is certain is that he became trapped by his own hostile images.[1318] 'A man cannot be too careful,' as Oscar Wilde once wrote, in quite another context, 'in the choice of his enemies.' The Egyptian leader who was at first called 'Colonel Jimmy' because of his pro-American stance could not escape the framework he had created in which the United States was 'Public Enemy Number One', identified with all her lesser confederates' sins – as imperialist as the British, as socially retrograde as the Saudis, as Zionist as the Israelis.

***

This image of the United States had developed through wars, and perpetuated them in its turn. It underwent a substantial transformation in the four years between the Egyptian Revolution and the Suez Crisis. The original close relations between the Free Officers and US representatives soon degenerated, and the main reason seems to have been the inherent difficulty of remaining an ally both of Egypt and of Egypt's enemies, Britain and Israel. The critical disputes punctuating this deterioration developed over issues such as the British evacuation of the Canal Zone, the supply of arms to Egypt and potential peace negotiations with Israel. Such was the context for Nasser's move to nationalise the Suez Canal Company in July 1956.

The nationalisation was not, as popularly portrayed, a straightforward response to Dulles' withdrawal of Aswan Dam funding. That had been expected, and the Egyptian government had been studying the possibility of nationalisation over the previous two years. However, the timing of Nasser's announcement appears to have been precipitate, and was probably a response to the wording of Dulles' statement. He objected not only to the perceived insults to the Egyptian economy and the suggestion that Sudanese interests had been inadequately considered, but most of all to what he interpreted as an open invitation for the Egyptian people to overthrow his regime. Nasser believed the Americans and British were bitterly hostile, but he thought that fear of world public opinion would restrain them from military attack. Convinced Britain would refuse to co-operate with Israel, he barely considered the scenario that Israel might act alone.

Nothing during the summer and autumn of 1956 changed the Egyptian President's views. He courted international sympathy, attempting to divide the United States from her allies. Notwithstanding obvious evidence of Franco-British belligerence and co-ordinated military planning, he continued to believe that the likelihood of war was decreasing and that it could ultimately be avoided. Moreover, he still saw the threat presented by Israel as essentially local. As a result, the Egyptian regime completely misinterpreted the Israeli offensive when it began on 29 October. The initial assumption was that it constituted a limited border incursion, and even when its true scale became clear, the possibility of collusion by the Western powers does not appear to have been raised before the Anglo-French ultimatum made it glaringly obvious. This was despite the receipt of warnings from multiple sources, including the Egyptian Embassy in Paris, which were cursorily dismissed as implausible.

Even after the ultimatum, the belief that Britain, at least, was far too competent (and too concerned with her image in the Arab world) to co-operate with Israel appears to have encouraged Nasser to believe that Eden must be bluffing, which may have made him more sanguine about his decision to reject the proffered terms. At any rate, the Egyptians were once again extremely surprised when British aircraft actually began to drop bombs on Cairo. Thus their initial response was confused and disorganised. However, surrender, which would clearly destroy the regime, was never seriously considered as an option, guerrilla warfare seeming a preferable alternative. US opposition to the attack was an unlooked-for blessing. Nevertheless, the United States was still viewed as Egypt's enemy, seeking to take over the British role in the Middle East. It was not until the early 1960s that Kennedy's change of policy began to undo some of the damage. And even this initiative was cut short when a new crisis arose in the Arab world, the consequences of which were to cement the image of America as Nasser's fatal foe.

***

The Egyptian military intervention in Yemen had a number of causes. Initially, some of these seem trivial – an old man's poem, a revolutionary's plea, a series of small augmentations resulting eventually, almost accidentally, in the commitment of 50,000 men. However, this interpretation is misleading. The dispatch of troops to Yemen was clearly a deliberate decision made by Nasser, with the input of close associates such as Amer and Sadat. Domestic pressures were a factor in that decision. The Egyptian regime depended on the Arab nationalist legitimacy that it had itself helped to create. Assisting Arab revolutions was an important aspect of this legitimacy, particularly given the need to regain lost ground in the wake of the Syrian secession. Once the intervention had begun, Nasser's prestige became ever more closely bound up with its success. Moreover, the army, the mainstay of the regime, had developed an independent interest in remaining in Yemen. However, one might have expected these factors to be outweighed by the disastrous effects on the Egyptian economy, and the apparent hopelessness of the task. It is therefore necessary to pinpoint why the failure of the Yemeni revolution would have been perceived as such a disastrous defeat for Cairo.

The simple strategic viewpoint suggests that Yemen was a pawn in a broader confrontation between Egypt and Saudi Arabia, and it was this confrontation that made the issue so important. However, that does not tell the whole story. First, the Yemenis themselves were mistakenly ignored. The strength of the royalist tribes was severely undervalued, due to their lack of cultural sophistication and the belief that Arab peoples (as opposed to rulers) would favour revolution. When Yemeni groups did attempt to take an independent line, they were seen as ungrateful, treacherous and manipulated by outside powers. Second, it is necessary to explain why Saudi Arabia was perceived as such a salient enemy in the first place. This was due partly to ideological differences and competition for Arab legitimacy, but the increasing virulence of the confrontation can only be explained in terms of the image of Saudi Arabia as a hostile conspirator with the West against Egypt, triggered by the Syrian secession of 1961 and constantly reinforced by developments in Yemen itself. The image induced both an overestimation of Saudi hostility (expressed in the belief that Saud would intervene if Nasser did not) and an underestimation of Saudi power. As a result, Cairo could not trust Riyadh enough to follow through with attempts at disengagement – and, in any case, the potential consequences of failing to do so seemed unlikely to be fatal.

As the decade advanced, Saudi Arabia was in some respects overtaken by Britain as an enemy in the Yemen arena. Britain, due to historical precedent and her presence in Aden, was seen as a hostile, imperialist conspirator endangering the Yemeni revolution, but her position was also perceived as weakened by it – creating a further incentive for the Egyptians to remain. The 1966 White Paper was interpreted to reinforce existing images, being seen as both a sign that Britain was on the defensive and an indication that she would plot to reorganise the Arabian Peninsula before she left – with the assistance not only of Saudi Arabia, but also of the United States.

The development of the Yemen conflict over five years had put an intolerable strain on the USA's anomalous position as a friend of both Egypt and the enemies with whom she was engaged in active confrontation. The perception of the US as a powerful enemy was increasingly reinforced by a growing belief in her conspiratorial intentions. Ordinary American support for British and Saudi allies, when they were actively engaged in assisting the Imam's party and thus subject to retaliation from Cairo, veered on occasion a little too close to outright confrontation. This was exacerbated by ongoing Arab-Israeli tensions. In the Egyptian mind, the United States, as the most powerful of the allies, came to be fatally tainted by the charges of imperialism and Zionism that had previously tended to be levelled against her lesser partners. In general, therefore, before the 1967 War changed everything, the Egyptian regime was mistrustful of all negotiations, grimly preparing to remain in Yemen for the foreseeable future.

***

The war of June 1967 is often cited as a classic example of international brinkmanship – an Awful Warning for those leaders who consider that a game of 'Chicken' constitutes clever diplomacy.[1319] However, this is inadequate. Nasser's initial mobilisation in Sinai is often attributed to false Soviet reports of Israeli troop concentrations, but these reports were contradicted almost immediately. The image of an aggressive Israel caused Cairo to lay excessive emphasis on threats against Damascus issuing from Tel Aviv; while the belief that the confrontation with Washington was coming to a head suggested that the USA might dictate an Israeli strike on Syria in order to embarrass Egypt. The Soviet Union's marked emphasis on the warning of troop movements was an opportunity not to be missed. It seemed to imply an invitation for Egypt to confront her enemies with Soviet diplomatic support – although Nasser did not expect military help against Israel unless the US launched an improbable military intervention of her own. Each step subsequently taken by Cairo therefore constituted a deliberately calculated risk.

The Arab regional context was significant. The problem of radical Syria was the initial cause of the tension. Criticism from his 'reactionary' enemies incited Nasser to some of his rasher initial moves, and their grudging shift to a more supportive stance as the crisis mounted increased his confidence in the ability of the united Arabs to confront Israel. The internal structure of the Egyptian regime was also a key factor. Its centralised authoritarianism meant that domestic propaganda influenced those whose duty it was to collect military information on Israel, causing them to underestimate its potential, and the elite to believe that error. The split with Marshal Amer limited Nasser's access to reliable information on the relative strengths of his own armed forces and those of the Israelis – although it does not seem to have been such a critical constraint on his decision-making as is sometimes suggested. More important was the way in which Nasser's image of the United States as an all-powerful adversary encouraged a dramatic underestimation of Israel's capacity for independent and effective military action.

After the Six Day War had proven the magnitude of that mistake, Nasser's choices were limited. He had to maintain his position in Egypt in the face of a major blow to his legitimacy, while seeking to regain the lost Sinai territory. At home, he was faced with a real threat of unrest from the army and from disaffected groups, particularly students. Together with the growing threat of Palestinian and Syrian radicalism, this limited his ability to make diplomatic concessions. However, the unfavourable Cold War context, which promoted a hostile US attitude and strict limits to Soviet assistance, equally constrained his military options. In this atmosphere of crisis, other former enemies became irrelevant, as the Egyptian regime focused much more narrowly on the perceived aggressive intentions of Israel and the United States. Despite increasingly desperate attempts (such as the 'Big Lie' that US and British planes had assisted the Israeli attack) to preserve the existing image, the 1967 defeat did ultimately cause Israel to be seen as more militarily capable and independent of American support.

These changed perceptions help to explain Nasser's attitude during the War of Attrition. Although attrition was a rational strategy to maintain pressure on a more powerful enemy and involve the superpowers, it could not solve Egypt's basic problems. Nasser was realistic about his poor military chances, but deeply sceptical about the prospects of a political solution. This was partly because of internal and regional constraints, but he also passed up potential opportunities for compromise that might not have involved excessive domestic costs. Cairo's fundamental pessimism was based upon an image of Israel as expansionist, arrogant, and abetted by United States. A hostile Washington establishment was seen as both unable and unwilling to press Tel Aviv to withdraw from the occupied territories. Even Nasser's acceptance of the Rogers ceasefire initiative in July 1970 was not based on any fundamental change in his image of the USA, still perceived to be entirely aligned with Israel. It was merely a tactical move to improve Egypt's chances in any future confrontation – which remained a very distant prospect at the time of the President's death.

***

The longer Nasser's legacy to Egypt and to the world is examined, the more paradoxical it appears. The bare mention of his name can still provoke a passionate debate in the cafés of Old Cairo. Colonel Nasser came to prominence as the leader of a nationalist revolution protesting against domestic oppression and corruption, foreign influence and the surrender of Arab territory to the state of Israel. By the time of his death, he had himself become an absolute ruler, cowing the Egyptian intelligentsia and imprisoning his former Muslim Brotherhood allies in concentration camps. The new government and swelling bureaucracy were not noted for their financial probity. Far-reaching Soviet penetration of the Egyptian army and administration had aspects in common with the heavy hand of British colonialism. Moreover, while the monarchy had allowed Palestine to be taken by the Zionists, it was Nasser, the supposed Arab Nationalist Hero, who – having squabbled with every other Arab country and failed spectacularly at unification with Syria – lost Egypt's own Sinai territory, not to mention the Holy Sites of Jerusalem.

However, that is not the whole story. Compared with the totalitarian excesses of such Arab dictators as Hafez al-Asad, Saddam Hussein, or even his own zealous acolyte Mu'ammar Gaddafi, Nasser's absolute rule was relatively restrained. He occasionally expressed rather unrealistic hopes of creating a democratic multi-party state with a genuine opposition. It just always seemed that these had to be deferred for the duration of the current crisis – until the revolution had been consolidated, or the land redistribution completed, or the CIA conspiracy exposed, or the Israeli occupation ended. Though some of those close to Nasser were corrupt, it is not suggested that he used his own position for financial gain. He enjoyed a quiet family life, he had few expensive pleasures and his favourite dinner consisted of chicken and rice prepared in the Egyptian style. (Indeed, he served little else in his home – to the deep distress of those of his revolutionary colleagues who had learned to appreciate finer fare.) The Soviet involvement in Egypt, as Moscow later admitted, brought it no permanent advantage, while Nasser wheedled out of the USSR not only costly development projects like the Aswan Dam, but also the most advanced Soviet weaponry yet provided to a non-communist country.

Finally, although Nasser's practical contribution to the Arab nationalist project was unimpressive, to say the least, his ideological influence was unparalleled. In 15 short years, he presided over a fundamental reorientation of the Arab world, setting in motion a chain of events still gathering momentum in the early twenty-first century. Nasser defined the nature of the Arab revolution. He defined it as secular, expelling his erstwhile Islamist allies into the wilderness of radical conspiracies. And, step by unwilling step, he defined it as anti-American, fostering an enduring legacy of distrust and resentment across the Middle East and beyond.

***

Today, as the content of Arab identity is reconsidered, in relation to both Western democracy and radical Islam, Nasser's legacy develops a startling contemporary resonance. Parallels between the Anglo-French intervention in the Suez War half a century ago and the current presence of coalition forces in Iraq are commonly drawn in both the Western and the Arab press. Although this analogy is in many ways deeply flawed – for example, the global position of the United States today is very different to that of Britain in the aftermath of the Second World War – one aspect does hold true. The potential for the highly emotive issue of Iraq to become a rallying point of solidarity and identity across the region at a grassroots level is becoming ever clearer. There has even been a resurgence in the popularity of loathed former Iraqi President Saddam Hussein, who tried to take on Nasser's mantle as the leader of secular Arab nationalism from the moment he came to power in the wake of the 1978 'Camp David' Accords, when Nasser's successor Sadat was accused of betraying the Palestinian cause by signing a separate peace with Israel.

The idea of the Arab countries as a unified entity – in spiritual, if not in political terms – seems to be undergoing a revival. It is a trend that was never predicted by those scholars who believed that Nasser's humiliating defeat in 1967, followed by his death three years later, had fatally impaired the ideology of Arabism. In much the same way as Nasser's radical radio station, *Voice of the Arabs*, swept across the region in the wake of the cheap transistor, the Arab world is once more being brought together by new media, ranging from satellite television to the internet. Phrases like 'the Arab street' are again bandied about, as advances in technology allow common language and a reawakened sense of common identity to translate into a common – and largely anti-Western – stance on the issues of the day. The comparison is far from perfect. *Voice of the Arabs* was an overt vehicle for Egyptian state influence and often ridiculously inaccurate. Channels such as *Al-Jazeera*, by contrast, although they are sometimes accused of a biased political agenda, pride themselves on their precision concerning matters of fact and their criticism of corrupt Arab rulers.[1320]

The most important difference, however, relates to the role of Islam. Nasserist Arab nationalism was generally secular. The first major modern Islamist movement, the Muslim Brotherhood, founded in pre-revolutionary Egypt by Hassan al-Banna, was bitterly opposed to secularism, drawing no distinction between the religious and the political spheres. Nasser's regime banned the Brotherhood in 1954. Many of its members were imprisoned and tortured, including the pivotal ideologue, Sayyid Qutb, who was eventually hanged in 1966. In his cell, he wrote 'In the Shade of the Koran', a massively influential work in which he labelled as unbelievers those 'ignorant' Muslims who oppressed their fellows. The charge of apostasy – and the violent *jihād* (holy war) that it was seen to justify – was directed not only against Nasser, but also against the corrupt and Westernised society by which he was surrounded. Islamism was divorced from Arabism in Nasser's prison camps.[1321]

Nasser's major contribution to contemporary Islamic thought was thus inadvertently to radicalise it. This tendency was accelerated after the shocking Arab defeat of 1967, for which the Egyptian regime was widely held responsible. The 'setback' fatally injured the legitimacy of secular Arabism, facilitating the rise of the Islamist alternative in the 1970s. Imprisoned members of the Muslim Brotherhood, who 11 years previously had longed to fight for their country in the Suez War, now heard of the Israeli victory 'with a mixture of shock and gloating'.[1322] Today, Islamism – in all its variety of forms – remains a much more vital force than Arabism. Even so, in the post-Cold War world, Islamic and Arab identities are once more being joined in alliance. They meet on different terms. Arabism is now the poor cousin, seeking to cadge some of Islamism's mounting social capital. Arabism no longer presents a secular alternative; instead, the revived potency of Arab identity as a source of allegiance is bound up with a new emphasis on its Islamic components. Nonetheless, Nasser's legacy is still visible in the least contentious common ground shared by the forces of Arab and Islamic solidarity: their deep suspicion of the West.

Notes

1 Proper nouns are not transliterated in this book unless they form part of a longer phrase or sentence in Arabic. Place names follow contemporary media usage, while personal and organisational names use either the standard Egyptian spelling or, if known, the preferred spelling of the individual or body in question. Unavoidably, there are sometimes variations in the spelling of names in quoted material.

2 The ambiguous role of Nasser's friend and rival Marshal Abdel Hakim Amer is discussed at length in later chapters.

3 On the composition of this core elite, see Hinnebusch, R. *Egyptian Politics under Sadat* (Cambridge University Press, 1985), pp. 15–16; Auda, G. 'The State of Political Control: The Case of Nasser 1960–1967', *The Arab Journal of the Social Sciences*, 2.1 (1987), p. 102.

4 Amin Howeidy Interview.

5 Heikal, M. H. *Autumn of Fury* (London: Andre Deutsch, 1983), pp. 37–8; Dia al-Din Dawud Interview; Frankel, N. 'Interviews with Ismail Fahmy, Ashraf Ghorbal and Mohamed Riad', *American Arab Affairs*, 31 (1990), p. 99.

6 Kenneth Boulding predicts that images will diverge farther from reality under authoritarianism, because feedback from lower levels of the elite is indirect and largely controlled by the upper levels. Boulding, K. E. *The Image* (University of Michigan: Ann Arbor, 1956), p. 100.

7 McLaurin, R. D., Mughisuddin, M. and Wagner, A. A. *Foreign Policy Making in the Middle East* (New York: Praeger, 1977), p. 42; Dabous, S. 'Nasser and the Egyptian Press', *In* Tripp, C. (ed.) *Contemporary Egypt: Through Egyptian Eyes* (London: Routledge, 1993); Ahmed Said Interview.

8 Heikal's role presents a particular difficulty for researchers. He is the ultimate source of a powerful 'official history' of the events of the Nasser era, which infuses the subsequent recollections even of direct participants. Moreover, some of his anecdotes, while too good to ignore, seem rather too good to be true.

9 Larson, D. W. *Origins of Containment* (Princeton University Press, 1985), pp. 60–1.

10 Specifically, the nature of the speaker or author, his relationship with the intended audience, and contemporary domestic and international imperatives. A claim is more likely to be true if it is consistently expressed to a variety of different audiences over a long period of time.

11 Insiders with the most intimate knowledge of the decision process also have the strongest incentives to be insincere, seeking to defend or aggrandise themselves and their associates. However, where their statements can be checked by others, authors also have an incentive to avoid the *appearance* of insincerity. Moreover, they do not have equal incentives to be insincere with regard to all issues. Therefore, when details within a particular document seem irrelevant to the purposes of the author, it may be possible to discount the influence of bias. Interpretative inferences can consequently

be drawn within the framework of an intuitive 'logic-of-the-situation approach'. George, A. L. *Propaganda Analysis* (Evanston: Row Peterson, 1959), p. 4.

12 Stephens, R. *Nasser: A Political Biography* (London: Penguin, 1971); Nutting, A. *Nasser* (London: Constable, 1972). Stephens' analysis is particularly thorough and insightful.

13 Aburish, S. K. (2004). *Nasser: The Last Arab*. Duckworth, London.

14 For the domestic angle, see Dekmejian, R. H. *Egypt under Nasir* (Albany: State University of New York Press, 1971); Vatikiotis, P. J. *Nasser and His Generation* (London: Croom Helm, 1978).

15 See Takeyh, R. *The Origins of the Eisenhower Doctrine* (London: Macmillan, 2000); Alterman, J. B. *Egypt and American Foreign Assistance, 1952–6* (New York: Palgrave Macmillan, 2002); Pearson, J. *Sir Anthony Eden and the Suez Crisis* (London: Palgrave Macmillan, 2003); Thornhill, M.T. *Road to Suez: Battle of the Canal Zone, 1951–54* (forthcoming, 2006).

16 See Jones, C. *Britain and the Yemen Civil War, 1962–1965* (Brighton: Sussex Academic Press, 2004); McNamara, R. *Britain, Nasser and the Balance of Power in the Middle East* (London: Frank Cass, 2003); Mawby, S. 'The Clandestine Defence of Empire', *Intelligence and National Security*, 17.3 (2002); Fain, W. T. 'Unfortunate Arabia', *Diplomacy & Statecraft*, 12.2 (2001).

17 See Bowen, J. *Six Days* (London: Pocket Books, 2003); Oren, M. B. *Six Days of War* (Oxford University Press, 2002).

18 On the dynamics of crisis decision-making, see Brecher, M. and Geist, B. *Decisions in Crisis* (Berkeley: University of California Press, 1980); Shlaim, A. *The United States and the Berlin Blockade, 1948–1949* (Berkeley: University of California Press, 1983); Frankel, J. *The Making of Foreign Policy* (Oxford University Press, 1963).

19 An 'enemy' is here defined simply as any state that is seen as having substantially hostile intentions toward the actor. It is argued that the focus in much of the existing literature on highly specific 'ideal-type' enemies is overly limiting. See Cottam, R. W. *Foreign Policy Motivation* (University of Pittsburgh Press: 1977); Shimko, K. L. *Images and Arms Control* (University of Michigan: Ann Arbor, 1991); Cottam, M. L. *Images and Intervention* (University of Pittsburgh Press: 1994); Herrmann, R. K. and Fischerkeller, M. P. 'Beyond the Enemy Image and Spiral Model', *International Organization*, 49.3 (1995).

20 For discussions of this 'cognitive' approach, see Holsti, O. R. 'Foreign Policy Formation Viewed Cognitively', *In* Axelrod, R. M. (ed.) *Structure of Decision* (Princeton University Press, 1976); Tetlock, P. E. and McGuire, C. 'Cognitive Perspectives on Foreign Policy', *In* Long, S. (ed.) *Political Behavior Annual* (Boulder: Westview Press, 1986); Goldstein, J. and Keohane, R. O. *Ideas and Foreign Policy* (New York: Cornell University Press, 1993).

21 Jervis, R. *Perception and Misperception in International Politics* (Princeton University Press, 1976), p. 3.

22 It is often argued that cultural factors explain the notorious prevalence of conspiracy theories in the Middle East. Daniel Pipes identifies President Nasser in particular as having a 'conspiratorial mentality'. Pipes, D. *The Hidden Hand* (London: Macmillan, 1996), p. 36. It seems possible, however, that universal cognitive tendencies might provide a more satisfactory explanation.

23 Jervis points out that the perception of hostility is central to the image of the opponent. 'To decide that the other is no longer hostile, or perhaps never has been hostile, requires that many other beliefs must also be changed. So when the other acts with restraint... the actor would be more likely to change his view of the other's strength than of its intentions.' Jervis, *Perception and Misperception*, p. 299. Indeed, as Holsti argues, *any* action may be ultimately interpreted as hostile when the opponent 'is viewed within the framework of an "inherent bad faith" model'. Under these circumstances, 'the image of the enemy is clearly self-perpetuating, for the model itself denies the existence of data that could invalidate it'. Holsti, O. R. 'Cognitive Dynamics and Images of the Enemy', *Journal of International Affairs*, 21.1 (1967), p. 17.

24 On this issue, see Vertzberger, Y. *The World in their Minds* (Stanford University Press, 1990), p. 17; Stein, J. G. and Welch, D. A. 'Rational and Psychological Approaches to the Study of International Conflict', *In* Geva, N. and Mintz, A. (eds) *Decision-Making on War and Peace* (London: Boulder, 1997), p. 55; Wohlforth, W. C. *The Elusive Balance* (Ithaca: Cornell University Press, 1993), p. 294; Boulding, K. E. 'National Images and International Systems', *Journal of Conflict Resolution*, 3.2 (1959), p. 13; Jervis, R. 'Hypotheses on Misperception', *World Politics*, 20.3 (1968), pp. 465–6; Jervis, *Perception and Misperception*, p. 308.

25 10/3/53, *BBC Summary of World Broadcasts* [BBC-SWB]: 343.

26 Quoted in Nutting, *Nasser*, p. 37.

27 Lucas, W. S. *Divided We Stand* (London: Hodder and Stoughton, 1991), p. 13; Sayed-Ahmed, M. A. W. *Nasser and American Foreign Policy, 1952–1956* (London: LAAM, 1989), pp. 46–7.

28 Thornhill, M. T. 'Britain, the United States and the Rise of an Egyptian Leader', *English Historical Review*, 69 (2004), p. 892.

29 Sadat, A. *In Search of Identity* (London: Collins, 1978), p. 108; Heikal, M. H. *Nasser: The Cairo Documents* (London: New English Library, 1972), pp. 45–7.

30 Mohi El Din, K. *Memories of a Revolution* (Cairo: AUC Press, 1995), p. 79; Thornhill, 'Britain, the United States and the Rise of an Egyptian Leader', p. 894; Hamed Mahmoud Interview; Khaled Mohieddin Interview.

31 Sayed-Ahmed, *Nasser and American Foreign Policy*, pp. 41–3; Lucas, *Divided We Stand*, p. 14; Copeland, M. *The Game of Nations* (London: Weidenfeld and Nicolson, 1969), p. 53.

32 Tharwat Okasha Interview.

33 Holland, M. F. *America and Egypt: From Roosevelt to Eisenhower* (Westport: Praeger, 1996), p. 23.

34 Eveland, W. *Ropes of Sand* (London: W.W. Norton, 1980), p. 97; Gordon, J. *Nasser's Blessed Movement* (Oxford University Press, 1992), pp. 162–4.

35 *The Fifty Years War: Israel and the Arabs*, Interview Transcripts, Private Papers Collection, Middle East Centre, St Antony's College, University of Oxford [FYW]: Mohsen Abdel Khalek Interview.

36 Tawil, M. *La'bat al-umam wa 'abd al-nāsir* (Cairo: Al-Maktab al-Misriyy al-Hadith, 1986), p. 49; Eveland, *Ropes of Sand*, p. 99.

37 Alterman, *Egypt and American Foreign Assistance*, p. 3.

38 FYW: Kamal al-Din Hussein Interview.

39 Sadat, A. *Revolt on the Nile* (London: Allan Wingate, 1957), p. 124.

40 Heikal, *Cairo Documents*, pp. 44–7.
41 *Foreign Relations of the United States* [FRUS]: 1952–54: IX-1004.
42 National Archives [NA]: CAB151/153.
43 Lucas, *Divided We Stand*, p. 16, p. 38; Sayed-Ahmed, *Nasser and American Foreign Policy*, pp. 44–5, p. 61. This is confirmed by Egyptian archival sources and histories. Alterman, *Egypt and American Foreign Assistance*, p. xxiii; Hamrush, A. *Qiṣṣat thawrat 26 yūlīyū* (Cairo: Madbouli, 1983) Vol. 1, p. 182; Tawil, *La'bat al-umam*, pp. 390–1. Even Amin Howeidy, who is keen to emphasise that Nasser did not 'co-operate' with the CIA, admits the importance of the contacts. 'He listened to them and he wanted to use them to give some of his messages to their decision-makers.' Howeidy Interview.
44 Eveland, *Ropes of Sand*, p. 146.
45 Jankowski, J. *Nasser's Egypt, Arab Nationalism and the United Arab Republic* (Boulder: Lynne Rienner, 2002), p. 24.
46 Kent, J. *Egypt and the Defence of the Middle East, Part III, 1953–1956* (London: HMSO, 1998), pp. 21–2.
47 Heikal, *Cairo Documents*, p. 44.
48 Mohi El Din, *Memories of a Revolution*, p. 60; Nasser, G. A. *The Philosophy of the Revolution* (Buffalo: Smith, Keynes and Marshall, 1959).
49 Heikal, M. H. *Cutting the Lion's Tail* (London: Andre Deutsch, 1986), p. 41.
50 Sayed-Ahmed, *Nasser and American Foreign Policy*, pp. 47–8.
51 Sadat, *Revolt on the Nile*, p. 103.
52 Okasha Interview; Nutting, *Nasser*, p. 21; Nasser, *Philosophy*, pp. 29–30.
53 22/7/54, BBC-SWB: 486.
54 Dessouki, A. E. H. 'Nasser and the Struggle for Independence', *In* Louis, W. R. and Owen, R. (eds) *Suez 1956: The Crisis and Its Consequences* (Oxford: Clarendon Press, 1989), p. 34.
55 8/9/52, FRUS: 1952–54: IX-1006.
56 Howeidy, A. 'Nasser and the Crisis of 1956', *In* Louis and Owen (eds), *Suez 1956*, p. 164.
57 Kyle, K. *Suez: Britain's End of Empire in the Middle East* (London: I. B. Tauris, 2003), p. 48.
58 BBC-SWB: 325; FYW: Kamal al-Din Hussein Interview; Abu al-Fadl, A. F. *Kuntu nā'iban li ra'īs al-mukhabarāt* (Cairo: Dar al-Shorouk, 2001), p. 95.
59 Fawzi, M. *Suez 1956: An Egyptian Perspective* (London: Shorouk International, 1988), p. 25.
60 NA: FO371/102764.
61 NA: FO371/102766. See also Nutting, *Nasser*, pp. 74–5; Lloyd, S. *Suez 1956* (London: Jonathan Cape, 1978), p. 15.
62 Mohi El Din, *Memories of a Revolution*, p. 131.
63 BBC-SWB: 331.
64 Shuckburgh, E. *Descent to Suez* (London: Weidenfeld and Nicolson, 1986), pp. 232–3.
65 Heikal, *Lion's Tail*, p. 49; Howeidy Interview.
66 BBC-SWB: 511.
67 Esmat Abdel Magid Interview.
68 Calvocoressi, P. *Suez: Ten Years After* (London: BBC, 1967), p. 33.
69 10/3/53, BBC-SWB: 343.
70 FYW: Khalek Interview.

71 20/11/53, BBC-SWB: 418.
72 Alterman, *Egypt and American Foreign Assistance*, p. 75.
73 FRUS: 1952–54: IX–1304.
74 Aronson, G. *From Sideshow to Center Stage: US Policy Toward Egypt 1946–1956* (Boulder: Lynne Rienner, 1986) pp. 52–3.
75 'He sent an expedition to Washington to have weapons,' recounts Amin Howeidy. 'They stayed there for one month. After the month, they told them, we will give you some pistols.' Howeidy Interview. See also FYW: Kamal al-Din Hussein Interview.
76 Holland, *America and Egypt*, p. 42.
77 Holland, *America and Egypt*, p. 57; Thornhill, 'Rise of an Egyptian Leader', pp. 919–20; Gordon, *Nasser's Blessed Movement*, p. 180.
78 Sayed-Ahmed, *Nasser and American Foreign Policy*, p. 91.
79 28/9/54, FRUS: 1952–54: IX-1364.
80 Burns, W. J. *Economic Aid and American Foreign Policy Toward Egypt, 1955–1981* (Albany: State University of New York Press, 1985), p. 23.
81 Heikal, *Cairo Documents*, pp. 54–5. See also Tawil, *La'bat al-umam*, pp. 395–7.
82 Eveland, *Ropes of Sand*, p. 101.
83 Mohammed Fayek Interview; FYW: Khalek Interview.
84 Copeland, *Game of Nations*, p. 56.
85 Sayed-Ahmed, *Nasser and American Foreign Policy*, p. 97.
86 FYW: Kamal al-Din Hussein Interview.
87 Morgan, J. *The Backbench Diaries of Richard Crossman* (London: Hamish Hamilton and Jonathan Cape, 1981), p. 287.
88 Riad, M. *The Struggle for Peace in the Middle East* (London: Quartet Books, 1981), p. 7.
89 FYW: Zakaria Mohieddin and Shams Badran Interviews; Tawil, *La'bat al-umam*, pp. 44–6; Sayed-Ahmed, *Nasser and American Foreign Policy*, p. 98.
90 18/8/53, BBC-SWB: 389; Stephens, *Nasser*, pp. 81–2.
91 FRUS: 1952–54: IX-632.
92 Mohieddin Interview.
93 FRUS: 1952–54: IX-560.
94 Oren, M. B. 'Secret Egypt-Israel Peace Initiatives Prior to the Suez Campaign', *Middle Eastern Studies*, 26.3 (1990), p. 353.
95 Shlaim, A. *The Iron Wall* (London: Penguin, 2000), pp. 78–80, p. 120.
96 FYW: Abdel Rahman Sadeq Interview.
97 FYW: Zakaria Mohieddin Interview. See also Khaled Mohieddin Interview; FYW: Kamal al-Din Hussein Interview.
98 FYW: Mohsen Abdel Khalek Interview.
99 Aburish, *Nasser*, p. 60.
100 29/4/54, BBC-SWB: 463; Nasser, G. A. 'The Egyptian Revolution', *Foreign Affairs*, 33.1 (1954), p. 211.
101 FYW: Zakaria Mohieddin Interview.
102 Aburish, *Nasser*, p. 70.
103 BBC-SWB: 502.
104 FRUS: 1952–54: IX-904.
105 Sheffy, Y. 'Unconcern at Dawn, Surprise at Sunset', *Intelligence and National Security*, 5.3 (1990), p. 15.

106 Tawil, *La'bat al-umam*, p. 399.
107 25/2/55, BBC-SWB: 548.
108 Heikal, *Cairo Documents*, p. 56.
109 FYW: Kamal al-Din Hussein Interview.
110 Lloyd, *Suez 1956*, p. 27.
111 Heikal, *Cairo Documents*, pp. 81–3.
112 Lucas, *Divided We Stand*, p. 41.
113 Heikal, *Lion's Tail*, p. 65.
114 BBC-SWB: 621.
115 FRUS: 1955–57: XIV-411.
116 Trevelyan, H. *The Middle East in Revolution* (London: Macmillan, 1970), p. 57; Trevelyan, H. *Public and Private* (London: Hamish Hamilton, 1980), p. 80.
117 Heikal, *Cairo Documents*, p. 84. See also Oren, M. B. 'A Winter of Discontent', *International Journal of Middle Eastern Studies*, 22.2 (1990), pp. 175–7.
118 Mohieddin Interview; Podeh, E. 'The Drift towards Neutrality: Egyptian Foreign Policy during the Early Nasserist Era, 1952–55', *Middle Eastern Studies*, 32.1 (1996), pp. 162–3; Kedourie, E. 'Egypt, the Arab States and the Suez Expedition', *In* Wilson, K. M. (ed.) *Imperialism and Nationalism in the Middle East* (London: Mansell Publishing, 1983), p. 127.
119 Barnett, M. N. *Dialogues in Arab Politics* (New York: Columbia University Press, 1998), p. 107.
120 Said Interview.
121 BBC-SWB: 535; Podeh, 'Drift towards Neutrality', p. 167.
122 Seale, P. *The Struggle for Syria* (London: Tauris, 1987), pp. 223–4.
123 *Al-Gomhouriyya*, 9/2/55, BBC-SWB: 542.
124 Shuckburgh, *Descent*, p. 249.
125 FRUS: 1955–57: XIV-35.
126 Kent, *Egypt and the Defence of the Middle East*, p. 401.
127 28/3/55, BBC-SWB: 557.
128 FRUS: 1955–57: XIV-123.
129 27/1/56, BBC-SWB: 642.
130 Sadat editorial in *Al-Gomhouriyya*, 22/2/56, BBC-SWB: 650.
131 Heikal, *Cairo Documents*, p. 55; Baghdadi, A. L. *Mudhakkirāt* (Cairo: Al-Maktab al-Hadith, 1977), Vol. 1, p. 197; Riad, *Struggle for Peace*, p. 7.
132 Doran, M. 'Egypt: Pan-Arabism in Historical Context', *In* Brown, L. C. (ed.) *Diplomacy in the Middle East* (London: I. B. Tauris, 2001), p. 107. See also Freiberger, S. Z. *Dawn over Suez* (Chicago: Ivan R. Dee, 1992), p. 102; Takeyh, *Origins of the Eisenhower Doctrine*, p. 74.
133 Hoda Abdel Nasser Interview; FYW: Kamal al-Din Hussein and Khalek Interviews.
134 Trevelyan, *Middle East in Revolution*, p. 36.
135 FRUS: 1955–57: XIV-31; FYW: Zakaria Mohieddin and Khalek Interviews.
136 Fayek Interview.
137 Talaat Mosallem Interview; FYW: Kamal al-Din Hussein Interview; Sayed-Ahmed, *Nasser and American Foreign Policy*, p. 107.
138 8/3/55, BBC-SWB: 549.
139 Howeidy Interview; FYW: Zakaria Mohieddin, Kamal al-Din Hussein and Khalek Interviews; Sadat, J. *A Woman of Egypt* (New York: Simon and Schuster, 1987), p. 154.

140 Heikal, *Lion's Tail*, p. 67.
141 FYW: Kamal al-Din Hussein Interview.
142 23/3/55, BBC-SWB: 556.
143 Sayed-Ahmed, *Nasser and American Foreign Policy*, p. 109; Aburish, *Nasser*, p. 74.
144 FRUS: 1955–57: XIV-97, 98.
145 Lucas, *Divided We Stand*, p. 47.
146 28/3/55, BBC-SWB: 557.
147 FRUS: 1955–57: XIV-123.
148 BBC-SWB: 608.
149 Heikal, *Cairo Documents*, pp. 59–63; Baghdadi, *Mudhakkirāt*, Vol. 1, pp. 203–5.
150 FRUS: 1955–57: XIV-321.
151 Shlaim, *Iron Wall*, pp. 126–7.
152 FRUS: 1955–57: XIV-123.
153 FRUS: 1955–57: XIV-62, 67; Alterman, *Egypt and American Foreign Assistance*, p. 111.
154 23/5/55, BBC-SWB: 572.
155 FRUS: 1955–57: XIV-195.
156 FRUS: 1955–57: XIV-416, 428.
157 FRUS: 1955–57: XV-32.
158 Alterman, *Egypt and American Foreign Assistance*, p. 117.
159 Kyle, *Suez*, p. 71.
160 Takeyh, *Origins of the Eisenhower Doctrine*, pp. 78–9; Shamir, S. 'The Collapse of Project Alpha', *In* Louis and Owen (eds), *Suez 1956*, pp. 87–8; Oren, 'Secret Egypt-Israel Peace Initiatives', p. 365.
161 6/7/55, BBC-SWB: 585; FRUS: 1955–57: XIV-321.
162 Sheffy, 'Unconcern at Dawn', pp. 16–17.
163 FYW: Zakaria Mohieddin Interview.
164 FRUS: 1955–57: XV-67.
165 13/3/56, FRUS: 1955–57: XV-211.
166 Sheffy, 'Unconcern at Dawn', pp. 16–24. See also Bandmann, Y. 'The Egyptian Armed Forces during the Kadesh Campaign', *In* Troen and Shemesh (eds), *Suez-Sinai Crisis*, p. 79.
167 13/5/56, BBC-SWB: 673.
168 Zeevy, R. 'The Military Lessons of the Sinai Campaign', *In* Troen and Shemesh (eds), *Suez-Sinai Crisis*, p. 61, p. 70.
169 Alterman, *Egypt and American Foreign Assistance*, p. 97.
170 Heikal, *Cairo Documents*, p. 67. He was not wrong that certain American officials were considering 'finding an alternative to Nasser somewhere'. But he was mistaken about the Dam. If the Americans concluded that he 'was really lost to the West', they thought 'it would be much better to give the Dam to a successor'. NA: FO371/113738.
171 FRUS: 1955–57: XV-21, 46; Burns, *Economic Aid*, p. 61.
172 FYW: Zakaria Mohieddin Interview.
173 FRUS: 1955–57: XV-111-2.
174 See FRUS: 1955–57: XV-357; Takeyh, *Origins of the Eisenhower Doctrine*, p. 117; Kent, *Egypt and the Defence of the Middle East*, p. 507.
175 Shuckburgh, *Descent*, p. 281.
176 NA: FO371/113738.
177 Heikal, *Cairo Documents*, pp. 85–6.

178 Nutting, A. *No End of a Lesson* (London: Constable, 1967), pp. 34–5, corrected by Kyle, *Suez*, p. 99.
179 Dorril, S. *MI6* (London: Fourth Estate, 2000), p. 613.
180 LUCKY BREAK is generally said to have been a member of Nasser's inner circle, although it has also been suggested that it was 'taps on cables running under the Suez Canal', or even an SIS fiction. However, its information was relayed and relied on at the highest levels, inspiring 'Omega' and possibly even encouraging Eden secretly to authorise certain SIS officers to investigate the possibility of assassinating Nasser. Thornhill, M. T. 'Trevelyan, Humphrey', In *Oxford Dictionary of National Biography* (Oxford University Press, 2004); Lucas, W. S. 'The Missing Link?' *In* Kelly, S. and Gorst, A. (eds) *Whitehall and the Suez Crisis* (London: Frank Cass, 2000), p. 119; Dorril, *MI6*, p. 614; Lucas, *Divided We Stand*, p. 101.
181 Shuckburgh, *Descent*, pp. 345–6.
182 NA: FO371/113738.
183 Nutting, *Nasser*, p. 123.
184 Lucas, *Divided We Stand*, p. 119.
185 Heikal, *Lion's Tail*, pp. 104–5; Lucas, *Divided We Stand*, pp. 116–18.
186 FRUS: 1955–57: XV-235.
187 NA: FO371/113738.
188 Fain, 'Unfortunate Arabia', p. 128.
189 FRUS: 1955–57: XV-363.
190 Heikal, *Lion's Tail*, pp. 104–5.
191 FRUS: 1955–57: XV-252.
192 Kyle, K. 'Britain's Slow March to Suez', *In* Tal, D. (ed.) *The 1956 War* (London: Frank Cass, 2001), p. 96.
193 Heikal, *Cairo Documents*, p. 87.
194 Nutting, *No End of a Lesson*, p. 34.
195 19/6/56, BBC-SWB: 683.
196 Aldrich, R. J. *The Hidden Hand: Britain, America and Cold War Secret Intelligence* (London: John Murray, 2001), p. 477; Sami Sharaf Interview; Dorril, *MI6*, p. 610; Imam, S. *Ḥusayn al-shāfi'i wa asrār thawrat yūlīyū wa ḥukm al-sadāt* (Cairo: Maktab Awziris, 1993), p. 73.
197 Okasha Interview.
198 See Fayek Interview; Cooper, *Lion's Last Roar*, p. 90; Heikal, *Cairo Documents*, p. 56.
199 FRUS: 1955–57: XV-351; BBC-SWB: 673.
200 Lucas, *Divided We Stand*, pp. 121–2. See also Pineau, C. *1956/Suez* (Paris: Éditions Robert Laffont, 1976), pp. 39–41; Howeidy Interview; Calvocoressi, *Suez*, p. 37; Heikal, *Cutting the Lion's Tail*, p. 108.
201 BBC-SWB: DS5; *Majmū'āt khuṭab wa tasrīḥāt wa bayānāt al-ra'īs jamāl 'abd al-nāṣir* (Cairo: Ha'ia al-Isti'lamat), Vol. 1, pp. 547–64.
202 Abdel Hamid Abubakr Interview; Abu-Bakr, A. H. *Qanāt al-sūīs wa al-ayām allatī hazzat al-dunīā* (Cairo: Dar al-Ma'arif, 1987) pp. 26–9.
203 Heikal, M. H. *Sphinx and Commissar* (London: Collins, 1978), p. 67.
204 Heikal, *Cairo Documents*, p. 89, p. 92.
205 Gopal, S. 'India, the Crisis and the Non-Aligned Nations', *In* Louis and Owen (eds), *Suez 1956*, p. 174.
206 Calvocoressi, *Suez*, p. 44.

207 Heikal, M. H. 'Egyptian Foreign Policy', *Foreign Affairs*, 56.4 (1978), p. 714.
208 Baghdadi, *Mudhakkirāt*, Vol. 1, p. 318.
209 Heikal, *Cairo Documents*, p. 93. See also Fayek Interview; Mar'i, 'Political Papers', pp. 359–61.
210 Heikal, *Cairo Documents*, p. 70.
211 Nasser had used the threat of establishing diplomatic relations with communist China against the US government since October 1953. Cooper, *Lion's Last Roar*, pp. 92–3.
212 FRUS: 1955–57: XV-399.
213 FRUS: 1955–57: XV-484.
214 Calvocoressi, *Suez*, pp. 41–2.
215 Howeidy Interview.
216 Nutting, *Nasser*, p. 139.
217 Howeidy Interview. See also Mahmoud Interview; Baghdadi, *Mudhakkirāt*, Vol. 1, p. 318.
218 Uruq, M. *Qirā'a fī awrāq 'alī ṣabrī* (Cairo: Dar al-Mustaqbal al-Arabiyy, 1992) p. 113; Fawzi, M. *Thiwār yūlīyū yitaḥaddithūn* (Cairo: Al-Zahra lil-I'lam al-Arabiyy, 1987), p. 100; Kyle, *Suez*, p. 119; Okasha (2004) Vol. 1, p. 207.
219 24/7/54, BBC-SWB: 487.
220 17/11/54, BBC-SWB: 520.
221 Calvocoressi, *Suez*, p. 43.
222 Fayek Interview.
223 Samd al-Din, I., Said Selim, M. and Khadduri, W. *Kayf yiṣna' al-qarār fī al-waṭan al-'arabiyy* (Cairo: Markaz Dirasat al-Wahida al-Arabiyya, 1980), pp. 86–97; Baghdadi, *Mudhakkirāt*, Vol. 1, p. 318; Mahmoud Interview; Hamrush Interview.
224 Uruq, *Awrāq 'alī ṣabrī*, p. 113.
225 Kyle, *Suez*, p. 120.
226 Heikal, *Lion's Tail*, p. 133.
227 Baghdadi, *Mudhakkirāt*, Vol. 1, p. 318; Imam, *Ḥusayn al-shāfi'i*, p. 69. See also Fawzi, *Thiwār yūlīyū*, p. 100.
228 Kyle, *Suez*, p. 120.
229 Mahmoud Interview; Samd al-Din et al., *Kayf yiṣna' al-qarār*, pp. 99–101.
230 Howeidy Interview; Fayek Interview.
231 Abubakr Interview; Mar'i, S. 'Sayyid Mar'i's Political Papers', *In* Troen and Shemesh (eds), *Suez-Sinai Crisis*, pp. 359–61.
232 Lucas, *Divided We Stand*, p. 139.
233 FRUS: 1955–57: XV-467.
234 FRUS: 1955–57: XV-502.
235 Dodds-Parker, D. *Political Eunuch* (London: Springwood Books, 1986), p. 97.
236 Rucher, L. 'The Soviet Union and the Suez Crisis', *In* Tal (ed.), *1956 War*.
237 Trevelyan, *Middle East in Revolution*, p. 55.
238 FRUS: 1955–57: XV-484.
239 26/7/56, BBC-SWB: DS5; *Majmū'āt khuṭab*, Vol. 1, pp. 547–64.
240 Baghdadi, *Mudhakkirāt*, Vol. 1, p. 318; Calvocoressi, *Suez*, pp. 41–2.
241 Uruq, *Awrāq 'alī ṣabrī*, p. 114. Trevelyan used the same phrase. NA: PREM11/1098.

242   24/7/56, BBC-SWB: DS3.
243   Heikal, *Cairo Documents*, p. 74.
244   26/7/56, BBC-SWB: DS5; *Majmū'āt khuṭab*, Vol. 1, pp. 547–64.
245   Nutting, *No End of a Lesson*, p. 45.
246   26/7/56, BBC-SWB: DS5; *Majmū'āt khuṭab*, Vol. 1, pp. 547–64.
247   Fawzi, *Suez 1956*, pp. 31–2.
248   Heikal, *Cairo Documents*, p. 89.
249   Heikal, *Cairo Documents*, pp. 90–1; Heikal, M. H. *Milaffāt al-sūīs* (Cairo: Al-Ahram, 1996), pp. 462–4.
250   Sheffy, 'Unconcern at Dawn', p. 20 fn53.
251   Mohieddin Interview.
252   Mar'i, 'Political Papers', pp. 359–61.
253   Howeidy Interview.
254   Heikal, *Cairo Documents*, pp. 90–1. See also Heikal, *Milaffāt*, pp. 462–4; Baghdadi, *Mudhakkirāt*, Vol. 1, pp. 319–20; Howeidy Interview.
255   Heikal, *Lion's Tail*, p. 122.
256   28/7/56, BBC-SWB: DS6.
257   FRUS: 1955–57: XVI-31.
258   Heikal, *Cairo Documents*, pp. 90–1; Heikal, *Milaffāt*, pp. 462–4.
259   Howeidy Interview; FRUS: 1955–57: XVI-31; Mohieddin Interview.
260   Heikal, *Cairo Documents*, pp. 90–1; Heikal, *Milaffāt*, pp. 462–4.
261   Heikal, *Cairo Documents*, p. 92.
262   Calvocoressi, *Suez*, p. 44.
263   Calvocoressi, *Suez*, p. 44.
264   See Baghdadi, *Mudhakkirāt*, Vol. 1, pp. 319–20; Nutting, *Nasser*, pp. 147–8; Howeidy Interview.
265   Howeidy Interview.
266   Heikal, *Cairo Documents*, pp. 90–1; Heikal, *Milaffāt*, pp. 462–4.
267   Baghdadi, *Mudhakkirāt*, Vol. 1, p. 327; Heikal, *Cairo Documents*, p. 93.
268   Heikal, *Cairo Documents*, pp. 90–1; Heikal, *Milaffāt*, pp. 462–4.
269   Mar'i, 'Political Papers', p. 362.
270   Kyle, *Suez*, p. 134, p. 142.
271   Kyle, *Suez*, p. 143, p. 257.
272   Howeidy, 'Nasser and the Crisis', p. 171.
273   Sayed-Ahmed, *Nasser and American Foreign Policy*, pp. 128–30.
274   Baghdadi, *Mudhakkirāt*, Vol. 1, p. 331.
275   Heikal, *Cairo Documents*, p. 101; Kyle, *Suez*, pp. 183–5, p. 196.
276   Eayrs, J. *The Commonwealth and Suez* (Oxford University Press, 1964), p. 41.
277   Fawzi, *Suez 1956*, pp. 49–50; Nutting, *Nasser*, p. 151.
278   NA: PREM11/1100.
279   Mar'i, 'Political Papers', p. 363.
280   NA: PREM11/1100. See also Menzies, R. G. *Afternoon Light* (London: Cassell, 1967), pp. 164–8.
281   BBC-SWB: DS47; *Majmū'āt khuṭab*, Vol. 1, p. 590.
282   Dodds-Parker Papers: MC: D2/5/2C/8.
283   Holland, *America and Egypt*, p. 112.
284   Heikal, *Cairo Documents*, p. 103.
285   Kyle, *Suez*, p. 221.
286   BBC-SWB: DS47; *Majmū'āt khuṭab*, Vol. 1, p. 595.

287 Kyle, *Suez*, p. 288.
288 23/9/56, NA: PREM11/1102.
289 Lucas, *Divided We Stand*, p. 220.
290 NA: PREM11/1098.
291 Kyle, *Suez*, p. 147. See NA: FO371/121662; Dodds-Parker Papers: MC: D2/5/2C/8.
292 NA: PREM11/1098.
293 Catterall, P. *The Macmillan Diaries: The Cabinet Years, 1950–1957* (London: Macmillan, 2003), p. 578.
294 Clark, W. *From Three Worlds* (London: Sidgwick & Jackson, 1986), p. 170.
295 NA: PREM11/1098.
296 Lucas, *Divided We Stand*, pp. 142–3.
297 Eden to Macmillan, 23/9/56, NA: PREM11/1102.
298 See Bower, T. *The Perfect English Spy* (London: Mandarin, 1996), pp. 186–93; Kyle, *Suez*, p. 191, p. 211, pp. 218–19; Wright, P. *Spycatcher* (New York: Viking, 1987), p. 160; Lucas, *Divided We Stand*, p. 181, pp. 193–5; Dorril, *MI6*, pp. 631–9, p. 694; Goldsworthy, D. *British Documents on the End of Empire: The Conservative Government and the End of Empire, 1951–57* (London, HMSO, 1994), pp. 100–2.
299 Andrew, C. and Mitrokhin, V. *The Mitrokhin Archive II* (London: Allen Lane, 2005), pp. 148–9. See also Rucher, 'Soviet Union', p. 77.
300 Thornhill, 'Alternatives to Nasser', pp. 18–22.
301 Dodds-Parker Papers: MC: D2/9/1MS/1-2, Oral History Interview. See also Dodds-Parker, *Political Eunuch*, pp. 102–3.
302 Bower, *Perfect English Spy*, pp. 200–1; Dorril, *MI6*, p. 628; Kyle, *Suez*, p. 148; Fielding, X. *One Man in His Time* (London: Macmillan, 1990) pp. 104–5.
303 NA: FO371/125423; Dorril, *MI6*, pp. 658–9; Pearson, *Sir Anthony Eden*, p. 84.
304 See Shaw (1996) pp. 92–4.
305 Fullick, R. and Powell, G. *Suez: The Double War* (London: Leo Cooper, 1990), pp. 46–7.
306 He adds that Nasser was suspicious of these reports at first, suspecting 'that they were being planted by the CIA to make Egypt frightened of continuing its attacks on Britain'. Heikal, *Cairo Documents*, p. 99, p. 105; Heikal, *Lion's Tail*, p. 175.
307 Lucas, *Divided We Stand*, p. 163.
308 BBC-SWB: DS18.
309 Heikal, *Lion's Tail*, p. 148.
310 Kyle, *Suez*, p. 222.
311 Trevelyan, *Public and Private*, p. 79; NA: FO371/118999.
312 Calvocoressi, *Suez*, p. 45.
313 Dorril, *MI6*, p. 631.
314 NA: PREM11/1100.
315 Howeidy Interview; Gamal Naguib Interview.
316 Baghdadi, *Mudhakkirāt*, Vol. 1, p. 327.
317 Mar'i, 'Political Papers', pp. 362–3.
318 Kyle, *Suez*, p. 188, p. 226.
319 See Eayrs, *Commonwealth and Suez*, pp. 49–50, p. 69; Gopal, 'India', p. 180.
320 12/8/56, BBC-SWB: DS18.

321   Heikal, *Milaffāt*, p. 825.
322   Heikal, *Cairo Documents*, p. 105.
323   Fayek Interview.
324   Ashton, N. J. *Eisenhower, Macmillan and the Problem of Nasser* (London: Macmillan, 1996), p. 92.
325   Troen and Shemesh (eds), *Suez-Sinai Crisis*, p. 377. See also Abu al-Fadl, *Kuntu nā'iban*, pp. 103–4; Mosallem Interview.
326   NA: FO371/118999.
327   Troen and Shemesh, *Suez-Sinai Crisis*, p. 152; Bandmann, 'Egyptian Armed Forces', pp. 79–80.
328   Heikal, *Lion's Tail*, p. 176.
329   Sheffy, 'Unconcern at Dawn', pp. 29–32.
330   Sadat, *Woman of Egypt*, p. 158.
331   FRUS: 1955–57: XVI-408.
332   Sheffy, 'Unconcern at Dawn', p. 33, p. 41.
333   See Kyle, *Suez*, pp. 338–51.
334   Heikal, *Cairo Documents*, p. 105.
335   Howeidy Interview.
336   Heikal, *Lion's Tail*, p. 177.
337   Baghdadi, A. L. 'Abd al-Latif al-Bughdadi's Memoirs', *In* Troen and Shemesh (eds), *Suez-Sinai Crisis*, p. 337; Baghdadi, *Mudhakkirāt*, Vol. 1, pp. 335–6.
338   Heikal, *Cairo Documents*, p. 106; Heikal, *Lion's Tail*, p. 178.
339   Eayrs, *Commonwealth and Suez*, p. 204; Kyle, *Suez*, pp. 358–9.
340   Fayek Interview.
341   Heikal, *Lion's Tail*, p. 179.
342   Rucher, 'Soviet Union', p. 78.
343   Dodds-Parker, *Political Eunuch*, p. 105.
344   Shuckburgh, *Descent*, p. 362.
345   Heikal, *Milaffāt*, p. 520, p. 823.
346   Baghdadi, *Mudhakkirāt*, Vol. 1, p. 328; Shemesh, M. 'Egypt: From Military Defeat to Political Victory', *In* Troen and Shemesh (eds), *Suez-Sinai Crisis*, p. 152.
347   Sheffy, 'Unconcern at Dawn', p. 40.
348   Heikal, *Cairo Documents*, p. 106.
349   Eveland, *Ropes of Sand*, p. 226.
350   Heikal, *Lion's Tail*, p. 179.
351   Okasha Interview.
352   Howeidy Interview. Amin Howeidy claims to have heard the story directly from the press attaché.
353   Fayek Interview.
354   Heikal, *Cairo Documents*, pp. 108–9.
355   6/12/56, *Egyptian Gazette*. Quoted in Bandmann, 'Egyptian Armed Forces', p. 85.
356   Mar'i, 'Political Papers', pp. 364–5.
357   Baghdadi, 'Memoirs', p. 338; Baghdadi, *Mudhakkirāt*, Vol. 1, pp. 337–8.
358   Mar'i, 'Political Papers', pp. 364–5.
359   NA: FO371/121783.
360   Moheeb Helal Interview.

361   Quoted in Kyle, *Suez*, p. 368.
362   Baghdadi, 'Memoirs', pp. 338–9; Baghdadi, *Mudhakkirāt*, Vol. 1, p. 339.
363   Heikal, *Cairo Documents*, pp. 108–9.
364   Howeidy, A. *Ḥurūb 'abd al-nāṣir* (Beirut: 1979), p. 92.
365   Baghdadi, 'Memoirs', pp. 339–40; Baghdadi, *Mudhakkirāt*, Vol. 1, pp. 340–1.
366   Calvocoressi, *Suez*, p. 48.
367   Baghdadi, 'Memoirs', pp. 339–40; Baghdadi, *Mudhakkirāt*, Vol. 1, pp. 340–1.
368   Mahmoud Interview.
369   Mosallem Interview.
370   Mar'i, 'Political Papers', pp. 366–7.
371   Howeidy Interview.
372   Baghdadi, 'Memoirs', pp. 339–40; Baghdadi, *Mudhakkirāt*, Vol. 1, pp. 340–1.
373   FRUS: 1955–57: XVI-458.
374   Heikal, *Lion's Tail*, p. 186.
375   Bandmann, 'Egyptian Armed Forces', p. 96.
376   Heikal, *Cairo Documents*, pp. 110–11.
377   Mahmoud Interview.
378   Fayek Interview; Howeidy Interview.
379   Heikal, *Lion's Tail*, p. 186.
380   Abu al-Fadl, *Kuntu nā'iban*, pp. 103–4.
381   Mahmoud Interview.
382   BBC-SWB: DS88.
383   Baghdadi, 'Memoirs', pp. 340; Baghdadi, *Mudhakkirāt*, Vol. 1, p. 341.
384   *Majmū'āt khuṭab*, Vol. 1, pp. 606–7.
385   FRUS: 1955–57: XVI-472.
386   This account is largely based on Baghdadi, *Mudhakkirāt*, Vol. 1, pp. 344–54, translated in Baghdadi, 'Memoirs', pp. 341–8. But see also Heikal, *Cairo Documents*, pp. 110–11; Fawzi, *Thiwār yūlīyū*, p. 101; Aburish, *Nasser*, p. 119; Nutting, *Nasser*, p. 166; Kyle, *Suez*, pp. 418–19, pp. 445–6.
387   Baghdadi, 'Memoirs', pp. 347–8; Baghdadi, *Mudhakkirāt*, Vol. 1, pp. 352–4.
388   Calvocoressi, *Suez*, p. 45.
389   Schramm, W. *One Day in the World's Press* (California: Stanford, 1959), p. 83.
390   Heikal, *Lion's Tail*, p. 195; Heikal, *Cairo Documents*, p. 113.
391   Mohieddin Interview.
392   FRUS: 1955–57: XVI-458.
393   Browne, H. *Flashpoints: Suez and Sinai* (London: Longman, 1971), p. 72.
394   FRUS: 1955–57: XVI-472.
395   Sayed-Ahmed, *Nasser and American Foreign Policy*, p. 143.
396   FRUS: 1955–57: XVI-486, 492.
397   FRUS: 1955–57: XVI-492.
398   Kyle, *Suez*, p. 455.
399   Heikal, *Lion's Tail*, pp. 187–8.
400   Howeidy Interview.
401   Alleras, I. 'Eisenhower and the Sinai Campaign of 1956', *In* Tal (ed.), *1956 War*.
402   Kyle, *Suez*, p. 482.
403   18/11/56, BBC-SWB: DS102.
404   Nasser, *Philosophy of the Revolution*, pp. 59–62, pp. 74–6. The other two circles were the Arab and Islamic worlds.

405   Stephens, *Nasser*, pp. 285–6. See also Yapp, M. E. *The Near East since the First World War* (London: Longman, 1996), pp. 114–15.
406   FYW: Kamal al-Din Hussein Interview.
407   See Hinnebusch, *Egyptian Politics*, pp. 15–16; Ayubi, S. *Nasser and Sadat* (Washington: University Press of America, 1994), pp. 12–14.
408   Said Interview.
409   Dabous, 'Egyptian Press', p. 100, pp. 106–8.
410   Heikal, *Autumn of Fury*, p. 30; *Who's Who in the Arab World, 1967–8, 2nd Edition* (Beirut: Publitec Publications), p. 1029; FRUS: 1964–68: XVIII-232.
411   Ayubi, *Nasser and Sadat*, p. 143.
412   Ayubi, *Nasser and Sadat*, p. 14.
413   Badeau, *Middle East Remembered*, pp. 236–8; Hoda Nasser Interview. See also Korn, D. A. *Stalemate* (Boulder: Westview, 1992), pp. 81–2; Sharaf Interview; Hamrush Interview.
414   Dabous, 'Egyptian Press', p. 110, p. 115.
415   Sadat, *Revolt on the Nile*, pp. 17–18; Sadat, *Identity*, p. 101; Okasha Interview.
416   Abdel Magid Farid Interview.
417   Stephens, *Nasser*, p. 79.
418   Aburish, *Nasser*, p. 91; Hoda Nasser Interview; FYW: Mohammed Fawzi Interview.
419   Hussein Shafei Interview; Yehia Gamal Interview.
420   Okasha Interview.
421   Okasha Interview; Hassan Issa Interview.
422   Fayek Interview; Sadat, *Identity*, p. 79.
423   Makram Mohammed Ahmed Interview; Heikal, *Sphinx and Commissar*, p. 78.
424   Badeau, *Middle East Remembered*, p. 225; Goldschmidt, A. *Biographical Dictionary of Modern Egypt* (Cairo: AUC Press, 2000), p. 23.
425   Farid Interview.
426   Fawzi, *Thiwār yūlīyū*, p. 71. See also Salah al-Din Hadidi Interview; Okasha Interview.
427   Saad al-Din Shazly Interview.
428   Imam, A. *'Abd al-nāṣir: kayf ḥakama miṣr?* (Cairo: Madbouli al-Saghir, 1996), pp. 104–5; Shafei Interview.
429   Podeh, E. *The Decline of Arab Unity* (Brighton: Sussex Academic Press, 1999), pp. 98–9.
430   Mahmoud Interview.
431   For accounts of the crisis, see Imam, *Husayn al-shāfi'i*, p. 121; Nasr, S. *Mudhakkirāt* (Cairo: Dar al-Khiyal, 1999), Vol. 3, p. 24; Baghdadi, *Mudhakkirāt*, Vol. 2, p. 165; Fawzi, Muhammad *Harb al thalāth sanawāt, 1967–1970* (Cairo: Dar al-Mustaqbal al-Arabiyy, 1983), pp. 31–40.
432   Farid Interview.
433   To avoid confusion, for dates subsequent to September 1961, this book generally refers to 'Egypt', although some quoted sources continue to use the country's official name.
434   Shafei Interview.
435   Fayek Interview. See Imam, A. *'Alī ṣabrī yitadhāhir* (Cairo: Tasmim al-Ghalaf al-Funan, 1987), pp. 81–2; Howeidy, A. *Ma' 'abd al-nāṣir* (Cairo: Dar Al-Mustaqbal al-Arabiyy, 1985), p. 139.

436 Farid, A. M. *et al.* 'Nasser: A Reassessment', *Arab Papers*, 8 (1981), p. 4.
437 FYW: Mohammed Fawzi Interview.
438 Farid Interview. See also Ahmed Abdel Halim Interview; Fawzi, *Harb al thalāth sanawāt*, p. 51.
439 Baghdadi, *Mudhakkirāt*, Vol. 2, pp. 189–91.
440 Kerr, M. H. *The Arab Cold War* (Oxford University Press, 1971), p. 39; Stephens, *Nasser*, pp. 379–80.
441 29/12/61, BBC-SWB: ME833.
442 Badeeb, S. M. *The Saudi-Egyptian Conflict over North Yemen* (Boulder: Westview Press, 1986), p. 132.
443 Heikal, *Cairo Documents*, p. 187.
444 1/12/61, BBC-SWB: ME811.
445 23/12/61, BBC-SWB: ME829.
446 28/7/62, BBC-SWB: ME1007.
447 *Al-Ahram*, 4/7/61, BBC-SWB: ME681.
448 NA: CO936/721.
449 22/12/61, BBC-SWB: ME830; FRUS: 1961–63: XVII-193.
450 *Al-Ahram*, 29/6/64, BBC-SWB: ME1591
451 14/11/61, BBC-SWB: ME794.
452 18/8/62, BBC-SWB: ME1024; 5/7/62, BBC-SWB: ME987.
453 For background, see Dresch, P. *A History of Modern Yemen* (Cambridge University Press, 2000), p. 87.
454 27/12/62, BBC-SWB: ME1133.
455 Kerr, M. H. 'Coming to Terms with Nasser', *International Affairs*, 43.1 (1967), p. 75.
456 See Bass, W. *Support Any Friend* (Oxford University Press, 2003), p. 70, p. 96.
457 FRUS: 1964–68: XVII-47, 54.
458 FRUS: 1964–68: XVII-101. Nasser, however, remained sensitive on this topic. 'There is nothing about which we are afraid to speak,' he reiterated, publicly defending these letters. 25/7/61, BBC-SWB: ME699.
459 Burns, *Economic Aid*, p. 134.
460 FRUS: 1964–68: XVII-107, 151.
461 FRUS: 1964–68: XVII-309.
462 FRUS: 1961–63: XVIII-31; Heikal, *Cairo Documents*, p. 200.
463 Dresch, *Modern Yemen*, p. 86.
464 *Al-Gomhouriyya*, 27/12/61, BBC-SWB: ME826.
465 Heikal, *Cairo Documents*, p. 193.
466 27/12/61, BBC-SWB: ME833.
467 Habib, T. *Milaffat thawrat yūlīyū* (Cairo: Al-Ahram, 1997), p. 240. For a similar line, see Imam, *'Abd al-nāṣir*, p. 334; Sharaf, Mahmoud and Fayek Interviews; Heikal, *Cairo Documents*, p. 194.
468 13/10/62, BBC-SWB: ME1074.
469 *Al-Ahram*, 19/10/62, BBC-SWB: ME1079.
470 9/1/63, BBC-SWB: ME1146; *Majmū'āt khuṭab*, Vol. 4, pp. 299–308.
471 Badeau, *Middle East Remembered*, p. 199; Sharaf Interview.
472 Heikal, *Cairo Documents*, p. 36. See Trevelyan, *Public and Private*, p. 78; Dann, U. *King Hussein and the Challenge of Arab Radicalism* (New York: Oxford University Press, 1989), p. 169; Jankowski, *Nasser's Egypt*, p. 73.
473 Trevaskis, K. *Shades of Amber* (London: Hutchinson, 1968), p. 180.

474 Stephens, *Nasser*, pp. 386–8; Halliday, F. *Arabia without Sultans* (London: Saqi Books, 2002), p. 102.
475 O'Ballance, E. *The War in the Yemen.* (London: Faber and Faber, 1971), p. 64; FRUS: 1961–63: XVIII-38.
476 Alaini, Baydani and Said Interviews.
477 BBC-SWB: ME1011, 1014.
478 25/9/62, BBC-SWB: ME1056.
479 For further analysis, see Stookey, R. W. *The Politics of the Yemen Arab Republic* (Boulder: Westview Press, 1978), p. 231; Dresch, *Modern Yemen*, p. 89. The views of contemporary Western observers can be found in FRUS: 1961–63: XVIII-38, 81; Gandy, C. 'A Mission to Yemen', *British Journal of Middle Eastern Studies*, 25.2 (1998), p. 257; NA: FO371/162948.
480 For the Yemeni perspective, see Maqalah, A. A. *'Abd al-nasir wa al-yaman* (Cairo: Markaz al-Hadaara al-Arabiyya, 2000), pp. 101–2; Alaini Interview; Rosser, K. 'Education, Revolt and Reform in Yemen', unpublished M.Phil. thesis, University of Oxford (1998), p. 55. Egyptian sources include Heikal, M. H. *1967 – sanawāt al-ghalayān* (Cairo: Al-Ahram, 1988), pp. 621–2; Nasr, *Mudhakkirāt*, Vol. 2, pp. 331–2; Dib, F. *'Abd al-nāṣir wa ḥarb al-taḥrīr al-yamanī* (Cairo: Dar al-Mustaqbal al-Arabiyy, 1990), p. 84.
481 Abdel Rahman Baydani Interview.
482 FRUS: 1961–63: XVIII-119.
483 Sherif, Hadidi and Said Interviews.
484 Howeidy Interview.
485 Alaini Interview.
486 28/9/62, BBC-SWB: ME1059; Dresch, *Modern Yemen*, p. 89.
487 Alaini Interview; O'Ballance, *War in the Yemen*, p. 75.
488 Badeeb, *Saudi-Egyptian Conflict*, pp. 34–5, p. 118.
489 O'Ballance, *War in the Yemen*, p. 65, p. 84.
490 Badeeb, *Saudi-Egyptian Conflict*, p. 37.
491 BBC-SWB: ME1068.
492 NA: CO1015/2150.
493 Noman, A. and Almadhagi, K. *Yemen and the United States* (London: Tauris, 1996), p. 32; Stookey, *Politics of the Yemen*, p. 231.
494 Nasr, *Mudhakkirāt*, Vol. 2, p. 333; Habib, *Milaffat*, p. 240.
495 BBC-SWB: ME1103.
496 *Voice of the Arabs*, 28/9/62, BBC-SWB: ME1059.
497 BBC-SWB: ME1071.
498 See Howeidy, A. *50 'āman min al-awāṣif* (Cairo: Al-Ahram, 2002), p. 97.
499 Quoted in Vatikiotis, *Nasser and His Generation*, p. 173 fn9.
500 See Rahmy, A. A. R. *The Egyptian Policy in the Arab World* (Washington, DC: University Press of America, 1983), pp. 105–6; Habib, *Milaffat*, p. 241; Baydani Interview; Farid Interview; Heikal, *Sanawāt al-ghalayān*, pp. 627–8.
501 Alaini Interview; Alaini, M. *Fifty Years in Shifting Sands* (An-Nahar Publications, in press), p. 42.
502 Sadat, *Identity*, p. 162.
503 Fawzi, *Thiwār yūlīyū*, p. 57.
504 Imam, *Ḥusayn al-shāfi'i*, p. 89.
505 See Fawzi, *Thiwār yūlīyū*, p. 126; Ahmed Interview; Mahmoud Interview; Nasr, *Mudhakkirāt*, Vol. 2 pp. 332–4; Imam, *'Abd al-nāṣir*, p. 339.

506 Badeeb, *Saudi-Egyptian Conflict*, p. 133.
507 Wahab Interview. See also Fawzi, *Thiwār yūlīyū*, p. 71.
508 Heikal, M. H. *Li-miṣr ila li-'abd al-nāṣir* (Cairo: Al-Ahram, 1987), p. 55. Confirmed by Badeau, *Middle East Remembered*, p. 223; Sadat, *Identity*, p. 162.
509 Alaini, *Fifty Years*, p. 66.
510 Howeidy Interview.
511 *Address by President Gamal Abdel Nasser at the Palestinian National Congress* (Cairo, 1965).
512 Rahmy, *Egyptian Policy*, p. 98; Habib, *Milaffat*, p. 244; Baydani Interview; Sharaf Interview.
513 Howeidy Interview.
514 Badeau, J. S. 'USA and UAR: A Crisis in Confidence', *Foreign Affairs*, 43.2 (1965), p. 287.
515 Rahmy, *Egyptian Policy*, p. 98; Maqalah, *Abd al-nasir*, pp. 38–9; FRUS: 1961–63: XVIII-69.
516 Shafei Interview; Howeidy Interview; Mahmoud Interview.
517 Vatikiotis, *Nasser and His Generation*, p. 311; Dawisha, 'Middle East', p. 217; Fawzi, *Thiwār yūlīyū*, p. 126; Habib, *Milaffat*, p. 241, p. 244.
518 Sharaf Interview; Shazly Interview.
519 Trevaskis, *Shades of Amber*, p. 187.
520 Badeeb, *Saudi-Egyptian Conflict*, p. 133.
521 Heikal, 'Egyptian Foreign Policy', p. 722.
522 27/12/62, BBC-SWB: ME1133.
523 FRUS: 1961–63: XVIII-63; BBC-SWB: ME1062.
524 Mahmoud Interview; Issa Interview.
525 *Al-Ahram*, 28/12/62, BBC-SWB: ME1135.
526 Shazly, Sharaf, Fayek, Wahab, Hadidi and Hamrush Interviews; Sadat, *Identity*, p. 162.
527 Gamal Interview.
528 Noman and Almadhagi, *Yemen and the US*, p. 33, p. 59; 20/8/62, BBC-SWB: ME1027.
529 FRUS: 1961–63: XVIII-353.
530 Sami Sharaf, sometimes called Nasser's 'dirty tricks' operator, admits that he managed such contacts until February 1963. Sharaf Interview.
531 9/1/63, BBC-SWB: ME1146, *Majmū'āt khuṭab*, Vol. 4, pp. 299–308.
532 23/12/62, BBC-SWB: ME1133, *Majmū'āt khuṭab*, Vol. 4, p. 260.
533 O'Ballance, *War in the Yemen*, pp. 84–7. The Yemenis themselves had almost no aircraft. NA: DEFE13/398.
534 NA: CO1015/2150.
535 Trevaskis Papers: MSS Brit Emp s.546 2/6, s.367 6/1.
536 Gandy, 'Mission to Yemen', p. 253.
537 Trevaskis Papers: MSS Brit Emp s.546 2/6; Dorril, *MI6*, p. 679.
538 NA: FO371/162948, 162953.
539 Stookey, *Politics of the Yemen*, p. 231.
540 22/5/63, BBC-SWB: ME1255.
541 27/12/62, BBC-SWB: ME1133. See also FRUS: 1961–63: XVIII-76.
542 Dawisha, 'Middle East', p. 216.
543 Nasser quoted in *The Times*, 5/3/68.

544 Habib, *Milaffat*, p.241; Nasr, *Mudhakkirāt*, Vol. 2, pp. 332–4.
545 Heikal, *Li-miṣr*, p. 55.
546 Rahmy, *Egyptian Policy*, p. 195.
547 Alaini, *Fifty Years*, p. 42; Mohsen Alaini Interview.
548 BBC-SWB: ME1092.
549 Badeeb, *Saudi-Egyptian Conflict*, p. 133. See also Nasr, *Mudhakkirāt*, Vol. 2, pp. 332–4; Habib, *Milaffat*, p. 240.
550 BBC-SWB: ME1068; Dawisha, 'Middle East', p. 216; O'Ballance, *War in the Yemen*, p. 78.
551 Trevaskis Papers: MSS Brit Emp s. 367 5/9.
552 Trevaskis, *Shades of Amber*, p. 169.
553 Jones, *Britain and the Yemen Civil War*, p. 24, pp. 33–4.
554 Heikal, *Cairo Documents*, p. 194. See also Dib, '*Abd al-nāṣir*, p. 78.
555 FRUS: 1961–63: XVIII-63.
556 Mahmoud Interview; Issa Interview; 29/9/62, *Akhbar al-Yawm*, BBC-SWB: ME1061.
557 5/10/62, BBC-SWB: ME1067; 30/11/62, BBC-SWB: ME1115.
558 Shafei Interview.
559 *Al-Ahram*, 28/12/62, BBC-SWB: ME1135.
560 7/2/63, FRUS: 1961–63: XVIII-151.
561 3/12/63, FRUS: 1961–63: XVIII-376.
562 Heikal, *Autumn of Fury*, p. 32.
563 23/12/62, BBC-SWB: ME1133; Dawisha, A.I. 'Intervention in the Yemen', *Middle East Journal*, 29.1 (1975), pp. 50–1.
564 21/5/63, BBC-SWB: ME1254.
565 FRUS: 1961–63: XVIII-353, 394; O'Ballance, *War in the Yemen*, p. 108.
566 Badeau, *Middle East Remembered*, p. 215.
567 18/12/62, BBC-SWB: ME1130; NA: PREM11/3878.
568 18/12/62, BBC-SWB: ME1130.
569 2/1/63, BBC-SWB: ME1140.
570 Alaini Interview.
571 Mahmoud Interview.
572 FRUS: 1961–63: XVIII-126.
573 See FRUS: 1964–68: XVIII-141, 176, 186.
574 The temple of Dendur is now in the Metropolitan Museum of Art, New York. FRUS: 1961–63: XVIII-328; Bass, *Support Any Friend*, p. 64.
575 BBC-SWB: ME1298.
576 BBC-SWB: ME1414.
577 Shafei Interview.
578 Baydani Interview.
579 Mourad Ghalib Interview.
580 FRUS: 1964–68: XVIII-96.
581 Assessment based on Mahmoud, Farid, Issa, Gamal and Fayek Interviews; Dawisha, 'Middle East', p. 207, p. 222; Rahmy, *Egyptian Policy*, pp. 203–7.
582 FRUS: 1961–63: XVIII-77 fn2.
583 Gandy, 'Mission to Yemen', pp. 267–8.
584 For details, see Jones, *Britain and the Yemen Civil War*, pp. 30–2, pp. 53–5; Dresch, *Modern Yemen*, p. 91.
585 NA: PREM11/3878.

586 NA: CAB128/36-7; Macmillan Diary, 22/10/62, MSS in Bodleian Library, Oxford.
587 Gandy, 'Mission to Yemen', pp. 267–8.
588 NA: CAB129/112; Macmillan Diary, 17/2/63.
589 NA: FO371/168786.
590 Bower, *Perfect English Spy*, p. 244, pp. 247–8.
591 NA: CO1015/2150; DEFE13/398, PREM11/3878, PREM11/4357.
592 See Fielding, *One Man in His Time*, pp. 131–5; Jones, *Britain and the Yemen Civil War*, pp. 38–9, p. 50.
593 Trevaskis Papers: MSS Brit Emp s. 367 5/9.
594 'The new Governor was a little shocked at the way we deal with things, which was not quite in accord with his Foreign Office training,' Trevaskis had written in 1961. 'Nevertheless, we are rapidly educating him and I have no doubt that by the time he leaves he will be one of us.' Trevaskis Papers: MSS Brit Emp s. 546 2/6.
595 Trevaskis Papers: MSS Brit Emp s. 367 6/1.
596 Fielding, *One Man in His Time*, p. 140; Balfour-Paul, G. *The End of Empire in the Middle East* (Cambridge University Press, 1991), p. 80.
597 NA: FO371/162953.
598 NA: FO371/162948.
599 Jones, *Britain and the Yemen Civil War*, p. 77.
600 9/1/63, BBC-SWB: ME1146; *Majmū'āt khuṭab*, Vol. 4, pp. 299–308.
601 NA: PREM11/4173.
602 Ashton, N. J. *Kennedy, Macmillan and the Cold War* (London: Palgrave Macmillan, 2002), p. 103.
603 9/8/63, BBC-SWB: ME1321; *Majmū'āt khuṭab*, Vol. 4, p. 489.
604 Issa Interview; NA: PREM11/3878.
605 Ashton, N. J. 'A "Special Relationship" Sometimes in Spite of Ourselves', *Journal of Imperial and Commonwealth History*, 33.2 (2005), p. 230; Stephens, *Nasser*, p. 392.
606 19/12/62, BBC-SWB: ME1131.
607 FRUS: 1961–63: XVIII-68.
608 9/1/63, BBC-SWB: ME1146; *Majmū'āt khuṭab*, Vol. 4, pp. 299–308.
609 Heikal, *Sanawāt al-ghalayān*, p. 651, pp. 926–27.
610 FRUS: 1961–63: XVIII-294, 305.
611 6/11/62, BBC-SWB: ME1092. See also his speech of 22/5/63, BBC-SWB: ME1255.
612 Figures synthesised from FRUS: 1964–68: XVIII-105; Dresch, *Modern Yemen*, p. 102; Stookey, *Politics of the Yemen*, p. 238; Witty, D. M. 'A Regular Army in Counter-Insurgency Operations', *Journal of Military History*, 65.2 (2001), p. 424.
613 Habib, *Milaffat*, p. 243; Farid Interview; Naguib Interview.
614 Generals Murtagi and Shazly in Habib, *Milaffat*, p. 241; Heikal, *Sphinx and Commissar*, p. 148.
615 NA:PREM11/3878; O'Ballance, *War in the Yemen*, p. 91.
616 Habib, *Milaffat*, pp. 241–3.
617 Quoted in Gamasy, M. A. G. *The October War* (Cairo: AUC Press, 1993), p. 18.
618 See De La Billière, P. *Looking for Trouble* (London: HarperCollins, 1994), pp. 203–5; Mawby, 'Clandestine Defence', pp. 122–4; Jones, *Britain and the*

Yemen Civil War, pp. 134–9; Bower, *Perfect English Spy*, pp. 247–52; Dorril, *MI6*, pp. 684–6.

619   Smiley, D. *Arabian Assignment* (London: Leo Cooper, 1975), p. 154.

620   NA: FO371/178594.

621   NA: FO371/174627.

622   26/4/64, BBC-SWB: ME1540; *Majmū'āt khuṭab*, Vol. 4, pp. 561–7; 27/4/64, BBC-SWB: ME1538; 28/4/64, BBC-SWB: ME1539.

623   Rahmy, *Egyptian Policy*, p. 125; FRUS: 1964–68: XVIII-35.

624   Ahmed Interview; Sherif Interview.

625   Badeeb, *Saudi-Egyptian Conflict*, p. 133.

626   Jones, C. 'Among Ministers, Mavericks and Mandarins', *Middle Eastern Studies*, 40.1 (2004) pp. 106–112, p. 121.

627   1/5/64, BBC-SWB: ME1544; FRUS: 1964–68: XXI-336.

628   De La Billière, *Looking for Trouble*, p. 205, p. 223.

629   NA: DEFE13/570.

630   NA: FO371/178594.

631   22/7/64, BBC-SWB: ME1613.

632   15/9/64, BBC-SWB: ME1657.

633   Nasr, *Mudhakkirāt*, Vol. 3, p. 61.

634   23/12/64, BBC-SWB: ME1743; *Majmū'āt khuṭab*, Vol. 5, p. 108.

635   Badeau, *Middle East Remembered*, p. 229.

636   FRUS: 1964–68: XVIII-208; XXI-367.

637   Shazly Interview.

638   Ahmed Interview; FRUS: 1961–63: XVIII-141.

639   Badeeb, *Saudi-Egyptian Conflict*, pp. 133–4.

640   4/2/65, BBC-SWB: ME1776.

641   FRUS: 1964–68: XXI-367.

642   Stookey, *Politics of the Yemen*, p. 232; Noman and Almadhagi, *Yemen and the US*, p. 40.

643   FRUS: 1964–68: XVIII-329.

644   Alaini Interview; Alaini, *Fifty Years*, pp. 60–6. For an Egyptian account, see Nasr, *Mudhakkirāt*, Vol. 3 pp. 79–86.

645   FRUS: 1964–68: XVIII-253.

646   *Al-Ahram*, 6/5/66, BBC-SWB: ME2156.

647   18/8/65, BBC-SWB: ME1939.

648   Mahmoud Interview.

649   FRUS: 1964–68: XXI-382; Stephens, *Nasser*, p. 419.

650   Badeeb, *Saudi-Egyptian Conflict*, p. 83.

651   Alaini Interview. See Dresch, *Modern Yemen*, p. 105.

652   FRUS: 1964–68: XXI-258. A conciliatory attitude to Saudi Arabia was of course a key Egyptian bargaining tool in US food aid negotiations.

653   FRUS: 1964–68: XXI-382.

654   FRUS: 1964–68: XVIII-253.

655   Sadat, *Identity*, p. 161; Stephens, *Nasser*, pp. 416–17; Rahmy, *Egyptian Policy*, pp. 203–7; Shazly, Hadidi and Mosallem Interviews.

656   FRUS: 1964–68: XXI-395, 398.

657   Heikal, *Li-miṣr*, p. 55.

658   Ahmed Interview.

659   *Majmū'āt khuṭab*, Vol. 5, p. 537. See Rahmy, *Egyptian Policy*, pp. 154–6.

660 23/12/66, BBC-SWB: ME2351.
661 25/9/66, BBC-SWB: ME2275.
662 FRUS: 1964–68: XVIII-290.
663 Alaini, *Fifty Years*, p. 72; Alaini Interview; Baydani Interview.
664 O'Ballance, *War in the Yemen*, p. 159, p. 164.
665 FRUS: 1964–68: XVIII-378.
666 Farid Interview; Kerr, *Arab Cold War*, pp. 110–11.
667 Hassan Sabri Al-Kholi, FRUS: 1964–68: XXI-386.
668 FRUS: 1964–68: XXI-391.
669 29/4/66, BBC-SWB: ME2150. See also Dawisha, 'Intervention', pp. 57–8.
670 22/3/66, BBC-SWB: ME2120.
671 FRUS: 1964–68: XXI-398.
672 BBC-SWB:ME2152, *Majmū'āt khuṭab*, Vol. 5, pp. 554–5; 24/11/66, BBC-SWB: ME2327.
673 FRUS: 1964–68: XVIII-386.
674 23/12/66, BBC-SWB: ME2351.
675 Badeeb, *Saudi-Egyptian Conflict*, p. 39; O'Ballance, *War in the Yemen*, pp. 172–3.
676 FRUS: 1964–68: XVIII-386.
677 Kerr, *Arab Cold War*, p. 113; Rahmy, *Egyptian Policy*, p. 172.
678 24/11/66, BBC-SWB: ME2327.
679 NA: PREM13/704.
680 22/2/66, BBC-SWB: ME2097.
681 FRUS: 1964–68: XXI-395.
682 NA: PREM13/704.
683 Alaini Interview.
684 22/2/67, BBC-SWB: ME2401; *Wathā'iq*, Vol. 1, p. 71.
685 FRUS: 1964–68: XXI-408.
686 Rahmy, *Egyptian Policy*, pp. 154–6; Mahgoub Interview.
687 O'Ballance, *War in the Yemen*, pp. 155–7.
688 FRUS: 1964–68: XXI-395.
689 See Dresch, *Modern Yemen*, p. 107.
690 Trevelyan, *Public and Private*, p. 62.
691 See Nasr, *Mudhakkirāt*, Vol. 3, p. 61.
692 22/2/67, BBC-SWB: ME2401; *Wathā'iq 'abd al-nāṣir* (Cairo: ACPSS), Vol. 1, p. 71.
693 22/2/67, BBC-SWB: ME2401.
694 22/7/66, BBC-SWB: ME2221, *Wathā'iq*, Vol. 1, p. 71.
695 15/5/67, BBC-SWB: ME2467.
696 Parker, R. B. *The Politics of Miscalculation in the Middle East* (Bloomington: Indiana University Press, 1993), p. 104; Gerges, F. A. *The Superpowers and the Middle East* (Boulder: Westview Press, 1994), pp. 175–6.
697 Burns, *Economic Aid*, pp. 154–5.
698 FRUS: 1964–68: XVIII-117.
699 Korn, *Stalemate*, p. 21; Burns, *Economic Aid*, pp. 155–9.
700 Badeau, *Middle East Remembered*, p. 195.
701 Parker, *Politics of Miscalculation*, p. 105; Burns, *Economic Aid*, p. 159.
702 23/12/64, BBC-SWB: ME1743.
703 FRUS: 1964–68: XVIII-117.

704   FRUS: 1964–68: XVIII-194.
705   FRUS: 1964–68: XVIII-253.
706   Burns, *Economic Aid*, p. 126.
707   Badeau 'USA and UAR', pp. 284–5.
708   FRUS: 1964–68: XVIII-234.
709   Burns, *Economic Aid*, p. 134, p. 145.
710   Dekmejian, *Egypt under Nasir*, p. 235.
711   FRUS: 1964–68: XVIII-302.
712   Farid Interview.
713   FRUS: 1964–68: XVIII-321.
714   FRUS: 1964–68: XVIII-393.
715   FRUS: 1964–68: XVIII-392.
716   Heikal, *Cairo Documents*, p. 187.
717   Korn, *Stalemate*, p. 22.
718   FRUS: 1964–68: XVIII-229.
719   See interviews with Kim Roosevelt and Donald Bergus, quoted in Burns, *Economic Aid*, p. 139; interview with former CIA officer James Critchfield, quoted in Aburish, *Nasser*, p. 209.
720   Bower, *Perfect English Spy*, p. 229.
721   Badeau, *Middle East Remembered*, p. 179, p. 191. My italics.
722   Burns, *Economic Aid*, p. 168.
723   Dekmejian, *Egypt under Nasir*, p. 235; Kepel, G. *Muslim Extremism in Egypt* (Berkeley: University of California Press, 2003), p. 33. This incident ultimately led to the hanging of the radical Islamist ideologue Sayyid Qutb in 1966.
724   FRUS: 1964–68: XVIII-396.
725   FRUS: 1964–68: XVIII-232, 371.
726   FRUS: 1964–68: XVIII-341. On Birdsall, see Korn, *Stalemate*, p. 22; Howeidy Interview; Sharaf Interview.
727   Heikal, *Cairo Documents*, p. 199; Heikal, *Sphinx and Commissar*, p. 150, p. 154; Heikal, *Autumn of Fury*, p. 32; Imam, *'Abd al-nāṣir*, p. 336.
728   22/2/67, BBC-SWB: ME2401.
729   FRUS: 1964–68: XXI-440.
730   FRUS: 1964–68: XXI-439.
731   FRUS: 1964–68: XVIII-417.
732   Halim, A. 'Al-*kh*ibra al-'arabiyya fī al-harb, *Al-Siyasa Al-Dawliyya*, 34 (1998), p. 104.
733   See Dresch, *Modern Yemen*, p. 105 fn41; Bower, *Perfect English Spy*, p. 251.
734   Noman and Almadhagi, *Yemen and the US*, pp. 80–1; FRUS: 1964–68: XXI-441.
735   FRUS: 1964–68: XVIII-417.
736   25/2/67, BBC-SWB: ME2403. See also Vatikiotis, *Nasser and His Generation*, p. 238.
737   FRUS: 1964–68: XVIII-394.
738   BBC-SWB: ME1709, *Majmū'āt khuṭab*, Vol. 5, p. 65.
739   FRUS: 1961–63: XVIII-270; Noman and Almadhagi, *Yemen and the US*, pp. 57–8; Little, D. 'The New Frontier on the Nile', *The Journal of American History*, 75.2 (1988), p. 521.
740   FRUS: 1964–68: XXI-378, 383.

741 Badeau, *Middle East Remembered*, p. 223.
742 FRUS: 1964–68: XVIII-232.
743 FRUS: 1964–68: XVIII-306; Habib, *Milaffat*, p. 241.
744 Hadidi Interview.
745 Hamrush Interview; Stookey, R. W. *America and the Arab States* (New York: Wiley, 1975), p. 183.
746 26/5/66, BBC-SWB: ME2172.
747 FRUS: 1964–68: XVIII-296.
748 24/11/66, BBC-SWB: ME2327.
749 BBC-SWB: ME2152.
750 1/5/67, *Wathā'iq*, Vol. 1, p. 163; BBC-SWB: ME2456; 22/2/67, *Wathā'iq*, Vol. 1, p. 72; BBC-SWB: ME2401. The final Arabic phrase, *'fājir 'āhir'*, is highly offensive, and even Nasser seems to have thought better of using it. 'As the English call him', he added hastily.
751 22/2/67, *Wathā'iq*, Vol. 1, pp. 68–71; BBC-SWB: ME2401; 15/5/67, BBC-SWB: ME2467.
752 4/2/67, BBC-SWB: ME2385.
753 15/5/67, BBC-SWB: ME2467.
754 1/5/67, *Wathā'iq*, Vol. 1, p. 163; BBC-SWB: ME2456.
755 Dekmejian, *Egypt under Nasir*, p. 238.
756 Parker, R. B. *The Six-Day War* (Gainesville: University Press of Florida, 1996), p. 219.
757 Sharaf Interview.
758 Parker, *Politics of Miscalculation*, p. 106.
759 24/2/67, BBC-SWB: ME2402; Heikal, M. H. *Naḥnu wa amrīka* (Cairo: Dar al-Asr al-Hadith, 1968), pp. 7–17.
760 22/5/67, BBC-SWB: ME2473.
761 28/5/67, *Wathā'iq*, Vol. 1, p. 205; *International Documents on Palestine, 1967* (Beirut: Institute for Palestine Studies, 1970) [IDP], p. 563.
762 Versions of this conversation are reproduced in Nasr, *Mudhakkirāt*, Vol. 3, p. 221; Sadat, *Identity*, p. 173; Riad, *Struggle for Peace*, p. 23.
763 Howard, M. and Hunter, R. 'Israel and the Arab World: The Crisis of 1967', *Adelphi Papers* 41 (1967), pp. 11–13.
764 22/2/67, *Wathā'iq*, Vol. 1, p. 67, BBC-SWB: ME2401.
765 26/5/66, *Wathā'iq*, Vol. 1, p. 181; BBC-SWB: ME2477.
766 4/2/67, BBC-SWB: ME2385. See also Mahmoud Interview.
767 3/6/66, BBC-SWB: ME2179.
768 Burdett, W. *Encounter with the Middle East* (New York: Atheneum, 1969), p. 240.
769 24/5/66, BBC-SWB: ME2171.
770 Sadat, *Identity*, p. 172. See also Farid Interview. His ally Badran denies Amer ever made such a statement. Habib, *Milaffat*, p. 320.
771 Riad, *Struggle for Peace*, p. 23.
772 Frankel, 'Interviews', p. 101.
773 NA: PREM13/1826.
774 18/5/67, BBC-SWB: ME2470.
775 For an opposing view, see Hadidi, S. D. *Shāhid 'ala ḥarb 1967* (Cairo: Dar al-Shorouk), pp. 13–89; Fawzi, *Harb al thalāth sanawāt*, p. 53; Hadidi Interview.

776 FRUS: 1964–68: XIX-44, 76. See Bergus, D. C. 'The View from Washington', *In* Parker (ed.), *Six-Day War*, p. 217.
777 Ahmad Samih Khalidi, quoted in Draper, T. *Israel and World Politics* (New York: Viking Press, 1968), pp. 71–2.
778 4/11/66, BBC-SWB: ME2310.
779 Frankel, 'Interviews', p. 101; Farid Interview.
780 Rikhye, I. J. *The Sinai Blunder* (London: Frank Cass, 1980), p. 71.
781 Ashraf Ghorbal, quoted in Frankel, 'Interviews', p. 94.
782 Sadat, *Identity*, p. 174.
783 FYW: Salah Bassiouny Interview.
784 Parker, *Politics of Miscalculation*, p. 79. Ambassador Hassan Issa agrees. Issa Interview.
785 Copeland, *Game of Nations*, p. 238.
786 24/11/66, BBC-SWB: ME2327.
787 Heikal, M. H. *1967 – al-infijār* (Cairo: Al-Ahram, 1990), p. 208.
788 26/3/67, *Al-Hawadis*.
789 15/5/67, BBC-SWB: ME2467.
790 22/5/67, *Wathā'iq*, Vol. 1, p. 175; BBC-SWB: ME2473.
791 Fawzi, *Harb al thalāth sanawāt*, p. 27.
792 Gawrych, G. W. *The Albatross of Decisive Victory* (Westport: Greenwood Press, 2000), p. 82.
793 Frankel, 'Interviews', p. 93.
794 Parker, *Politics of Miscalculation*, p. 40.
795 FRUS: 1964–68: XVIII-404.
796 Parker, *Politics of Miscalculation*, p. 90.
797 Naguib Interview.
798 22/5/67, BBC-SWB: ME2473, *Wathā'iq*, Vol. 1, p. 173; 26/5/67, *Wathā'iq*, Vol. 1, p. 180, BBC-SWB: ME2477.
799 See also Brown, L. C. 'Nasser and the June War: Plan or Improvisation?' *In* Seikaly, S., Baalbaki, R. and Dodd, P. (eds) *Quest for Understanding* (Beirut: AUB Press, 1991).
800 FYW: Mohammed Fawzi Interview.
801 FRUS: 1964–68: XIX-5.
802 Parker, *Politics of Miscalculation*, pp. 5–6; Andrew, C. and Gordievsky, O. *KGB* (London: Sceptre, 1990), p. 501.
803 Parker, *Politics of Miscalculation*, p. 62.
804 Hadidi Interview.
805 See Sadat, *Identity*, p. 172; Fayek Interview; FYW: Mohammed Fawzi and Shams Badran Interviews.
806 Oren, *Six Days*, pp. 58–9.
807 23/7/67, BBC-SWB: ME2525.
808 Gamasy, *October War*, pp. 21–2.
809 FYW: Mohammed Fawzi Interview.
810 See Brams, S. J. 'To Mobilize or not to Mobilize', *International Studies Quarterly*, 43.4 (1999), p. 633; Oren, *Six Days*, p. 14; Bar-Joseph, U. 'Rotem: The Forgotten Crisis', *Journal of Contemporary History*, 31.3 (1996), p. 547, p. 563.
811 FRUS: 1964–68: XIX-5.
812 Fawzi, *Harb al thalāth sanawāt*, pp. 71–2; FYW: Mohammed Fawzi Interview.

813 Oren, *Six Days*, pp. 62–3.
814 Parker, *Politics of Miscalculation*, p. 228.
815 FYW: Shams Badran Interview.
816 Hadidi Interview.
817 Quoted in Brown, L. C. 'Origins of the Crisis', *In* Parker (ed.), *Six-Day War*, pp. 41–2.
818 13/5/67, IDP p. 7.
819 See 13/5/67, *The New York Times*.
820 Fayek Interview.
821 21/5/67, FRUS: 1964–68: XIX-28.
822 FYW: Salah Bassiouny Interview.
823 Safran, N. *From War to War* (New York: Pegasus, 1969), pp. 277–8; Heikal, *Sphinx and Commissar*, p. 170, p. 181.
824 Rikhye, *Sinai Blunder*, p. 16.
825 FYW: Mohammed Fawzi Interview; Riad, *Struggle for Peace*, p. 18.
826 Rikhye, *Sinai Blunder*, p. 21.
827 Parker, *Politics of Miscalculation*, p. 47.
828 FYW: Mohammed Fawzi Interview; Oren, *Six Days*, p. 67.
829 Heikal, *Li-misr*, p. 117.
830 Fawzi, *Harb al thalāth sanawāt*, p. 69.
831 Rikhye, *Sinai Blunder*, p. 51.
832 Fawzi, *Harb al thalāth sanawāt*, p. 73; FYW: Mohammed Fawzi Interview.
833 FYW: General Noufal Interview. For General Murtagi's contrasting account, see Parker, *Politics of Miscalculation*, p. 74.
834 Rikhye, *Sinai Blunder*, p. 19, p. 37. See also IDP, pp. 211–15, U Thant's *Report on the Withdrawal of UNEF*, 26/6/67.
835 FYW: General Noufal Interview; Gamasy, *October War*, pp. 38–9.
836 Howard and Hunter, 'Israel and the Arab World', p. 17.
837 FYW: General Fawzi Interview.
838 Rikhye, *Sinai Blunder*, p. 49.
839 FYW: Shams Badran Interview.
840 26/5/67, *Wathā'iq*, Vol. 1, p. 180; BBC-SWB: ME2477.
841 FRUS: 1964–68: XIX-54. See Bergus, 'View from Washington', p. 219.
842 Sadat, *Identity*, p. 172.
843 Heikal, *Li-misr*, pp. 117–18.
844 22/5/67, *Wathā'iq*, Vol. 1, p. 175; BBC-SWB: ME2473.
845 Bowen, *Six Days*, p. 51.
846 Gamal Interview.
847 FYW: Ahmed Fakhr Interview; Sharaf Interview.
848 BBC-SWB: ME2482.
849 Quoted in Parker, *Politics of Miscalculation*, p. 47.
850 Rikhye, *Sinai Blunder*, p. 72; Parker, *Politics of Miscalculation*, p. 228.
851 Sadat, *Identity*, p. 172; Burdett, *Encounter*, p. 239; 23/7/67, BBC-SWB: ME2525.
852 FYW: Shams Badran Interview.
853 BBC-SWB: ME2471.
854 Laqueur, W. *The Road to War* (London: Weidenfeld and Nicolson, 1968), pp. 90–1.
855 Parker, *Politics of Miscalculation*, p. 228.
856 Parker, *Politics of Miscalculation*, p. 75.

857   Hadidi Interview.
858   Fawzi, *Thiwār yūlīyū*, pp. 177–8; Safran, *War to War*, p. 288.
859   Fawzi, *Harb al thalāth sanawāt*, pp. 79–80.
860   BBC-SWB: ME2473. See also Mor, B. D. 'Nasser's Decision-Making in the 1967 Middle East Crisis', *Journal of Peace Research*, 28.4 (1991), p. 371.
861   Gamal Interview.
862   21/5/67, FRUS: 1964–68: XIX-28.
863   Farid, Naguib and Wahab Interviews.
864   25/5/67, FRUS: 1964–68: XIX-61.
865   Sadat, *Identity*, p. 172.
866   Gamasy, *October War*, p. 76.
867   Transcript, Robert S. McNamara Oral History, Special Interview I, 3/26/93, by Robert Dallek, Internet Copy, LBJ Library.
868   FRUS: 1964–68: XIX-77. See also Quandt, W. B. *Decade of Decisions* (Berkeley: University of California Press, 1977), p. 49.
869   Dawn, E. 'The Egyptian Remilitarisation of Sinai', *Journal of Contemporary History*, 3.3 (1968), p. 201.
870   Hadidi Interview; FYW: Mohamed Abdel Ghani Gamasy Interview.
871   Bowen, *Six Days*, p. 57.
872   FRUS: 1964–68: XIX-28.
873   Gamasy, *October War*, p. 23.
874   Hadidi Interview; Gamasy, *October War*, p. 41.
875   Burdett, *Encounter*, p. 241.
876   Fawzi, *Harb al thalāth sanawāt*, p. 111.
877   Fawzi, *Harb al thalāth sanawāt*, pp. 99–104.
878   Fawzi, *Harb al thalāth sanawāt*, p. 109; Oren, *Six Days*, p. 92.
879   Shazly Interview.
880   Said Interview; 2/8/03, *Al-Bayan* (UAE) p. 20.
881   Fawzi, *Harb al thalāth sanawāt*, p. 113.
882   Gamasy, *October War*, p. 42. Confirmed by Sharaf and Fayek Interviews.
883   Said and Shazly Interviews.
884   FYW: Ahmed Fakhr Interview.
885   FYW: Shams Badran Interview.
886   Auda, 'State of Political Control', p. 108; Dekmejian, *Egypt under Nasir*, p. 239.
887   Sadat, *Identity*, p. 161, p. 169. See also Fayek Interview.
888   Shafei Interview.
889   Hadidi Interview; Fawzi, *Thiwār yūlīyū*, p. 177.
890   FYW: Mohammed Fawzi Interview; Fawzi, *Harb al thalāth sanawāt*, pp. 113–14.
891   Quoted in Brown, 'Origins of the Crisis', pp. 44–5. See FYW: Salah Bassiouny Interview.
892   Farid Interview; Stephens, *Nasser*, p. 484.
893   Oren, *Six Days*, p. 120.
894   Fayek Interview.
895   Sharaf Interview; Habib, *Milaffat*, pp. 338–9.
896   Salah Nasr suggests that Sharaf actually destroyed the tape of this meeting at Nasser's behest. Nasr, *Mudhakkirāt*, Vol. 3, p. 227.
897   FYW: Shams Badran Interview. See also Farid Interview.
898   FRUS: 1964–68: XIX-78.
899   NA: FCO17/489.

900 Naguib Interview.
901 FYW: General Noufal Interview.
902 *Wathā'iq*, Vol. 1, p. 175; BBC-SWB: ME2473.
903 28/5/67, *Wathā'iq*, Vol. 1, p. 192; IDP p. 553.
904 *Wathā'iq*, Vol. 1, p. 224; IDP p. 579.
905 22/5/67, BBC-SWB: ME2473.
906 26/5/67, *Wathā'iq*, Vol. 1, p. 182; BBC-SWB: ME2477.
907 Hussein of Jordan, *My 'War' with Israel* (London: Peter Owen, 1969), pp. 43–6; Oren, *Six Days*, p. 132.
908 IDP pp. 578–9.
909 Quoted in Churchill, R. S. and W. S. *The Six Day War* (London: Heinemann, 1967), p. 60.
910 2/6/67, *Al-Ahram*, BBC-SWB: ME2482.
911 Heikal, *Li-miṣr*, p. 118; Stephens, *Nasser*, p. 481.
912 *Wathā'iq*, Vol. 1, p. 203.
913 Hussein, *My 'War'*, p. 49; FYW: King Hussein Interview.
914 23/7/67, BBC-SWB: ME2525; Sadat, *Identity*, p. 174; FYW: Mohammed Fawzi Interview.
915 Sharaf Interview.
916 Mahmoud Interview.
917 Fayek, Ghalib and Farid Interviews; Elwi-Saif, M. 'Nasser's Perception of 1967 Crisis', paper presented at a conference on *The United States, the Middle East and the 1967 Arab-Israeli War* (US State Department, January 12–13, 2004), p. 23.
918 Even more oddly, the Iraqi Prime Minister was airborne at the same time, escorted by Vice President Hussein Shafei on a trip Nasser himself apparently approved. See Fawzi, *Thiwār yūlīyū*, p. 29, p. 187; Fayek Interview; Imam, *Ḥusayn al-shāfi'i*, p. 115.
919 FYW: General Noufal, Shams Badran and Mohammed Fawzi Interview.
920 Fawzi, *Thiwār yūlīyū*, p. 174; Elwi-Saif, 'Nasser's Perception', p. 22.
921 Elwi-Saif, 'Nasser's Perception', pp. 22–3; Sharaf Interview.
922 Oren, *Six Days*, p. 159.
923 Heikal, *Li-miṣr*, p. 118.
924 Fayek, Halim and Hoda Nasser Interviews; Aburish, *Nasser*, p. 259.
925 Ghalib Interview. For minutes of the Badran-Kosygin meetings, see Howeidy, *50 'āman*, pp. 407–35.
926 FYW: Shams Badran and Mohammed Fawzi Interviews; Ghalib Interview.
927 Nasr, *Mudhakkirāt*, Vol. 3, pp. 219–20; Imam, *'Abd al-nāṣir*, p. 362; FYW: Salah Bassiouny Interview; Brown, 'Origins of the Crisis', p. 44.
928 Wahab Interview.
929 *Wathā'iq*, Vol. 1, p. 195; IDP p. 555.
930 FRUS: 1964–68: XIX-107 fn2.
931 Safran, *War to War*, pp. 296–7.
932 FRUS: 1964–68: XIX-107 fn2.
933 Heikal, *Cairo Documents*, p. 221.
934 Korn, *Stalemate*, pp. 17–18.
935 Riad, *Struggle for Peace*, p. 20; FYW: Mohammed Fawzi Interview.
936 Riad, *Struggle for Peace*, p. 21.
937 See Cockburn, A. and L. *Dangerous Liaison* (London: Bodley Head, 1992), p. 147.

206   *Notes*

938   Shlaim, *Iron Wall*, p. 241.
939   Robert S. McNamara Oral History, Special Interview I, 3/26/93, by Robert Dallek, Internet Copy, LBJ Library.
940   See Korn, *Stalemate*, pp. 17–18; McNamara, R. 'Britain, Nasser and the Outbreak of the Six Day War', *Journal of Contemporary History*, 35.4 (2000), pp. 634–8; Gat, M. 'Let Someone Else do the Job', *Diplomacy & Statecraft*, 14.1 (2003); Quandt, W. B. 'Lyndon Johnson and the June 1967 War', *Middle East Journal*, 46.2 (1992) p. 199.
941   Parker, *Politics of Miscalculation*, p. 121.
942   Brecher and Geist, *Decisions in Crisis*, p. 149, p. 346.
943   Wahab Interview.
944   Riad, *Struggle for Peace*, p. 22.
945   Mutawi, S. A. *Jordan in the 1967 War* (Cambridge University Press, 1987), p. 109.
946   FYW: King Hussein Interview.
947   Parker, *Politics of Miscalculation*, pp. 235–8, p. 242; NA: FCO39/250.
948   FRUS: 1964–68: XIX-129.
949   25/3/68, Farid, A. M. *Nasser: The Final Years* (Reading: Ithaca, 1994), p. 127.
950   Nutting, *Nasser*, p. 430.
951   FRUS: 1964–68: XIX-500.
952   Wahab Interview.
953   Quoted in Bowen, *Six Days*, p. 290.
954   Heikal, *Sphinx and Commissar*, p. 190.
955   Hershberg, J. G. 'The Soviet Bloc and the Aftermath of the June 1967 War: Selected Documents from East-Central European Archives', papers distributed at a conference on *The United States, the Middle East and the 1967 Arab-Israeli War* (US State Department, January 12–13, 2004), p. 41.
956   FYW: King Hussein Interview; Heikal, *Cairo Documents*, p. 39; Farid, *Final Years*, p. 1.
957   Mar'i, *Awrāq*, Vol. 2 p. 520, translated by Meital, Y. *Egypt's Struggle for Peace* (Gainesville: University Press of Florida, 1997), p. 13.
958   See FYW: Shams Badran and Mohammed Fawzi Interviews; Springborg, R. *Family, Power and Politics in Egypt* (Philadelphia: University of Pennsylvania Press, 1982), p. 175; Dawud Interview.
959   Quoted in Bowen, *Six Days*, p. 291.
960   Wahab Interview.
961   Dekmejian, *Egypt under Nasir*, p. 218.
962   Shazly Interview.
963   Okasha Interview.
964   Trevelyan, *Public and Private*, p. 82.
965   Farid Interview.
966   O'Ballance, E. *The Electronic War in the Middle East, 1968–70* (London: Faber and Faber, 1974), p. 19, p. 24.
967   Ayubi, *Nasser and Sadat*, p. 15; Shafei Interview; Imam, *Husayn al-shāfi'i*, p. 119.
968   Kishtainy, K. *Arab Political Humour* (London: Quartet Books, 1985), p. 157.
969   See Korn, *Stalemate*, p. 79; Heikal, M. H. *The Road to Ramadan* (London: Collins, 1975), p. 41.
970   Farid *et al.*, 'Nasser', p. 5.

971 9/5/67, BBC-SWB: ME2488; *Wathā'iq*, Vol. 1, p. 232.

972 23/7/68, BBC-SWB: ME2830.

973 Farid, *Final Years*, p. 2.

974 Mar'i, *Awrāq*, Vol. 3, p. 570; Heikal, *Autumn of Fury*, p. 114.

975 Dekmejian, *Egypt under Nasir*, p. 279; McLaurin *et al.*, *Foreign Policy Making*, p. 51; Fayek Interview.

976 Heikal, *Autumn of Fury*, p. 33; Springborg, *Family, Power and Politics*, pp. 181–3.

977 FRUS: 1964–68: XX-167, 327; Springborg, *Family, Power and Politics*, pp. 179–81.

978 Dabous, 'Egyptian Press', p. 100.

979 FRUS: 1964–68: XX-167.

980 FRUS: 1964–68: XIX-299.

981 Figures from Barnett, M. N. and Levy, J. S. 'Domestic Sources of Alliances and Alignments', *International Organization*, 45.3 (1991), pp. 382–3; Dessouki, A. E. H. and Labban, A. 'Arms Race, Defense Expenditures and Development', *Journal of South Asian and Middle Eastern Studies*, 4.3 (1981), p. 77; Farid, *Final Years*, p. 55; Heikal, *Cairo Documents*, p. 46.

982 Kerr, *Arab Cold War*, p. v.

983 Frankel, 'Interviews', p. 97.

984 Hoda Nasser Interview.

985 Mutawi, *Jordan*, p. 176; FRUS: 1964–68: XX-344.

986 Farid, *Final Years*, p. 48; Shlaim, A. 'His Royal Shyness: King Hussein and Israel', *The New York Review of Books*, 15 July 1999 (1999), p. 16.

987 Fayek Interview; Farid, *Final Years*, p. 112.

988 BBC-SWB: ME2494.

989 Wahab Interview; FRUS: 1964–68: XX-4, 74; McNamara, *Britain, Nasser and the Balance of Power in the Middle East*, p. 280.

990 8/12/67, BBC-SWB: ME2644.

991 Barnett, *Dialogues in Arab Politics*, p. 170.

992 Vatikiotis, *Nasser and His Generation*, p. 258; Meital, *Egypt's Struggle*, p. 12.

993 1/7/67, BBC-SWB: ME2506.

994 Gamasy, *October War*, p. 75.

995 Generals Badri, Mahgoub and Zohdy, quoted in Korn, *Stalemate*, p. 90.

996 Frankel, 'Interviews', p. 94.

997 See Heikal's 20/10/67 article on the modern and educated Israeli army, as well as Nasser's speeches of 10/3/68 and 2/11/69, BBC-SWB: ME2601; Meital, *Egypt's Struggle*, p. 12.

998 Farid, *Final Years*, p. 56.

999 Korn, *Stalemate*, p. 91.

1000 The allegation was indeed a lie, despite claims to the contrary in Green, S. *Taking Sides* (London: Faber & Faber, 1984), pp. 204–11. See Parker, *Politics of Miscalculation*, p. 108; FRUS: 1964–68: XIX-262.

1001 Korn, *Stalemate*, p. 24; Burns, *Economic Aid*, p. 170.

1002 Baghdadi, *Mudhakkirāt*, Vol. 2, pp. 284–9.

1003 NA: FCO17/599.

1004 Heikal, *Cairo Documents*, p. 222; Heikal, *Sphinx and Commissar*, p. 181; Riad, *Struggle for Peace*, p. 77; Howeidy Interview.

1005 Sadat, *Identity*, p. 175. See Hadidi Interview.

1006 Parker, *Politics of Miscalculation*, p. 224.
1007 FRUS: 1964–68: XIX-171 fn4.
1008 Churchill, *Six Day War*, p. 90.
1009 See Farid, *Final Years*, p. 19; NA: FCO17/598.
1010 Sadat, *Identity*, p. 178.
1011 *Wathā'iq*, Vol. 1, pp. 244–6, p. 226.
1012 Heikal, *Cairo Documents*, p. 223.
1013 FRUS: 1964–68: XIX-412.
1014 Heikal, *Cairo Documents*, p. 223.
1015 Farid, *Final Years*, p. 42; Wahab Interview.
1016 Farid, *Final Years*, p. 5.
1017 Dawud Interview.
1018 Farid, *Final Years*, p. 42.
1019 Korn, *Stalemate*, pp. 48–50.
1020 FYW: Mohammed Fawzi Interview.
1021 Naguib, Farid and Fayek Interviews.
1022 Heikal, *Sphinx and Commissar*, p. 183.
1023 31/10/67, FRUS: 1964–68: XIX-495.
1024 Sharaf Interview.
1025 Frankel, 'Interviews', pp. 92–4.
1026 Gamasy, *October War*, p. 98.
1027 FRUS: 1964–68: XX-337. It is not recorded that this learned exhortation made any deep impression.
1028 Howeidy Interview.
1029 Hershberg, 'Soviet Bloc', pp. 18–22; pp. 44–5.
1030 Korn, *Stalemate*, pp. 25–9.
1031 Riad, *Struggle for Peace*, p. 47; FYW: Salah Bassiouny Interview.
1032 Rabin, Y. *The Rabin Memoirs* (Berkeley: University of California Press, 1996), p. 137, p. 140.
1033 FRUS: 1964–68: XX-12.
1034 NA: FO17/757.
1035 NA: PREM13/2073.
1036 Stephens, *Nasser*, p. 523.
1037 Fayek Interview.
1038 Nasser could not even have left the country safely to go to Khartoum had he not arrested Amer in August. Shazly Interview.
1039 Korn, *Stalemate*, pp. 86–7.
1040 Farid, *Final Years*, p. 56.
1041 Hussein, *My 'War'*, p. 117; Mutawi, *Jordan*, pp. 175–6.
1042 Dawud Interview. SEC member Dia al-Din Dawud claims to have been present for this conversation.
1043 S/RES/242 (United Nations Security Council, 1967).
1044 Whetten, L. L. *The Canal War* (Cambridge: MIT Press, 1974), p. 57.
1045 Shlaim, *Iron Wall*, pp. 260–1.
1046 Heikal, *Cairo Documents*, p. 47.
1047 Issa, Farid and Wahab Interviews; Howeidy, *Ḥurūb*, p. 180.
1048 25/1/68, BBC-SWB: ME2681.
1049 14/9/67, BBC-SWB: ME2572.
1050 See Hershberg, 'Soviet Bloc', p. 17; Fayek Interview; Howeidy Interview; Korn, *Stalemate*, p. 93.

1051 Heikal, *Cairo Documents*, p. 50.
1052 Rosser, 'Education, Revolt and Reform', p. 69 fn38.
1053 10/11/67, BBC-SWB: ME2619.
1054 Quoted in Korn, *Stalemate*, p. 89.
1055 Farid, *Final Years*, p. 124.
1056 Helal, Halim and Shazly Interviews.
1057 Parker, *Politics of Miscalculation*, p. 126.
1058 Farid Interview.
1059 Ghalib Interview.
1060 FRUS: 1964–68: XX-167.
1061 Hershberg, 'Soviet Bloc', p. 15.
1062 Mosallem Interview.
1063 Hershberg, 'Soviet Bloc', p. 17.
1064 Heikal, *Road to Ramadan*, pp. 39–40.
1065 Howeidy Interview.
1066 FRUS: 1964–68: XX-13.
1067 Andrew and Gordievsky, *KGB*, p. 502; Ghalib Interview.
1068 NA: FCO17/525.
1069 McLaurin *et al.*, *Foreign Policy Making*, p. 75.
1070 Heikal, *Cairo Documents*, p. 58.
1071 Korn, *Stalemate*, pp. 96–7.
1072 FRUS: 1964–68: XIX-500.
1073 Sharaf Interview. Confirmed in Helal Interview.
1074 Howeidy Interview.
1075 NA: FCO17/525.
1076 Howeidy Interview.
1077 Mahmoud Interview.
1078 Helal Interview.
1079 Howeidy Interview.
1080 Hershberg, 'Soviet Bloc', p. 58.
1081 Heikal, *Cairo Documents*, pp. 44–50; BBC-SWB: ME2630; Parker, *Politics of Miscalculation*, p. 126.
1082 See Meital, *Egypt's Struggle*, p. 37; Touval, S. *The Peace Brokers* (Princeton University Press, 1982), p. 136.
1083 7/4/68, Farid, *Final Years*, p. 94. See Riad, *Struggle for Peace*, p. 75.
1084 Korn, *Stalemate*, p. 56.
1085 29/4/68, BBC-SWB: ME2758; *Wathā'iq*, Vol. 1, pp. 444–5.
1086 29/3/68, BBC-SWB: ME2735.
1087 5/2/68, Farid, *Final Years*, p. 112.
1088 Nasser's speeches of 23/11/67 and 29/4/68. BBC-SWB: ME2630, ME2758; *Wathā'iq*, Vol. 1, p. 445.
1089 Mosallem Interview.
1090 14/9/67, BBC-SWB: ME2572.
1091 29/12/67, BBC-SWB: ME2657.
1092 Howeidy Interview; Howeidy, *Ḥurūb*, p. 88, p. 219. Sami Sharaf confirms that relations between the CIA and the Egyptian government continued unchanged after 1967. Sharaf Interview.
1093 Ghalib Interview.
1094 FRUS: 1964–68: XIX-500.
1095 FRUS: 1964–68: XX-167.

1096   FRUS: 1964–68: XX-23, 31.
1097   FRUS: 1964–68: XX-13. See Schonmann, N. 'Tactics of Peace: The Role of Peace Overtures in Nasser's Postwar Foreign Policy Making', unpublished MA thesis, Tel Aviv University (2005), pp. 26–7; Korn, *Stalemate*, p. 49; Meital, *Egypt's Struggle*, p. 18, p. 48.
1098   FRUS: 1964–68: XX-34.
1099   Farid, *Final Years*, pp. 92–4. Confirmed in Howeidy Interview.
1100   FRUS: 1964–68: XX-91, 102.
1101   FRUS: 1964–68: XX-104.
1102   FRUS: 1964–68: XX-136.
1103   FRUS: 1964–68: XX-167.
1104   Farid, *Final Years*, p. 58.
1105   Hershberg, 'Soviet Bloc', p. 55.
1106   22/12/67, BBC-SWB: ME2654.
1107   5/2/68, Farid, *Final Years*, p. 111. See Naguib Interview.
1108   Farid, *Final Years*, p. 120, p. 96.
1109   *Wathā'iq*, Vol. 1, p. 227.
1110   Heikal, *Cairo Documents*, pp. 282–5.
1111   BBC-SWB: ME2630.
1112   28/7/67, *Al-Ahram*, BBC-SWB: ME2530.
1113   A comparison between Nasser's words to Anderson in November and his January meeting with Bergus resulted in a US report that 'we seem to be getting two separate sets of signals from the UAR'. FRUS: 1964–68: XIX-500; FRUS: 1964–68: XX-34; Meital, Y. 'The Khartoum Conference and Egyptian Policy after the 1967 War', *Middle East Journal*, 54.1 (2000), p. 71.
1114   Farid, A. M. *Min maḥāḍir ijtimā'āt 'abd al-nāṣir al-'arabiyya wa al-dawliyya* (Beirut: Dar al-Muthallath, 1979), p. 136.
1115   Farid, *Min maḥāḍir*, p. 119.
1116   Kerr, *Arab Cold War*, p. 131.
1117   Meital, *Egypt's Struggle*, p. 27.
1118   The phrase is Sami Sharaf's. Sharaf Interview.
1119   Fayek Interview.
1120   FRUS: 1964–68: XX-209.
1121   Kishtainy, *Arab Political Humour*, p. 158.
1122   6/11/69, BBC-SWB: ME3224.
1123   *Wathā'iq*, Vol. 1, p. 510.
1124   Gamasy, *October War*, p. 98; Ayubi, *Nasser and Sadat*, p. 61.
1125   NA: FCO17/638; Parker, *Politics of Miscalculation*, p. 129; Gamasy, *October War*, p. 105.
1126   Korn, *Stalemate*, p. 92.
1127   Parker, *Politics of Miscalculation*, p. 128.
1128   13/9/68, NA: FCO17/638.
1129   15/9/68, NA: FCO17/638.
1130   NA: FCO17/757.
1131   Korn, *Stalemate*, p. 93; O'Ballance, *Electronic War*, p. 41.
1132   NA: FCO17/757.
1133   See Parker, *Politics of Miscalculation*, p. 129; NA: FCO17/629.

1134 See Eran, O. 'Soviet Middle East Policy 1967–1973', *In* Rabinovich, I. and Shaked, H. (eds) *From June to October* (New Brunswick: Transaction Books, 1978), p. 33; Whetten, *Canal War*, p. 67, p. 74.

1135 NA: FCO17/638.

1136 12/9/68, FRUS: 1964–68: XX-251.

1137 *Wathā'iq*, Vol. 1, p. 511; BBC-SWB: ME2875, 2881.

1138 13/9/68, BBC-SWB: ME2875.

1139 Parker, *Politics of Miscalculation*, p. 130. See Korn, *Stalemate*, p. 94.

1140 NA: FCO17/629; FCO17/638; Shlaim, 'His Royal Shyness', p. 16.

1141 See NA: PREM13/2073; NA: FCO17/757.

1142 Korn, *Stalemate*, p. 70.

1143 23/8/68, BBC-SWB: ME2857.

1144 24/9/68, NA: PREM13/2073.

1145 FRUS: 1964–68: XX-258.

1146 See Bar-Siman-Tov, Y. *The Israeli-Egyptian War of Attrition, 1969–1970* (New York: Columbia University Press, 1980), p. 45; Whetten, *Canal War*, p. 62; Korn, *Stalemate*, pp. 106–7; Mosallem Interview.

1147 Sadat, *Identity*, p. 196.

1148 See Mosallem Interview; Parker, *Politics of Miscalculation*, p. 130.

1149 FRUS: 1964–68: XX-327.

1150 12/11/68, Farid, *Final Years*, pp. 101–3. See O'Ballance, *Electronic War*, p. 52.

1151 BBC-SWB: ME2942.

1152 Bar-Siman-Tov, *Israeli-Egyptian War*, p. 46; Herzog, C. *The Arab-Israeli Wars* (London: Arms and Armour Press, 1982), p. 201.

1153 Mosallem Interview.

1154 Korn, *Stalemate*, p. 106.

1155 BBC-SWB: ME2980; *Wathā'iq*, Vol. 2, p. 23. See also Korn, *Stalemate*, p. 108.

1156 FRUS: 1964–68: XX-367; O'Ballance, *Electronic War*, pp. 48–9.

1157 Riad, *Struggle for Peace*, p. 96.

1158 Farid, *Final Years*, p. 92, pp. 104–5, p. 197.

1159 3/1/69, BBC-SWB: ME2966.

1160 See Korn, *Stalemate*, p. 107; O'Ballance, *Electronic War*, p. 52, p. 62.

1161 Parker, *Politics of Miscalculation*, pp. 135–6.

1162 Korn, *Stalemate*, p. 108; O'Ballance, *Electronic War*, p. 57.

1163 *Wathā'iq*, Vol. 2, p. 76; BBC-SWB: ME3037.

1164 *Wathā'iq*, Vol.2, p.104; BBC-SWB: ME3039.

1165 BBC-SWB: ME3047.

1166 1/5/69, BBC-SWB: ME3064.

1167 NA: FCO17/759. See also FRUS: 1964–68: XX-327; Parker, *Politics of Miscalculation*, p. 136.

1168 Heikal, *Sphinx and Commissar*, p. 193. See also Ginor, I. 'Under the Yellow Helmet Gleamed Blue Russian Eyes', *Cold War History*, 3.1 (2002), p. 135; Sadat, *Identity*, p. 196; Ghalib Interview.

1169 BBC-SWB: ME3093.

1170 NA: FCO17/760.

1171 Gamasy, *October War*, pp. 107–9.

1172   These were summarised as early as 21 March by Heikal in *Al-Ahram*. BBC-SWB: ME3032.
1173   Gamasy, *October War*, p. 98, p. 107.
1174   Fayek Interview.
1175   Mar'i, *Awrāq*, Vol. 3, p. 570; Vatikiotis, *Nasser and His Generation*, p. 257.
1176   NA: FCO17/758.
1177   11/3/69, NA: PREM13/2609.
1178   Fayek Interview; Gamasy, *October War*, p. 107; Farid, *Final Years*, p. 136.
1179   Bar-Siman-Tov, *Israeli-Egyptian War*, pp. 53–8.
1180   6/6/69, BBC-SWB: ME3094.
1181   Mosallem Interview. See also Meital, *Egypt's Struggle*, p. 31; Korn, *Stalemate*, pp. 108–9, p. 166.
1182   Gamasy, *October War*, p. 107; Bar-Siman-Tov, *Israeli-Egyptian War*, pp. 50–1; Meital, *Egypt's Struggle*, p. 63.
1183   Parker, *Politics of Miscalculation*, p. 135.
1184   12/11/68, Farid, *Final Years*, pp. 101–3.
1185   NA: FCO17/757.
1186   BBC-SWB: ME3093.
1187   10/3/69, NA: PREM 13/2609.
1188   12/11/68, Farid, *Final Years*, pp. 101–3.
1189   See Bar-Siman-Tov, *Israeli-Egyptian War*, pp. 45–6.
1190   BBC-SWB: ME3064.
1191   O'Ballance, *Electronic War*, p. 65.
1192   Farid, *Final Years*, p. 113. See FRUS: 1964–68: XX-300.
1193   See FRUS: 1964–68: XX-327; NA: PREM13/2609.
1194   Kissinger, H. *The White House Years* (London: Weidenfeld and Nicolson, 1979), p. 360.
1195   Farid, *Final Years*, p. 137.
1196   11/9/69, NA: FCO17/760; Riad, *Struggle for Peace*, pp. 92–4.
1197   FRUS: 1964–68: XX-314, 323, 327.
1198   FRUS: 1964–68: XX-343.
1199   7/2/69, BBC-SWB: ME2996.
1200   NA: FCO17/758.
1201   10/3/69, NA: PREM13/2609.
1202   29/3/69, BBC-SWB: ME3037; *Wathā'iq*, Vol. 2, p. 81.
1203   Farid, *Final Years*, p. 134, p. 136.
1204   For example, see FRUS: 1964–68: XX-14.
1205   FRUS: 1964–68: XX-301, 337; Quandt, *Decade of Decisions*, pp. 66–7; Parker, *Politics of Miscalculation*, p. 132.
1206   See Meital, *Egypt's Struggle*, p. 38; Farid, *Final Years*, p. 92.
1207   Heikal, *Cairo Documents*, p. 53.
1208   NA: PREM13/2609.
1209   Ghorbal, A. *Ṣu'ūd wa inhiyār* (Cairo: Al-Ahram, 2004), p. 51. See also Quandt, *Decade of Decisions*, p. 85; Riad, *Struggle for Peace*, p. 99.
1210   Kissinger, *White House Years*, pp. 360–1.
1211   Gamasy, *October War*, p. 114.
1212   23/7/69, *Wathā'iq*, Vol. 2, p. 174; BBC-SWB: ME3134.
1213   O'Ballance, *Electronic War*, pp. 74–5.
1214   See Gamasy, *October War*, pp. 111–12; Korn, *Stalemate*, pp. 169–71; Parker, *Politics of Miscalculation*, p. 137; Herzog, *Arab-Israeli Wars*, p. 212.

1215 Farid, *Final Years*, p. x; O'Ballance, *Electronic War*, p. 92.
1216 Heikal, *Cairo Documents*, p. 62, p. 66; Trevelyan, *Public and Private*, p. 78.
1217 McLaurin *et al.*, *Foreign Policy Making*, p. 84.
1218 Korn, *Stalemate*, p. 174.
1219 21/11/69, BBC-SWB: ME3237.
1220 See Whetten, *Canal War*, p. 89; Bar-Siman-Tov, *Israeli-Egyptian War*, p. 96, p. 99; Shlaim, A. 'Failures in National Intelligence Estimates', *World Politics*, 28.3 (1976), p. 487.
1221 10/8/69, Farid, *Final Years*, p. 139. For the rejection, see Nasser's speech of 28/7/69, BBC-SWB: ME3134.
1222 Heikal, *Autumn of Fury*, p. 61.
1223 NA: FCO17/760; 29/8/69, BBC-SWB: ME3166.
1224 See NA: FCO17/760; Whetten, *Canal War*, p. 75; Korn, *Stalemate*, pp. 156–7.
1225 BBC-SWB: ME3224; *Wathā'iq*, Vol. 2, p. 210; Spiegel, S. L. *The Other Arab-Israeli Conflict* (University of Chicago Press, 1985), p. 186.
1226 Korn, *Stalemate*, pp. 163–4.
1227 For instance, see Meital, *Egypt's Struggle*, p. 67; Bar-Siman-Tov, *Israeli-Egyptian War*, p. 115.
1228 Korn, *Stalemate*, p. 159.
1229 NA: FCO17/760-1; CAB151/153; Quandt, *Decade of Decisions*, pp. 87–9.
1230 Farid, *Final Years*, p. 153.
1231 Whetten, *Canal War*, pp. 78–9.
1232 Safran, N. *Saudi Arabia* (New York: Cornell University Press, 1988), pp. 141–2.
1233 Kerr, *Arab Cold War*, p. 146.
1234 Farid Interview.
1235 Farid, *Final Years*, pp. 157–8. See Heikal, *Cairo Documents*, p. 74.
1236 Sharaf Interview.
1237 FRUS: 1964–68: XX-327.
1238 Trevelyan, *Public and Private*, p. 79.
1239 Meital, 'Khartoum Conference', p. 76.
1240 Barnett and Levy, 'Domestic Sources of Alliances', p. 384; Ciorciari, J. D. 'Saudi-U.S. Alignment after the Six-Day War', *Middle East Review of International Affairs*, 9.2 (2005), p. 13.
1241 Riad, *Struggle for Peace*, p. 119.
1242 Korn, *Stalemate*, pp. 175–6.
1243 See Gamasy, *October War*, p. 113; Gawrych, *Albatross*, p. 113; Ayubi, *Nasser and Sadat*, p. 142, p. 154.
1244 Sharaf, Fayek, Dawud, Howeidy and Hoda Nasser Interviews.
1245 Ayubi, *Nasser and Sadat*, p. 154.
1246 See Korn, *Stalemate*, pp. 184–5; Parker, *Politics of Miscalculation*, p. 141; Shlaim, 'Failures in National Intelligence', p. 492.
1247 1/1/1970, BBC-SWB: ME3269; 2/2/70, BBC-SWB: ME3296.
1248 Heikal, *Cairo Documents*, p. 81; Ghalib Interview; Korn, *Stalemate*, pp. 188–90.
1249 Ginor, 'Under the Yellow Helmet', p. 138.
1250 Korn, *Stalemate*, p. 198; O'Ballance, *Electronic War*, p. 114, p. 120; Kissinger, *White House Years*, p. 576.
1251 11/7/67, Hershberg, 'Soviet Bloc', p. 16. See Meital, *Egypt's Struggle*, p. 69.

1252   Ghalib Interview.
1253   Howeidy Interview.
1254   Shazly, Mosallem and Sharaf Interviews.
1255   Springborg, *Family, Power and Politics*, pp. 182–3.
1256   Gamasy, *October War*, p. 114.
1257   Korn, *Stalemate*, pp. 163–4.
1258   Ginor, 'Under the Yellow Helmet', p. 143.
1259   Korn, *Stalemate*, pp. 195–8, pp. 200–3.
1260   Whetten, *Canal War*, p. 97.
1261   Bar-Siman-Tov, *Israeli-Egyptian War*, pp. 159–64.
1262   4/3/70, BBC-SWB: ME3322.
1263   Gamasy, *October War*, p. 119.
1264   20/2/70, BBC-SWB: ME3312.
1265   10/4/70, BBC-SWB: ME3351.
1266   Korn, *Stalemate*, pp. 240–1. Summarised from Sisco's account in a declassified cable from the Cairo Embassy.
1267   Howeidy, A. *Al-furaṣ al ḏā'i'a* (Beirut: 1992) pp. 88–9. See Heikal's *Al-Ahram* editorial of 17/4/70, BBC-SWB: ME3357.
1268   BBC-SWB: ME3369.
1269   Ghorbal, *Ṣu'ūd*, pp. 19–20.
1270   *Wathā'iq*, Vol. 2, p. 372; BBC-SWB: ME3369.
1271   Korn, *Stalemate*, pp. 242–7; Touval, *Peace Brokers*, p. 175.
1272   *Wathā'iq*, Vol. 2, p. 458; Whetten, *Canal War*, p. 103.
1273   Korn, *Stalemate*, p. 253; Dawud Interview.
1274   BBC-SWB: ME3414.
1275   BBC-SWB: ME3422, 3428.
1276   *Wathā'iq*, Vol. 2, p. 488; BBC-SWB: ME3439.
1277   Karawan, I. A. 'Identity and Foreign Policy: The Case of Egypt', *In* Telhami, S. and Barnett, M. (eds) *Identity and Foreign Policy* (Ithaca: Cornell University Press, 2002) p. 160; Meital, *Egypt's Struggle*, p. 74.
1278   NA: FCO17/1161; Shazly Interview; Mosallem Interview.
1279   Issa Interview; Whetten, *Canal War*, p. 114.
1280   Gawrych, *Albatross*, p. 118; Korn, *Stalemate*, p. 250.
1281   For example, Whetten, *Canal War*, p. 103.
1282   Mar'i, *Awrāq*, Vol. 3, p. 604; Farid, Mosallem, Shazly and Ghalib Interviews.
1283   Heikal, *Cairo Documents*, p. 91.
1284   Sharaf Interview. See Riad, *Struggle for Peace*, pp. 143–6; Korn, *Stalemate*, p. 251.
1285   Sadat, *Identity*, pp. 198–9. Sadat, of course, had a political interest when he wrote this memoir in portraying Nasser as turning away from the USSR.
1286   Hamrush Interview; Naguib Interview; Meital, *Egypt's Struggle*, p. 73.
1287   Sadat, *Identity*, p. 198.
1288   24/7/70, BBC-SWB: ME3440.
1289   Farid, *Final Years*, p. 182.
1290   Riad, *Struggle for Peace*, p. 148.
1291   See Mar'i, *Awrāq*, Vol. 3, p. 604; Heikal, *Cairo Documents*, p. 89; Sharaf, Mahmoud and Dawud Interviews.

1292 Farid, *Final Years*, pp. 176–7. See also Fayek Interview.
1293 Heikal, M. H. and Ghareeb, E., 'Mohammed Hassanein Heykal Discusses War and Peace in the Middle East', *Journal of Palestine Studies* 1.1 (1971), p. 6.
1294 Quoted in Korn, *Stalemate*, p. 252.
1295 BBC-SWB: ME3440.
1296 NA: FCO17/1161.
1297 Whetten, *Canal War*, p. 128.
1298 Heikal, *Cairo Documents*, p. 15.
1299 Howeidy Interview; Gamasy, *October War*, p. 98; Mahmoud Interview.
1300 Heikal, *Sphinx and Commissar*, p. 198, p. 201; Korn, *Stalemate*, p. 269.
1301 Hamrush Interview.
1302 Farid Interview. See Imam, *Ḥusayn al-shāfi'i*, p. 132.
1303 Sharaf Interview.
1304 Farid Interview.
1305 Sharaf Interview.
1306 Fayek Interview.
1307 Farid, *Final Years*, p. 170.
1308 Heikal, *Cairo Documents*, p. 105.
1309 FYW: Jihan Sadat Interview.
1310 Korn, *Stalemate*, p. 273; Meital, *Egypt's Struggle*, pp. 99–100.
1311 Magid Interview.
1312 Shazly Interview. See Meital, *Egypt's Struggle*, p. 85; Howeidy Interview.
1313 Mosallem Interview.
1314 Quandt, *Decade of Decisions*, p. 112.
1315 Stephens, *Nasser*, pp. 549–50.
1316 Heikal, *Road to Ramadan*, p. 100.
1317 Heikal, *Cairo Documents*, p. 15.
1318 It is worth emphasising that, in their origin, these images were not unique to Nasser. The specific events to which he himself harked back – early demonstrations against colonialism; the British tanks surrounding the Abdin Palace in 1942; the creation of the state of Israel in 1948 – gained their symbolic resonance from the way in which they shaped the mentality of a generation, not of one man. See Ayubi, *Nasser and Sadat*; Stephens, *Nasser*; Nasser, G. A. 'Memoirs of the First Palestine War', *Journal of Palestine Studies*, 2.2 (1973); and of course Vatikiotis, *Nasser and His Generation*.
1319 See Lebow, R. N. *Between Peace and War* (Baltimore: Johns Hopkins University Press, 1981).
1320 See Miles, H. *Al-Jazeera* (London: Abacus, 2005).
1321 Sivan, E. *Radical Islam* (New Haven: Yale University Press, 1985), pp. 28–32. See also Kepel, *Muslim Extremism in Egypt*.
1322 Sivan, *Radical Islam*, p. 17.

Bibliography

Primary sources

Archival sources

Files from the series CAB, CO, DEFE, FCO, FO, PREM: The National Archives, Kew, London [NA].
Trevaskis Papers: Rhodes House, University of Oxford.
Dodds-Parker Papers: Magdalen College, University of Oxford.
Brian Lapping Associates, Interview Transcripts, *The Fifty Years War: Israel and the Arabs* [FYW]: Private Papers Collection, Middle East Centre, St Antony's College, University of Oxford.

Documents

BBC Summary of World Broadcasts, 1952–1970 [BBC-SWB].
Foreign Relations of the United States, 1952–1968 [FRUS].
International Documents on Palestine, 1967 (Beirut: Institute for Palestine Studies, 1970) [IDP].
Majmūʿāt khuṭab wa taṣrīḥāt wa bayānāt al-raʾīs jamāl ʿabd al-nāṣir (Cairo: Haʾia al-Istiʾlamat).
Wathāʾiq ʿabd al-nāṣir: khuṭab, aḥādīth, taṣrīḥāt (Cairo: Al-Ahram Centre for Political and Social Studies).
Who's Who in the Arab World, 1967–8, 2nd Edition (Beirut: Publitec Publications).
Eayrs, J. *The Commonwealth and Suez: A Documentary Survey* (Oxford University Press, 1964).
Farid, A. M. *Min maḥāḍir ijtimāʿāt ʿabd al-nāṣir al-ʿarabiyya wa al-dawliyya 1967–1970* (Beirut: Dar al-Muthallath, 1979).
Farid, A. M. *Nasser: The Final Years* (Reading: Ithaca, 1994).
Goldsworthy, D. *British Documents on the End of Empire: The Conservative Government and the End of Empire, 1951–57* (London: HMSO, 1994).
Heikal, M. H. *Naḥnu wa amrīka* (Cairo: Dar al-Asr al-Hadith, 1968).
Hershberg, J. G. 'The Soviet Bloc and the Aftermath of the June 1967 War: Selected Documents from East-Central European Archives', papers distributed at a conference on *The United States, the Middle East and the 1967 Arab-Israeli War* (US Department of State, January 12–13, 2004).
Kent, J. *Egypt and the Defence of the Middle East, Part III, 1953–1956* (London: HMSO, 1998).
Nasser, G. A. *Address by President Gamal Abdel Nasser at the Palestinian National Congress, May 31, 1965* (Cairo, 1965).
Nasser, H. G. A. *Maḥāḍir jalsāt al-lajna al-markaziyya al-ittiḥād al-ishtirākiyy al-ʿarabiyy* (Cairo: Al-Ahram Centre for Political and Social Studies).
Schramm, W. *One Day in the World's Press: Fourteen Great Newspapers on a Day of Crisis – November 2, 1956* (California: Stanford, 1959).

216

Author interviews

Abdel Hamid Abubakr, *aide to Mahmoud Younis in 1956* (Cairo, 7 April 2004: English).

Makram Mohammed Ahmed, *journalist for Al-Ahram in the Yemen War* (Cairo, 13 March 2004: English).

Mohsen Alaini, *Yemeni Foreign Minister then UN representative from 1962* (Cairo, 25 March 2004: English).

Abdel Rahman Baydani, *Yemeni Prime Minister from 1962* (Cairo, 8 April 2004: English).

Dia al-Din Dawud, *Minister of Social Affairs from 1967* (Cairo, 24 March 2004: Arabic).

Abdel Magid Farid, *General Secretary of the ASU from 1967* (London, 14 June 2004: English).

Mohammed Fayek, *Information Minister and Foreign Minister after 1967* (Cairo, 25 March 2004: English).

Yehia Gamal, *assistant to Nasser on Arab relations 1964–67* (Cairo, 18 April 2004: English).

Dr Mourad Ghalib, *Egyptian Ambassador to the USSR 1961–71* (Cairo, 19 December 2004: English).

Sir John Graham, *Assistant Private Secretary to the British Secretary of State for Foreign Affairs 1954–57* (Shipton, 19 July 2005: English).

General Salah al-Din Hadidi, *Commander of the Eastern Front 1964–66* (Cairo, 12 December 2004: English).

General Ahmed Abdel Halim, *Captain in Yemen War and Canal War* (Cairo, 1 April 2004: English).

Ahmed Hamrush, *former Free Officer and historian of the 26 July Revolution* (Cairo, 8 and 12 December 2004: English).

Admiral Moheeb Helal, *head of training at various naval bases in the 1960s* (Alexandria, 2 March 2004: English).

Dr Hoda Abdel Nasser, *daughter of the President, worked in his office after 1967* (Cairo, 1 March 2004: English).

Amin Howeidy, *Head of General Intelligence and Defence Minister from 1967* (Cairo, 27 March and 9 December 2004: English).

Ambassador Hassan Issa, *Diplomatic Service from 1960* (Cairo, 4 April 2004: English).

Dr Esmat Abdel Magid, *Diplomatic Service from the 1950s* (Cairo, 20 April 2004: English).

Hamed Mahmoud, *Governor of the Red Sea and Suez in the 1960s* (Cairo, 24 March 2004: English/Arabic).

Khaled Mohieddin, *RCC member and left-wing newspaper editor, exiled 1954–56* (Cairo, 9 April 2004: English).

General Talaat Mosallem, *Divisional Chief of Operations 1968–70* (Cairo, 8 December 2004: English).

Ambassador Gamal Naguib, *chef du cabinet to Foreign Minister Fawzi from 1967* (Cairo, 19 April 2004: English).

Dr Tharwat Okasha, *Free Officer and later Minister of Culture* (Cairo, 18 December 2004: English).

Ahmed Said, *Manager of the Voice of the Arabs radio station, 1953–67* (Cairo, 20 December 2004: Arabic).

Hussein Shafei, *RCC member, Minister and Vice President, 1961–68* (Cairo, 11 December 2004: Arabic/English).
Sami Sharaf, *close advisor to Nasser, Minister for Presidential Affairs, 1970* (Cairo, 28 March and 7 December 2004: English).
Marshal Saad El-Din Shazly, *Commander of Egyptian Special Forces 1967–69* (Cairo, 13 December 2004: English).
Youssef Sherif, *journalist for Rose al-Youssef in the Yemen War* (Cairo, 6 March 2004: Arabic).
Ambassador Mohammed Abdel Wahab, *Foreign Service from 1963* (Cairo, 30 March 2004: English).

Published interviews

Calvocoressi, P. *Suez: Ten Years After* (London: BBC, 1967).
Fawzi, M. *Thiwār yūlīyū yitahaddithūn* (Cairo: Al-Zahra lil-I'lam al-Arabiyy, 1987).
Fawzi, M. *Al-dubāt al-ahrār yitahaddithūn* (Cairo: Madbouli, 1990).
Frankel, N. 'Interviews with Ismail Fahmy, Ashraf Ghorbal and Mohamed Riad', *American Arab Affairs*, 31 (1990).
Habib, T. *Milaffat thawrat yūlīyū: shahādāt 122 min san'hā wa mu'āṣiriyyha* (Cairo: Al-Ahram, 1997).
Heikal, M. H. and Ghareeb, E., 'Mohammed Hassanein Heykal Discusses War and Peace in the Middle East (Interview)', *Journal of Palestine Studies*, 1.1 (1971).
Hussein of Jordan, *My 'War' with Israel: As Told to and with Additional Material by Vick Vance and Pierre Lauer* (London: Peter Owen, 1969).
Imam, A. *'Alī ṣabrī yitadhāhir* (Cairo: Tasmim al-Ghalaf al-Funan, 1987).
Imam, A. *'Abd al-nāṣir: kayf hakama miṣr?* (Cairo: Madbouli al-Saghir, 1996).
Imam, S. *Husayn al-shāfi'i wa asrār thawrat yūlīyū wa hukm al-sadāt* (Cairo: Maktab Awziris lil-Kutub wa al-Magalat,1993).
Jawadi, M. *Mudhakkirāt wuzarā' al-thawra.* (Cairo: Dar al-Shorouk, 1995).
Mansour, A. *Husayn al-shāfi'i: shāhid 'ala 'aṣr thawrat yūlīyū* (Cairo: Al-Maktab al-Misry, 2004).
Shlaim, A. 'His Royal Shyness: King Hussein and Israel', *The New York Review of Books*, 15 July 1999 (1999).

Memoirs

Abu al-Fadl, A. F. *Kuntu nā'iban li ra'īs al-mukhabarāt* (Cairo: Dar al-Shorouk, 2001).
Abu-Bakr, A. H. *Qanāt al-sūīs wa al-ayām allatī hazzat al-dunīā* (Cairo: Dar al-Ma'arif, 1987).
Ahmed, M. A. *Dhikrayāt harb al-yaman 1962–1967* (Cairo: Matba'at al-Ukhuwah, 1992).
Alaini, M. *Khamsūn 'āman fī al-rumāl al-mutaharrika* (Cairo: Dar al-Shorouk, 1999).
Alaini, M. *Fifty Years in Shifting Sands: Personal Experience in the Building of a Modern State in Yemen* (An-Nahar Publications, in press).
Amery, J. 'The Suez Group: A Retrospective on Suez', *In* Troen, S.I. and Shemesh, M. (eds) *The Suez-Sinai Crisis 1956: Retrospective and Reappraisal* (London: Frank Cass, 1990).

Badeau, J. S. 'USA and UAR: A Crisis in Confidence', *Foreign Affairs*, 43.2 (1965).

Badeau, J. S. *The Middle East Remembered* (Washington, DC: The Middle East Institute, 1983).

Baghdadi, A. L. *Mudhakkirāt* (Cairo: Al-Maktab al-Hadith, 1977).

Baghdadi, A. L. 'Abd al-Latif al-Bughdadi's Memoirs', *In* Troen, S. I. and Shemesh, M. (eds) *The Suez-Sinai Crisis 1956: Retrospective and Reappraisal* (London: Frank Cass, 1990).

Baydani, A. R. *Azmat al-umma al-'arabiyya wa thawrat al-yaman* (Cairo: 1984).

Bergus, D. C. 'The View from Washington', *In* Parker, R. B. (ed.) *The Six-Day War: A Retrospective* (Gainesville: University Press of Florida, 1996).

Bowie, R. R. 'Eisenhower, Dulles and the Suez Crisis', *In* Louis, W. R. and Owen, R. (eds) *Suez 1956: The Crisis and Its Consequences* (Oxford: Clarendon Press, 1989).

Brown, G. *In My Way: The Political Memoirs of Lord George-Brown* (London: Victor Gollancz Ltd, 1971).

Catterall, P. *The Macmillan Diaries: The Cabinet Years, 1950–1957* (London: Macmillan, 2003).

Clark, W. *From Three Worlds: Memoirs* (London: Sidgwick & Jackson, 1986).

Cooper, C. L. *The Lion's Last Roar: Suez 1956* (New York: Harper and Row, 1978).

Copeland, M. *The Game of Nations: The Amorality of Power Politics* (London: Weidenfeld and Nicolson, 1969).

Copeland, M. *Without Cloak or Dagger* (New York: Simon and Schuster, 1974).

De La Billière, P. *Looking for Trouble: An Autobiography – from the SAS to the Gulf* (London: HarperCollins, 1994).

Dib, F. *'Abd al-nāsir wa harb al-tahrīr al-yamanī* (Cairo: Dar al-Mustaqbal al-Arabiyy, 1990).

Dodds-Parker, D. *Political Eunuch* (London: Springwood Books, 1986).

Eveland, W. *Ropes of Sand: America's Failure in the Middle East* (London: W.W. Norton, 1980).

Fahmy, I. *Negotiating for Peace in the Middle East* (London: Croom Helm, 1983).

Fawzi, M. *Suez 1956: An Egyptian Perspective* (London: Shorouk International, 1988).

Fawzi, M. *Harb al thalāth sanawāt, 1967–1970* (Cairo: Dar al-Mustaqbal al-Arabiyy, 1983).

Fawzi, M. *Al-i'dād li mu'āraka al-tahrīr: 1967–1970* (Cairo: Dar al-Mustaqbal al-Arabiyy, 1999).

Gamasy, M. A. G. *The October War: Memoirs of Field Marshal El-Gamasy of Egypt* (Cairo: AUC Press, 1993).

Gandy, C. 'A Mission to Yemen: August 1962–January 1963', *British Journal of Middle Eastern Studies*, 25.2 (1998).

Ghalib, M. *Ma' 'abd al-nāsir wa al-sadāt* (Cairo: Al-Ahram, 2000).

Ghorbal, A. *Su'ūd wa inhiyār: 'alāqāt misr wa amrīka* (Cairo: Al-Ahram, 2004).

Glubb, J. B. *The Middle East Crisis: A Personal Interpretation* (London: Hodder & Stoughton, 1967).

Hadidi, S. D. *Shāhid 'ala harb 1967* (Cairo: Dar al-Shorouk).

Halim, A. A. 'Al-khibra al-'arabiyya fī al-harb', *Al-Siyasa Al-Dawliyya*, 34 (1998).

Hamrush, A. *Qissat thawrat 26 yūlīyū* (Cairo: Madbouli, 1983).

Hassouna, H. A. *The League of Arab States and Regional Disputes: A Study of Middle East Conflicts* (New York: Dobbs Ferry, 1975).

Heikal, M. H. *Nasser: The Cairo Documents* (London: New English Library, 1972).
Heikal, M. H. *The Road to Ramadan* (London: Collins, 1975).
Heikal, M. H. *Sphinx and Commissar: The Rise and Fall of Soviet Influence in the Arab World* (London: Collins, 1978).
Heikal, M. H. 'Egyptian Foreign Policy', *Foreign Affairs*, 56.4 (1978).
Heikal, M. H. *Autumn of Fury* (London: Andre Deutsch, 1983).
Heikal, M. H. *Cutting the Lion's Tail: Suez through Egyptian Eyes* (London: Andre Deutsch, 1986).
Heikal, M. H. *Li-miṣr ila li-'abd al-nāṣir* (Cairo: Al-Ahram, 1987).
Heikal, M. H. *1967 – sanawāt al-ghalayān* (Cairo: Al-Ahram, 1988).
Heikal, M. H. *1967 – al-infijār* (Cairo: Al-Ahram, 1990).
Heikal, M. H. *Milaffāt al-sūīs* (Cairo: Al-Ahram, 1996).
Howeidy, A. *Ḥurūb 'abd al-nāṣir* (Beirut: 1979).
Howeidy, A. *Ma' 'abd al-nāṣir* (Cairo: Dar Al-Mustaqbal al-Arabiyy, 1985).
Howeidy, A. 'Nasser and the Crisis of 1956', *In* Louis, W. R. and Owen, R. (eds) *Suez 1956: The Crisis and Its Consequences* (Oxford: Clarendon Press, 1989).
Howeidy, A. *Al-furaṣ al ḍā'i'a* (Beirut: 1992).
Howeidy, A. *50 'āman min al-awāṣif* (Cairo: Al-Ahram, 2002).
Johnston, C. H. *The View from Steamer Point: Being an Account of Three Years in Aden* (London: Collins, 1964).
Kissinger, H. *The White House Years* (London: Weidenfeld and Nicolson, 1979).
Ledger, D. *Shifting Sands: The British in South Arabia* (London: Peninsular Publishing, 1983).
Lloyd, S. *Suez 1956: A Personal Account* (London: Jonathan Cape, 1978).
Lunt, J. *The Barren Rocks of Aden* (London: Herbert Jenkins, 1966).
Macmillan, H. *At the End of the Day, 1961–1963* (London: Macmillan, 1973).
Magid, E. A. *Zaman al-inkisār wa al-intiṣār* (Cairo: Dar al-Shorouk, 1999).
Mar'i, S. *Awrāq siyāsiyya* (Cairo: Al-Maktab al-Misriyy al-Hadith, 1978).
Mar'i, S. 'Sayyid Mar'i's Political Papers', *In* Troen, S.I. and Shemesh, M. (eds) *The Suez-Sinai Crisis 1956: Retrospective and Reappraisal* (London: Frank Cass, 1990).
McDermott, G. *The Eden Legacy and the Decline of British Diplomacy* (London: Leslie Frewin, 1969).
Menzies, R. G. *Afternoon Light: Some Memories of Men and Events* (London: Cassell, 1967).
Mohi El Din, K. *Memories of a Revolution: Egypt 1952* (Cairo: AUC Press, 1995).
Morgan, J. *The Backbench Diaries of Richard Crossman* (London: Hamish Hamilton and Jonathan Cape, 1981).
Murtagi, A. M. *Al-farīq murtagī yarwi al-ḥaqā'iq* (Cairo: Al-Watan al-Arabiyy, 1973).
Nasr, S. *Mudhakkirāt* (Cairo: Dar al-Khiyal, 1999).
Nasser, G. A. 'The Egyptian Revolution', *Foreign Affairs*, 33.1 (1954).
Nasser, G. A. *The Philosophy of the Revolution* (Buffalo: Smith, Keynes and Marshall, 1959).
Nasser, G. A. 'Memoirs of the First Palestine War', *Journal of Palestine Studies*, 2.2 (1973).
Nu'man, A. M. *Mudhakkirāt* (Cairo: Madbouli).
Nutting, A. *No End of a Lesson: The Story of Suez* (London: Constable, 1967).
Nutting, A. *Nasser* (London: Constable, 1972).

Okasha, T. *Mudhakkirātī fi al-siyāsa wa al-thaqāfa* (Cairo: Dar al-Shorouk, 2004).

Pineau, C. *1956/Suez* (Paris: Éditions Robert Laffont, 1976).

Rabin, Y. *The Rabin Memoirs* (Berkeley: University of California Press, 1996).

Riad, M. *The Struggle for Peace in the Middle East* (London: Quartet Books, 1981).

Rikhye, I. J. *The Sinai Blunder: Withdrawal of the United Nations Emergency Force Leading to the Six-Day War of June 1967* (London: Frank Cass, 1980).

Sadat, A. *Revolt on the Nile* (London: Allan Wingate, 1957).

Sadat, A. *In Search of Identity: An Autobiography* (London: Collins, 1978).

Sadat, J. *A Woman of Egypt* (New York: Simon and Schuster, 1987).

Shazly, S. *The Crossing of Suez: The October War* (London: Third World Centre, 1980).

Shuckburgh, E. *Descent to Suez: Diaries 1951–56* (London: Weidenfeld and Nicolson, 1986).

Smiley, D. *Arabian Assignment* (London: Leo Cooper, 1975).

Trevaskis, K. *Shades of Amber: A South Arabian Episode* (London: Hutchinson, 1968).

Trevelyan, H. *The Middle East in Revolution* (London: Macmillan, 1970).

Trevelyan, H. *Public and Private* (London: Hamish Hamilton, 1980).

Uruq, M. *Qirā'a fī awrāq 'alī ṣabrī* (Cairo: Dar al-Mustaqbal al-Arabiyy, 1992).

Wright, P. *Spycatcher: The Candid Autobiography of a Senior Intelligence Officer* (New York: Viking, 1987).

Yost, C. W. 'The Arab-Israeli War: How It Began', *Foreign Affairs*, 42.2 (1968).

Secondary sources

Historical works

Abu-Izzedin, N. M. *Nasser of the Arabs: An Arab Assessment* (London: Third World Centre, 1975).

Abu-Lughod, I. *The Arab-Israeli Confrontation of June 1967: An Arab Perspective* (Evanston: Northwestern University Press, 1970).

Aburish, S. K. *Nasser: The Last Arab* (London: Duckworth, 2004).

Ajami, F. *The Arab Predicament: Arab Political Thought and Practice since 1967* (Cambridge University Press, 1981).

Aldrich, R. J. 'Intelligence, Anglo-American Relations and the Suez Crisis, 1956', *Intelligence and National Security*, 9.3 (1994).

Aldrich, R. J. *The Hidden Hand: Britain, America and Cold War Secret Intelligence* (London: John Murray, 2001).

Ali, K. H. *Muḥāribūn wa mufāwiḍūn.* (Cairo: Al-Ahram, 1986).

Alterman, J. B. *Egypt and American Foreign Assistance, 1952–6: Hopes Dashed* (New York: Palgrave Macmillan, 2002).

Amos, J. W. *Arab-Israeli Military/Political Relations: Arab Perceptions and the Politics of Escalation* (New York: Pergamon Press, 1979).

Andrew, C. and Gordievsky, O. *KGB: The Inside Story of its Foreign Operations from Lenin to Gorbachev* (London: Sceptre, 1990).

Andrew, C. and Mitrokhin, V. *The Mitrokhin Archive II: The KGB and the World* (London: Allen Lane, 2005).

Aronson, G. *From Sideshow to Center Stage: US Policy toward Egypt 1946–1956* (Boulder: Lynne Rienner, 1986).

Ashton, N. J. *Eisenhower, Macmillan and the Problem of Nasser: Anglo-American Relations and Arab Nationalism, 1955–59* (London: Macmillan Press, 1996).

Ashton, N. J. 'The Hijacking of a Pact: The Formation of the Baghdad Pact and Anglo-American Tensions in the Middle East, 1955–1958', *Review of International Studies*, 19.2 (1999).

Ashton, N. J. *Kennedy, Macmillan and the Cold War: The Irony of Interdependence* (London: Palgrave Macmillan, 2002).

Ashton, N. J. 'A "Special Relationship" Sometimes in Spite of Ourselves: Britain and Jordan, 1957–73', *Journal of Imperial and Commonwealth History*, 33.2 (2005).

Auda, G. 'The State of Political Control: The Case of Nasser 1960–1967', *The Arab Journal of the Social Sciences*, 2.1 (1987).

Ayubi, S. *Nasser and Sadat: Decision-making and Foreign Policy, 1970–1972* (Washington, DC: University Press of America, 1994).

Badeeb, S. M. *The Saudi-Egyptian Conflict over North Yemen, 1962–1970* (Boulder: Westview Press, 1986).

Balfour-Paul, G. *The End of Empire in the Middle East: Britain's Relinquishment of Power in her Last Three Arab Dependencies* (Cambridge University Press, 1991).

Bar-Joseph, U. 'Rotem: The Forgotten Crisis on the Road to the 1967 War', *Journal of Contemporary History*, 31.3 (1996).

Barnett, M. N. *Confronting the Costs of War: Military Power, State and Society in Egypt and Israel* (Princeton University Press, 1992).

Barnett, M. N. *Dialogues in Arab Politics: Negotiations in Regional Order* (New York: Columbia University Press, 1998).

Barnett, M. N. and Levy, J. S. 'Domestic Sources of Alliances and Alignments: The Case of Egypt, 1962–73', *International Organization*, 45.3 (1991).

Bar-Siman-Tov, Y. *The Israeli-Egyptian War of Attrition, 1969–1970: A Case-Study of Limited Local War* (New York: Columbia University Press, 1980).

Bass, W. *Support Any Friend: Kennedy's Middle East and the Making of the US-Israel Alliance* (Oxford University Press, 2003).

Bowen, J. *Six Days: How the 1967 War Shaped the Middle East* (London: Pocket Books, 2003).

Bower, T. *The Perfect English Spy: Sir Dick White and the Secret War, 1935–90* (London: Mandarin, 1996).

Brands, H. W. 'What Eisenhower and Dulles saw in Nasser: Personalities and Interests in US-Egyptian Relations', *American Arab Affairs*, 17 (1986).

Brecher, M. *The Foreign Policy System of Israel: Settings, Images, Process* (New Haven: Yale University Press, 1972).

Brecher, M. *Decisions in Israel's Foreign Policy* (New Haven: Yale University Press, 1974).

Brecher, M. and Geist, B. *Decisions in Crisis: Israel, 1967 and 1973* (Berkeley: University of California Press, 1980).

Brenchley, F. *Britain and the Middle East: An Economic History, 1945–87* (London: Lester Crook, 1989).

Brown, L. C. *International Politics and the Middle East: Old Rules, Dangerous Game* (London: I. B. Tauris, 1984).

Brown, L. C. 'Nasser and the June War: Plan or Improvisation?' *In* Seikaly, S., Baalbaki, R. and Dodd, P. (eds) *Quest for Understanding: Arabic and Islamic Studies in Memory of Malcolm H. Kerr.* (Beirut: American University of Beirut Press, 1991).

Brown, L. C. *Diplomacy in the Middle East: The International Relations of Regional and Outside Powers* (London: I. B. Tauris, 2001).

Browne, H. *Flashpoints: Suez and Sinai* (London: Longman, 1971).

Burdett, W. *Encounter with the Middle East: An Intimate Report on What Lies Behind the Arab-Israeli Conflict* (New York: Atheneum, 1969).

Burke, J. *Al-Qaeda: The True Story of Radical Islam* (London: Penguin, 2004).

Burns, W. J. *Economic Aid and American Foreign Policy Toward Egypt, 1955–1981* (Albany: State University of New York Press, 1985).

Childers, E. B. *The Road to Suez: A Study of Western-Arab Relations* (London: MacGibbon and Kee, 1962).

Churchill, R. S. and W. S. *The Six Day War* (London: Heinemann, 1967).

Ciorciari, J. D. 'Saudi-U.S. Alignment after the Six-Day War', *Middle East Review of International Affairs*, 9.2 (2005).

Clapham, C. *Foreign Policy Making in Developing States: A Comparative Approach* (Westmead: Saxon House, 1977).

Cockburn, A. and L. *Dangerous Liaison: The Inside Story of the US-Israeli Covert Relationship* (London: Bodley Head, 1992).

Cohen, M. J. and Kolinsky, M. *Demise of the British Empire in the Middle East: Britain's Responses to Nationalist Movements, 1943–55* (London: Frank Cass, 1998).

Cohen, R. *Culture and Conflict in Egyptian-Israeli Relations: A Dialogue of the Deaf* (Bloomington: Indiana University Press, 1990).

Dann, U. *King Hussein and the Challenge of Arab Radicalism: Jordan, 1955–1967* (New York: Oxford University Press, 1989).

Dawisha, A. I. 'Intervention in the Yemen: An Analysis of Egyptian Perceptions and Policies', *Middle East Journal*, 29.1 (1975).

Dawisha, A. I. *Egypt in the Arab World: The Elements of Foreign Policy* (New York: Wiley, 1976).

Dawisha, A. I. 'Perceptions, Decisions and Consequences in Foreign Policy: The Egyptian Intervention in the Yemen', *Political Studies*, 25.2 (1977).

Dawisha, A. I. *Islam in Foreign Policy* (Cambridge University Press, 1983).

Dawisha, A. I. *The Arab Radicals* (New York: Council on Foreign Relations, 1986).

Dawn, E. 'The Egyptian Remilitarisation of Sinai', *Journal of Contemporary History*, 3.3 (1968).

Deffarge, C. and Troeller, G. *Yemen 62–69: De la Révolution 'Sauvage' à la Trêve des Guerriers* (Paris: Robert Laffont, 1969).

Dekmejian, R. H. *Egypt under Nasir: A Study in Political Dynamics* (Albany: State University of New York Press, 1971).

Dessouki, A. E. H. and Labban, A. 'Arms Race, Defense Expenditures and Development: The Egyptian Case 1952–73', *Journal of South Asian and Middle Eastern Studies*, 4.3 (1981).

Draper, T. *Israel and World Politics: Roots of the Third Arab-Israeli War* (New York: Viking Press, 1968).

Dresch, P. *A History of Modern Yemen* (Cambridge University Press, 2000).

Doran, M. *Pan-Arabism before Nasser: Egyptian Power Politics and the Palestine Question* (Oxford University Press, 1999).

Dorril, S. *MI6: Fifty Years of Special Operations* (London: Fourth Estate, 2000).

Elwi-Saif, M. 'Nasser's Perception of 1967 Crisis', unpublished paper presented at a conference on *The United States, the Middle East and the 1967 Arab-Israeli War* (US Department of State, January 12–13, 2004).

Fain, W. T. 'Unfortunate Arabia: The United States, Great Britain and Yemen, 1955–63', *Diplomacy & Statecraft*, 12.2 (2001).

Farid, A. M., Stephens, R. and Auda, M. 'Nasser: A Reassessment', *Arab Papers*, 8 (1981).

Fielding, X. *One Man in His Time: The Life of Lieutenant-Colonel NLD ('Billy') McLean, DSO* (London: Macmillan, 1990).

Freiberger, S. Z. *Dawn over Suez: The Rise of American Power in the Middle East, 1953–1957* (Chicago: Ivan R. Dee, 1992).

Fullick, R. and Powell, G. *Suez: The Double War* (London: Leo Cooper, 1990).

Gat, M. 'Let Someone Else do the Job: American Policy on the Eve of the Six Day War', *Diplomacy & Statecraft*, 14.1 (2003).

Gat, M. 'The Great Powers and the Water Dispute in the Middle East: A Prelude to the Six Day War', *Middle Eastern Studies*, 41.6 (2005).

Gawrych, G. W. *The Albatross of Decisive Victory: War and Policy between Egypt and Israel in the 1967 and 1973 Arab-Israeli Wars* (Westport: Greenwood Press, 2000).

Gerges, F. A. *The Superpowers and the Middle East: Regional and International Politics, 1955–1967* (Boulder: Westview Press, 1994).

Gerges, F. A. 'The Kennedy Administration and the Egyptian-Saudi Conflict in Yemen: Co-opting Arab Nationalism', *Middle East Journal*, 49.2 (1995).

Ginat, R. *The Soviet Union and Egypt: 1945–55* (London: Frank Cass, 1993).

Ginor, I. ''Under the Yellow Helmet Gleamed Blue Russian Eyes': Operation Kavkaz and the War of Attrition, 1969–70', *Cold War History*, 3.1 (2002).

Golan, G. *Soviet Policies in the Middle East from World War Two to Gorbachev* (Cambridge University Press, 1990).

Golani, M. 'Chief of Staff in Quest of a War: Moshe Dayan Leads Israel into War', *Journal of Strategic Studies*, 24.1 (2001).

Goldschmidt, A. *Biographical Dictionary of Modern Egypt* (Cairo: AUC Press, 2000).

Gordon, J. *Nasser's Blessed Movement: Egypt's Free Officers and the July Revolution* (Oxford University Press, 1992).

Greffenius, S. *The Logic of Conflict: Making War and Peace in the Middle East* (New York: Armonk, 1993).

Green, S. *Taking Sides: America's Secret Relations with a Militant Israel 1948/1967* (London: Faber & Faber, 1984).

Hahn, P. L. *The United States, Great Britain and Egypt, 1945–56* (Chapel Hill: University of North Carolina Press, 1991).

Halliday, F. *Arabia without Sultans* (London: Saqi Books, 2002).

Harkabi, Y. *Arab Attitudes to Israel* (Jerusalem: Keter Publishing House, 1972).

Hasou, T. Y. *The Struggle for the Arab World: Egypt's Nasser and the Arab League* (London: KPI, 1985).

Herzog, C. *The Arab-Israeli Wars* (London: Arms and Armour Press, 1982).

Hinnebusch, R. 'From Nasser to Sadat: Elite Transformation in Egypt', *Journal of South Asian and Middle Eastern Studies*, 7.1 (1983).

Hinnebusch, R. *Egyptian Politics under Sadat: The Post-Populist Development of an Authoritarian-Modernizing State* (Cambridge University Press, 1985).

Hinnebusch, R. and Ehteshami, A. *The Foreign Policies of Middle Eastern States* (London: Lynne Rienner, 2002).

Holland, M. F. *America and Egypt: From Roosevelt to Eisenhower* (Westport: Praeger, 1996).

Howard, M. and Hunter, R. 'Israel and the Arab World: The Crisis of 1967', *Adelphi Papers*, 41 (1967).

Ismael, T. Y. *The UAR in Africa: Egypt's Policy under Nasser* (Evanston: Northwestern University Press, 1971).

Jankowski, J. *Nasser's Egypt, Arab Nationalism and the United Arab Republic* (Boulder: Lynne Rienner, 2002).

Jones, C. 'Among Ministers, Mavericks and Mandarins: Britain, Covert Action and the Yemen Civil War, 1962–64', *Middle Eastern Studies*, 40.1 (2004).

Jones, C. *Britain and the Yemen Civil War, 1962–1965: Ministers, Mercenaries and Mandarins: Foreign Policy and the Limits of Covert Action* (Brighton: Sussex Academic Press, 2004).

Karawan, I. A. 'Identity and Foreign Policy: The Case of Egypt', *In* Telhami, S. and Barnett, M. (eds) *Identity and Foreign Policy* (Ithaca: Cornell University Press, 2002).

Kelly, S. and Gorst, A. *Whitehall and the Suez Crisis* (London: Frank Cass, 2000).

Kepel, G. *Muslim Extremism in Egypt: The Prophet and the Pharaoh* (Berkeley: University of California Press, 2003).

Kerr, M. H. 'Coming to Terms with Nasser: Attempts and Failures', *International Affairs*, 43.1 (1967).

Kerr, M. H. *The Arab Cold War: Gamal 'Abd al-Nasir and His Rivals, 1958–1970* (Oxford University Press, 1971).

Khadduri, M. *Political Trends in the Arab World: The Role of Ideas and Ideals in Politics* (Baltimore: Johns Hopkins, 1970).

Khalidi, A. S. 'The War of Attrition', *Journal of Palestine Studies*, 3.1 (1973).

Kimche, D. *The Sandstorm: The Arab-Israeli War of 1967, Prelude and Aftermath* (London: Secker and Warburg, 1968).

Kishtainy, K. *Arab Political Humour* (London: Quartet Books, 1985).

Korany, B. and Dessouki, A. *The Foreign Policies of Arab States* (Boulder: Westview, 1984).

Korn, D. A. *Stalemate: The War of Attrition and Great Power Diplomacy in the Middle East, 1967–1970* (Boulder: Westview, 1992).

Kunz, D. B. *The Economic Diplomacy of the Suez Crisis* (Chapel Hill: University of North Carolina Press, 1991).

Kyle, K. *Suez: Britain's End of Empire in the Middle East* (London: I. B. Tauris, 2003).

Lall, A. *The UN and the Middle East Crisis, 1967* (New York: Columbia University Press, 1970).

Laqueur, W. *The Road to War: The Origin and Aftermath of the Arab-Israeli Conflict 1967–8* (London: Weidenfeld and Nicolson, 1968).

Lesch, D. W. 'Gamal Abd al-Nasir and an Example of Diplomatic Acumen', *Middle Eastern Studies*, 31.2 (1995).

Little, D. 'The New Frontier on the Nile: JFK, Nasser and Arab Nationalism', *The Journal of American History*, 75.2 (1988).

Louis, W. R. and Owen, R. *Suez 1956: The Crisis and Its Consequences* (Oxford: Clarendon Press, 1989).

Love, K. *Suez: The Twice-Fought War* (New York: McGraw-Hill, 1969).

Lucas, W. S. 'Redefining the Suez "Collusion"', *Middle Eastern Studies*, 26.1 (1990).

Lucas, W. S. *Divided We Stand: Britain, the US and the Suez Crisis* (London: Hodder and Stoughton, 1991).

Maqalah, A. A. *Abd al-Nasir wa al-Yemen* (Cairo: Markaz al-Hadaara al-Arabiyya, 2000).

Mawby, S. 'The Clandestine Defence of Empire: British Special Operations in Yemen 1951–64', *Intelligence and National Security*, 17.3 (2002).

McLaurin, R. D., Mughisuddin, M. and Wagner, A. A. *Foreign Policy Making in the Middle East: Domestic Influences on Policy in Egypt, Iraq, Israel and Syria* (New York: Praeger, 1977).

McNamara, R. 'Britain, Nasser and the Outbreak of the Six Day War', *Journal of Contemporary History*, 35.4 (2000).

McNamara, R. *Britain, Nasser and the Balance of Power in the Middle East 1952–1967: From the Egyptian Revolution to the Six Day War* (London: Frank Cass, 2003).

Meital, Y. *Egypt's Struggle for Peace: Continuity and Change, 1967–77* (Gainesville: University Press of Florida, 1997).

Meital, Y. 'The Khartoum Conference and Egyptian Policy after the 1967 War: A Re-examination', *Middle East Journal*, 54.1 (2000).

Meyer, G. E. *Egypt and the United States: The Formative Years* (Rutherford: Fairleigh Dickinson University Press, 1980).

Miles, H. *Al-Jazeera* (London: Abacus, 2005).

Morsy, L. A. 'American Support for the 1952 Egyptian Coup: Why?' *Middle Eastern Studies*, 31.2 (1995).

Mor, B. D. 'Nasser's Decision-Making in the 1967 Middle East Crisis: A Rational-Choice Explanation', *Journal of Peace Research*, 28.4 (1991).

Mutawi, S. A. *Jordan in the 1967 War* (Cambridge University Press, 1987).

Nasser, H. G. A. *Britain and the Egyptian Nationalist Movement 1936–1952* (Reading: Ithaca Press, 1994).

Nasser, M. K. 'Egyptian Mass Media under Nasser and Sadat: Two Models of Press Management and Control', *Journalism Monographs*, 124 (1990).

Nasser, W. A. *Al-masār wa al-maṣīr* (Cairo: Mahdet Misr, 2002).

Noman, A. and Almadhagi, K. *Yemen and the United States: A Study of a Small Power and Super-State Relationship 1962–1994* (London: Tauris Academic Studies, 1996).

O'Ballance, E. *The War in the Yemen.* (London: Faber and Faber, 1971).

O'Ballance, E. *The Electronic War in the Middle East, 1968–70* (London: Faber and Faber, 1974).

Oren, M. B. 'Escalation to Suez: The Egypt-Israel Border War, 1949–56', *Journal of Contemporary History*, 24.2 (1989).

Oren, M. B. 'Secret Egypt-Israel Peace Initiatives Prior to the Suez Campaign', *Middle Eastern Studies*, 26.3 (1990).

Oren, M. B. 'A Winter of Discontent: Britain's Crisis in Jordan', *International Journal of Middle Eastern Studies*, 22.2 (1990).

Oren, M. B. *Six Days of War: June 1967 and the Making of the Modern Middle East* (Oxford University Press, 2002).

Ovendale, R. *Britain, the United States and the Transfer of Power in the Middle East, 1945–1962* (London: Leicester University Press, 1996).

Parker, R. B. *The Politics of Miscalculation in the Middle East* (Bloomington: Indiana University Press, 1993).

Parker, R. B. *The Six-Day War: A Retrospective* (Gainesville: University Press of Florida, 1996).

Pearson, J. *Sir Anthony Eden and the Suez Crisis: Reluctant Gamble* (London: Palgrave Macmillan, 2003).

Pieragostini, K. *Britain, Aden and South Arabia: Abandoning Empire* (London: Macmillan, 1991).

Pipes, D. *The Hidden Hand: Middle East Fears of Conspiracy* (London: Macmillan, 1996).

Podeh, E. 'The Struggle over Arab Hegemony after the Suez Crisis', *Middle East Studies*, 29.1 (1993).

Podeh, E. 'The Drift towards Neutrality: Egyptian Foreign Policy during the Early Nasserist Era, 1952–55', *Middle Eastern Studies*, 32.1 (1996).

Podeh, E. *The Decline of Arab Unity: The Rise and Fall of the United Arab Republic* (Brighton: Sussex Academic Press, 1999).

Podeh, E. 'To Unite or Not to Unite – That is *Not* the Question: The 1963 Tripartite Unity Talks Reassessed', *Middle Eastern Studies*, 39.1 (2003).

Podeh, E. 'Suez in Reverse: The Arab Response to the Iraqi Bid for Kuwait, 1961–63', *Diplomacy and Statecraft*, 14.1 (2003).

Pridham, B. R. *Contemporary Yemen: Politics and Historical Background* (London: Croom Helm, 1984).

Quandt, W. B. *Decade of Decisions: American Policy toward the Arab-Israeli Conflict, 1967–76* (Berkeley: University of California Press, 1977).

Quandt, W. B. *The United States and Egypt* (Washington: Brookings Press, 1990).

Quandt, W. B. 'Lyndon Johnson and the June 1967 War: What Color Was the Light?' *Middle East Journal*, 46.2 (1992).

Quandt, W. B. *Peace Process: American Diplomacy and the Arab-Israeli Conflict since 1967* (Washington: Brookings Press, 2001).

Rabinovich, I. *The Road Not Taken: Early Arab-Israeli Negotiations* (Oxford University Press, 1991).

Rabinovich, I. and Shaked, H. *From June to October: The Middle East between 1967 and 1973* (New Brunswick: Transaction Books, 1978).

Rahmy, A. A. R. *The Egyptian Policy in the Arab World: Intervention in Yemen* (Washington, DC: University Press of America, 1983).

Rathmell, A. 'Brotherly Enemies: The Rise and Fall of the Syrian-Egyptian Intelligence Axis, 1954–1967', *Intelligence and National Security*, 31.1 (1998).

Richardson, L. 'Avoiding and Incurring Losses: Decision-Making in the Suez Crisis', *In* Stein, J. G. and Pauly, L. W. (eds) *Choosing to Co-operate: How States Avoid Loss* (Baltimore: John Hopkins, 1993).

Rosser, K. 'Education, Revolt and Reform in Yemen: The 'Famous Forty' Mission of 1947', unpublished M.Phil. thesis, University of Oxford (1998).

Rubin, B. 'America and the Egyptian Revolution, 1950–7', *Political Science Quarterly*, 97.1 (1982).

Rucher, L. 'The Soviet Union and the Suez Crisis', *In* Tal, D. *The War: Collusion and Rivalry in the Middle East* (London: Frank Cass, 2001).

Safran, N. *From War to War: The Arab-Israeli Confrontation, 1948–1967* (New York: Pegasus, 1969).

Safran, N. *Saudi Arabia: The Ceaseless Quest for Security* (New York: Cornell University Press, 1988).

Samd al-Din, I., Said Selim, M. and Khadduri, W. *Kayf yiṣna' al-qarār fī al-waṭan al-'arabiyy* (Cairo: Markaz Dirasat al-Wahida al-Arabiyya, 1980).

Sayed-Ahmed, M. A. W. *Nasser and American Foreign Policy, 1952–1956* (London: LAAM, 1989).

Sayigh, Y. 'Escalation or Containment? Egypt and the Palestine Liberation Army, 1964–67', *International Journal of Middle East Studies*, 30.1 (1998).

Sayigh, Y. and Shlaim, A. *The Cold War and the Middle East* (Oxford: Clarendon Press, 1997).

Schmidt, D. A. *Yemen: The Unknown War* (London: Bodley Head, 1968).

Schonmann, N. 'Tactics of Peace: The Role of Peace Overtures in Nasser's Postwar Foreign Policy Making', unpublished MA thesis, Tel Aviv University (2005).

Seale, P. *The Struggle for Syria* (London: Tauris, 1987).

Sela, A. *The Decline of the Arab-Israeli Conflict: Middle East Politics and the Quest for Regional Order* (Albany: State University of New York Press, 1998).

Shaked, H. and Rabinovich, I. *The Middle East and the United States: Perceptions and Policies* (New Jersey: Transaction Books, 1980).

Sharabi, H. B. *Nationalism and Revolution in the Arab World* (Princeton: D. Van Nostrand, 1966).

Shaw, T. *Eden, Suez and the Mass Media: Propaganda and Persuasion during the Suez Crisis* (London: I. B. Tauris, 1996).

Sheffy, Y. 'Unconcern at Dawn, Surprise at Sunset: Egyptian Intelligence Appreciation before the Sinai Campaign, 1956', *Intelligence and National Security*, 5.3 (1990).

Shlaim, A. 'Failures in National Intelligence Estimates', *World Politics*, 28.3 (1976).

Shlaim, A. 'Conflicting Approaches to Israel's Relations with the Arabs', *Middle East Journal*, 37.2 (1983).

Shlaim, A. 'The Protocol of Sevres, 1956: Anatomy of a War Plot', *International Affairs*, 73.3 (1997).

Shlaim, A. *The Iron Wall: Israel and the Arab World* (London: Penguin, 2000).

Shpiro, S. 'The CIA as Peace Broker?' *Survival*, 45.2 (2003).

Sivan, E. *Radical Islam: Medieval Theology and Modern Politics* (New Haven: Yale University Press, 1985).

Siverson, R. M. 'A Research Note on Cognitive Balance and International Conflict: Egypt and Israel in the Suez Crisis', *Western Political Quarterly*, 27.2 (1974).

Smith, S. C. 'Rulers and Residents: British Relations with the Aden Protectorate, 1937–59', *Middle Eastern Studies*, 31.3 (1995).

Smith, S. C. 'Revolution and Reaction: South Arabia in the Aftermath of the Yemeni Revolution', *In* Fedorowich, K. and Thomas, M. (eds) *International Diplomacy and Colonial Retreat* (London: Frank Cass, 2001).

Spiegel, S. L. *The Other Arab-Israeli Conflict: Making America's Middle East Policy, from Truman to Reagan* (University of Chicago Press, 1985).

Springborg, R. *Family, Power and Politics in Egypt: Sayed Bay Marei – His Clan, Clients and Cohorts* (Philadelphia: University of Pennsylvania Press, 1982).

Stein, J. G. and Tanter, R. *Rational Decision-Making: Israel's Security Choices, 1967* (Columbus: Ohio State University Press, 1980).

Stephens, R. *Nasser: A Political Biography* (London: Penguin, 1971).

Stookey, R. W. *America and the Arab States: An Uneasy Encounter* (New York: Wiley, 1975).

Stookey, R. W. *The Politics of the Yemen Arab Republic* (Boulder: Westview Press, 1978).

Takeyh, R. *The Origins of the Eisenhower Doctrine: The US, Britain and Nasser's Egypt* (London: Macmillan, 2000).

Tal, D. *The 1956 War: Collusion and Rivalry in the Middle East* (London: Frank Cass, 2001).

Tal, D. 'Israel's Road to the 1956 War', *International Journal of Middle East Studies*, 28.1 (1996).

Tawil, M. *La'bat al-umam wa 'abd al-nāsir* (Cairo: Al-Maktab al-Misriyy al-Hadith, 1986).

Thornhill, M. T. 'Alternatives to Nasser: Humphrey Trevelyan, Ambassador to Egypt.' *In* Kelly, S. and Gorst, A. *Whitehall and the Suez Crisis* (London: Frank Cass, 2000).

Thornhill, M. T. 'Britain, the United States and the Rise of an Egyptian Leader: the Politics and Diplomacy of Nasser's Consolidation of Power, 1952–4', *English Historical Review*, 69 (2004).

Touval, S. *The Peace Brokers: Mediators in the Arab-Israeli Conflict, 1948–1979* (Princeton University Press, 1982).

Tripp, C. *Contemporary Egypt: Through Egyptian Eyes: Essays in Honour of Professor P.J. Vatikiotis* (London: Routledge, 1993).

Troen, S. I. and Shemesh, M. *The Suez-Sinai Crisis 1956: Retrospective and Reappraisal* (London: Frank Cass, 1990).

Vatikiotis, P. J. *Nasser and His Generation* (London: Croom Helm, 1978).

Vatikiotis, P. J. *The History of Modern Egypt: From Muhammad Ali to Mubarak* (London: Weidenfeld and Nicolson, 1991).

Verrier, A. *Through the Looking Glass: British Foreign Policy in an Age of Illusions* (London: Jonathan Cape, 1983).

Walt, S. M. *The Origins of Alliances* (Ithaca: Cornell University Press, 1987).

Wilson, K. M. *Imperialism and Nationalism in the Middle East: The Anglo-Egyptian Experience 1882–1982* (London: Mansell Publishing, 1983).

Witty, D. M. 'A Regular Army in Counter-Insurgency Operations: Egypt in North Yemen, 1962–1967', *Journal of Military History*, 65.2 (2001).

Yapp, M. E. *The Near East since the First World War: A History to 1995*, 2nd edn (London: Longman, 1996).

Yizraeli, S. *The Remaking of Saudi Arabia: The Struggle between King Sa'ud and Crown Prince Faysal, 1953–1962* (Tel Aviv University: Dayan Center, 1977).

Select theoretical works

Axelrod, R. M. *Structure of Decision: The Cognitive Maps of Political Elites* (Princeton University Press, 1976).

Ayres, R. W. 'Mediating International Conflicts: Is Image Change Necessary?' *Journal of Peace Research*, 34.3 (1997).

Boulding, K. E. *The Image: Knowledge in Life and Society* (University of Michigan: Ann Arbor, 1956).

Boulding, K. E. 'National Images and International Systems', *Journal of Conflict Resolution*, 3.2 (1959).

Brams, S. J. 'To Mobilize or not to Mobilize: Catch-22s in International Crises', *International Studies Quarterly*, 43.4 (1999).

Cohen, R. *Threat Perception in International Crisis* (Madison: University of Wisconsin Press, 1979).

Cottam, M. L. *Images and Intervention: US Policies in Latin America* (University of Pittsburgh Press: 1994).

Cottam, R. W. *Foreign Policy Motivation: A General Theory and a Case Study* (University of Pittsburgh Press: 1977).

Farrell, J. C. and Smith, A. P. *Image and Reality in World Politics* (New York: Columbia, 1967).

Finlay, D. J., Holsti, O. R. and Fagen, R. R. *Enemies in Politics* (Chicago: Rand McNally, 1967).

Frankel, J. *The Making of Foreign Policy: An Analysis of Decision Making* (Oxford University Press, 1963).

George, A. L. *Propaganda Analysis: A Study of Inferences Made From Nazi Propaganda in World War II* (Evanston: Row Peterson, 1959).

George, A. L. 'The 'Operational Code': A Neglected Approach to the Study of Political Leaders and Decision-Making', *International Studies Quarterly*, 13.2 (1969).

Geva, N. and Mintz, A. *Decision-Making on War and Peace: The Cognitive-Rational Debate* (London: Boulder, 1997).

Goldstein, J. and Keohane, R. O. *Ideas and Foreign Policy: Beliefs, Institutions and Political Change* (New York: Cornell University Press, 1993).

Herrmann, R. K. and Fischerkeller, M. P. 'Beyond the Enemy Image and Spiral Model: Cognitive-Strategic Research after the Cold War', *International Organization*, 49.3 (1995).

Holsti, O. R. 'Cognitive Dynamics and Images of the Enemy', *Journal of International Affairs*, 21.1 (1967).

Jervis, R. 'Hypotheses on Misperception', *World Politics*, 20.3 (1968).

Jervis, R. *The Logic of Images in International Relations* (Princeton University Press, 1970).

Jervis, R. *Perception and Misperception in International Politics* (Princeton University Press, 1976).

Jervis, R. and Snyder, J. *Dominoes and Bandwagons: Strategic Beliefs and Great Power Competition in the Eurasian Rimland* (Oxford University Press, 1991).

Khong, Y. F. *Analogies at War: Korea, Munich, Dien Bien Phu, and the Vietnam Decisions of 1965* (Princeton University Press, 1992).

Larson, D. W. *Origins of Containment: A Psychological Explanation* (Princeton University Press, 1985).

Lebow, R. N. *Between Peace and War: The Nature of International Crisis* (Baltimore: Johns Hopkins University Press, 1981).

Rieber, R. W. *The Psychology of War and Peace: The Image of the Enemy* (New York: Plenum Press, 1991).

Shimko, K. L. *Images and Arms Control: Perceptions of the Soviet Union in the Reagan Administration* (University of Michigan: Ann Arbor, 1991).

Shlaim, A. *The United States and the Berlin Blockade, 1948–1949: A Study in Crisis Decision-Making* (Berkeley: University of California Press, 1983).

Sprout, H. and M. 'Environmental Factors in the Study of International Politics', *Journal of Conflict Resolution*, 1 (1957).

Stein, J. G. and Pauly, L. W. *Choosing to Co-operate: How States Avoid Loss* (Baltimore: Johns Hopkins, 1993).

Sylvan, D. A. and Voss, J. F. *Problem Representation in Foreign Policy Decision Making* (Cambridge University Press, 1998).

Tetlock, P. E. and McGuire, C. 'Cognitive Perspectives on Foreign Policy', *In* Long, S. (ed.) *Political Behavior Annual* (Boulder: Westview Press, 1986).

Vertzberger, Y. *The World in their Minds: Information Processing, Cognition, and Perception in Foreign Policy Decision Making* (Stanford University Press, 1990).

White, R. K. 'Misperception in the Arab-Israeli Conflict', *Journal of Social Issues*, 33.1 (1977).

Wohlforth, W. C. *The Elusive Balance: Power and Perceptions during the Cold War* (Ithaca: Cornell University Press, 1993).

Yee, A. S. 'The Causal Effects of Ideas on Policies', *International Organization*, 50.1 (1996).

Index